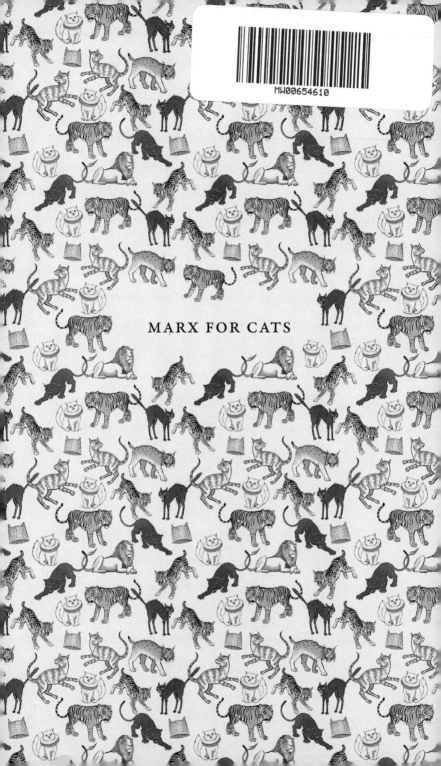

MARX FOR CATS

Marx
for Cats

A RADICAL BESTIARY

Leigh Claire La Berge

DUKE UNIVERSITY PRESS DURHAM AND LONDON 2023

© 2023 DUKE UNIVERSITY PRESS
All rights reserved
Printed in the United States of America on acid-free paper ∞
Project Editor: Lisa Lawley
Designed by Aimee C. Harrison
Typeset in Garamond Premier Pro by Copperline Book Services

Library of Congress Cataloging-in-Publication Data
Names: La Berge, Leigh Claire, author.
Title: Marx for cats : a radical bestiary / Leigh Claire La Berge.
Description: Durham : Duke University Press, 2023. |
Includes bibliographical references and index.
Identifiers: LCCN 2022056743 (print)
LCCN 2022056744 (ebook)
ISBN 9781478019251 (paperback)
ISBN 9781478016618 (hardcover)
ISBN 9781478023883 (ebook)
Subjects: LCSH: Social structure in literature. | Social classes in
literature. | Communism in literature. | Cats in literature. | Capitalism
in literature. | Literature—History and criticism. |
BISAC: PHILOSOPHY / General | PETS / Cats / General
Classification: LCC PN56.S654 L334 2023 (print) |
LCC PN56.S654 (ebook) | DDC 320.53/22—dc23/eng/20230718
LC record available at https://lccn.loc.gov/2022056743
LC ebook record available at https://lccn.loc.gov/2022056744

Cover art: Illustration by Trenton Duerksen;
visual effects by Andrew Strasser; creative direction
by Caroline Woolard.

For The Mitten and for Lion

CONTENTS

Part III. Our Dumb Beasts
THE RISE OF THE BOURGEOISIE AND
ITS APPROPRIATION OF CATS, 1800–1900

———————

Part IV. Every Paw Can Be a Claw
REVOLUTIONS WITH CATS, REVOLUTIONS
AGAINST CAPITALISM, 1900–2000

———————

ACKNOWLEDGMENTS

———————————

This book has its origins with Caroline Woolard in multiple ways. It was her idea to create the video series *Marx for Cats*: she was the producer; she found the collaborators; she got the grants; she hired the assistants; she got the project into artist residencies; and, finally, when she was queried about producing a book proposal for an art press, it was she who asked: Could *Marx for Cats* be a book? I was only the one who wrote it, and it turned out not to be an art book but one certainly motivated and influenced by my time in different art spaces.

The material that I've molded here into a historical narrative was developed in conversation with Thyrza Nichols Goodeve (and her six cats); with students, visitors, and J. Morgan Puett herself at Mildred's Lane; with glassblowers at Pilchuck; and with Athena Kokoronis at the Domestic Performance Agency. Those presentations occurred before the pandemic and they convinced me that this material could come alive in conversation with others. Presenting more developed material at the Zoom-mediated Red May festival during the pandemic was likewise important, and I thank Philip Wohlstetter for the opportunity to do so.

Several books have had an outsized influence this one. I have cited them in the text, but they should be acknowledged here as well for their combination of a sense of adventure, an astuteness of critique, and a creative latitude. These include *Fear of the Animal Planet: The Hidden History of Animal Resistance* by Jason Hribal; *Beasts of Burden: Animal and Disability Liberation* by Sunaura Taylor; *Red Rosa: A Graphic Biography of Rosa Luxemburg* by Kate Evans; and *Male Fantasies, Volume I: Women, Floods, Bodies, History* by Klaus Theweleit. Each of these books introduced me to a new model for presenting and analyzing a visual and conceptual archive.

A host of colleagues and friends have read bits and pieces of the manuscript along the way. I thank Erica Meiners, Isaac Kamola, Janet Neary, Alissa Karl, Max Haiven, Troy Vettese, Jason Hannan, Doug Barrett, Nathan Snaza, Sean Grattan, Jordan Meaner, Christopher Breu, Lika Volkova, Cecilia Sebastian, Jesse Schwartz, Or Zubalsky, Anna Kornbluh, Asmus Rungby, Faith Wilson Stein, Seth Kim-Cohen, Salomé Skvirsky, John Pat Leary, and the Comparative Theory group. Jordan Stein added several crucial references about nineteenth-century American print culture; Benjamin Kohlmann did so for twentieth-century German Marxist culture; Jonathan Flatley for twentieth-century Black radicalism. Jessie Kindig and I had several conversations that helped to transform the structure of my text from a monograph to a proper bestiary. Jarrett Moran helped me put the manuscript and its images into proper shape.

And then there are the randos: people on social media who have helped populate this archive and offered a menagerie of wonderful feline factoids and images. Many of these suggestions have found their way into this project's final form. During the pandemic, with so many archives closed, these (apparent) lovers of feline history offered me bits from their own collections; I thank them collectively.

This project has been supported by several City University of New York grants, including funds for publishing and research from the Professional Staff Congress, time away from teaching provided by the CUNY Graduate Center's Advanced Research Collaborative, and more time away from teaching as well as a wonderful scholarly atmosphere provided by Gary Wilder and the Graduate Center's Committee on Globalization and Social Change.

I thank the two anonymous reviewers of this manuscript: I have never received such generative and generous readers' reports in my many years of academic publishing. The comments these readers offered really did help this project leap from one level to the next in terms of their important specific comments as well as their larger structural suggestions. I thank Courtney Berger at Duke for finding such readers as well as for her support of this project from its early stages. And I thank the whole Duke team as well.

The majority of this book was written during the COVID-19 pandemic of 2020–21, and that writing would not have been possible without the spirit of Lion Woolard and without the childcare provided to him by Sam Lopez. I thank them both for filling our home with playfulness and joy.

My mother, Ann F. La Berge, not only read this manuscript but told me as a teenager, when I first became interested in social movements, that a friend of hers from graduate school in the 1970s had named her cat Angela Davis. That was my introduction to the Black Panthers. I thank her for that acquaintance as well as for a lifetime of sharing archives and animals with me; I've here combined two family interests.

Finally, this book is dedicated to two cats in my life, past and present. First, to the memory of The Mitten, who really was a naughty kitten, and who accompanied me on numerous physical and intellectual voyages. His spirit was as present in writing this book as his furry, concrete self had been the writing of in others. And second, to Lion, for many reasons. Meow.

INTRODUCTION

Cat out of
the Bag

*"To take 'liberties' with the signature of Marx is . . .
merely to enter the freedom of Marxism."*

—PERRY ANDERSON, *PASSAGES FROM
ANTIQUITY TO FEUDALISM*

 s she languished in a Berlin prison during World War I, Marxist revolutionary Rosa Luxemburg often thought of her cat: "At home so many times she knew how to lead me onto the right road with her long, silent look," Luxemburg reminisced.[1] She had first encountered the feline some years before, while teaching at a socialist party school, and adopted her and gave her a Hebraic name, Mimi, which means both *rebellion* and *bitter*. While her imprisonment dragged on with the war, Luxemburg no doubt felt both senses of the cat's name. Her voluminous

letters convey a sense of pain, yet Luxemburg never lost her rebellious disposition. She remained determined to continue the struggle and make the socialist revolution, which she helped to do upon her release, in Germany, in 1918–19.

Before and after her stint in prison, Luxemburg organized, taught, agitated, and theorized, and it was Mimi who was her comrade—a word whose derivation, from the Spanish *comrada*, for roommate, conveys here a distinct truth.[2] They lived together, read together, talked together, and received visitors together, including Vladimir Lenin, with whom Mimi "flirted" and who returned the affection. "I get up early, work, go for a stroll, and have conversations with Mimi," Luxemburg wrote to one lover.[3] "I kiss you, and so does Mimi," she offered another. "Mimi and I are alone together," she related to a friend. A student of botany, Luxemburg recorded that "we busied ourselves with the flowers, that is, Mimi and I, she is helping me skillfully the whole time." Mimi, too, had an epistolary habit: "There is always a big celebration at my house when a letter from you arrives. Even Mimi sniffs at it lovingly (she calls that 'reading the letter')," she responded to a political ally.

Rosa Luxemburg led a revolutionary life. But so did Mimi. And while the former's contribution to Marxist theory and practice is well known in the annals of radical history, the latter's is considered as merely an accompaniment, if it is considered at all. *Marx for Cats* amends such tendencies. Moving beyond any individual episode, person, beast, or even mode of production, this book presents a feline archive for the theorizing and writing of economic history.

The gambit of *Marx for Cats* is that the history of Western capitalism can be told through the cat and that doing so reveals a heretofore unrecognized animality at the heart of both Marx's critique and Western Marxist critique. That animality has most often been feline, and it has been present in how Marxists have represented what constitutes the economy and imagined how the economy could be transformed from a site of exploitation into one of equality. From capitalism's feudal prehistory to its contemporary financialization, those seeking to maintain economic power as well as those seeking to challenge it have recruited cats into their efforts. Medieval kings and lords styled themselves as lions; dissidents from the medieval order were identified through their relationships with domestic cats, who likewise were considered dissidents. The first real capitalist empire, Great Britain, adopted a leonine symbol, while some of the most powerful worker actions against capitalism have been known as wildcat strikes. In the eighteenth century, French and Haitian revolutionaries were denigrated as tigers by the conservatives who opposed them; in the twentieth century, the Black Panther Party insisted that capitalism was a fundamentally racist system and demanded its overthrow.

Like any text in the Marxist tradition, *Marx for Cats* gestures in two directions at once. In asking how our society is structured and for whom, Marxism turns toward economic history. And with the materials it finds there, it begins to conceive of how the present might have been different and how the future still could be. In offering a feline narrative of our economic past, I argue that Marxism not only has the potential to be an interspecies project but that it already is one. And in using that knowledge and those histories, presented here in cat form, I suggest that we may collectively plot a new future together, one that recognizes the work that cats have always done for Marxists and one that wonders: What political commitments can Marxists make to cats? This is less a radical history of a single species than a history of how felines and humans have made each other radical—both radically progressive and radically conservative.

Beginning its history in the eighth century CE and moving forward into our own day, *Marx for Cats* should be understood as what the philosopher Walter Benjamin called a *Tigersprung,* or a tiger's leap, into the past.[4] For Benjamin, the recollection of a historical moment functions as a kind of return to it. In the most revolutionary eruptions of both feudalism and capitalism—the peasant uprisings of the Middle Ages, the Paris Commune of the modern age, the queer and communist movements of the twentieth century—in each of these radical reformulations of economic power and possibility cats were present; indeed, they were often used for said reformulation. But cats have also been called on to oppose such movements, and some of economic history's most rapacious and atavistic rulers have passed their days in private menageries, staring into the eyes of big cats in kin-like fashion.

For Marx, too, the figure of the leap was an important one. But, for Marx, capital does the leaping. And capital leaps into the future, not the past, as it remakes the world through industry, wage labor, and revolution. Marx returned to the leap in multiple texts, writing in his magnum opus, *Capital*, for example, "So soon, in short, as the general conditions requisite for production by the modern industrial system have been established, this mode of production [capitalism] acquires an elasticity, a capacity for sudden extension by leaps and bounds."[5] Numerous Marxists, from Leon Trotsky to Mao Zedong to C. L. R. James, would follow Marx and use the leap in their analyses of capitalism and its overcoming.

Domestic cats leap as well, and their sense of poise and balance as they do so has long distinguished them among animals that cohabit with humans. Perhaps that's why Red Emma Goldman claimed she was like a cat: no matter where she was thrown from and regardless of where she was forced to jump, she always landed, according to Goldman herself, catlike, on her "paws."[6]

Marx for Cats combines these multiple figures and figurations of the leap in order to capture the moments in which cats and capitalism interact and intersect. In those interstices we may locate how felines have long been creatures of economic critique and communist possibility. We need only a certain punctuated history of capitalism to realize this feline truth, and mine is an illustrative, not exhaustive, telling. I have found the required history in disparate times and places—in church edicts and newspaper advertisements, in the texts of both realized and failed revolutions, in high theory and children's primers—and stitched it together. In presenting the past through this sometime disjointed feline narrative, I have followed Marx, who stressed the importance of understanding history not as a seamless continuum but rather as constituted by moments of break and rupture, of lurches forward and backward. If we are not careful to follow history's meandering path, we wind up with a bland conception of history-as-progress that amounts to, according to Marx, a scene in which "all cats become grey since all historical difference is abolished."[7] But if we follow the cats themselves, history hardly appears monochrome; we are presented with a calico palette in which those on society's margins and those fighting for a different social world have either sought out or been forced into the companionship of felines.

As a guide to capitalism's past, *cat* is hardly a transparent category, and in *Marx for Cats* it assumes three distinct roles. First, cats are witnesses to and perhaps makers of history: they have different and sometimes competing designs and desires. Cats benefit from certain historical situations—being welcomed indoors, for example—and suffer from others, such as the cat massacres that roiled late medieval and early modern Europe. When a new historical order is heralded in or an old one is banished, cats always seem to appear on the scene, where they take positions as both vanguard and rearguard. One could be forgiven for wondering whether cats are to nonhuman animals what the proletariat is to all other classes, namely, midwives of a different world.

Second, cats mark economic history as both icons, or symbols, and as indexes, or material residues of a past that really did happen. This is an archival project, and I could not find what was not there. When the first president of the United States, George Washington, styled himself as a new kind of leader during the American Revolution, he decorated himself with leonine sword. When radical printer Thomas Spence designed coins for a new socialist economy in eighteenth-century England, the one that celebrated freedom from slavery was stamped with a cat. The icon and the index can never be fully separated, and the symbolic feline history I uncover herein doubles as a material history in which those actors, both human and not, who undertook revolutionary activity left traces of a changed world in doing so.

And third, from Niccolò Machiavelli to Adam Smith, from Friedrich Engels to Louise Michel, from Rosa Luxemburg to John Maynard Keynes and, yes, Karl Marx himself, those who have studied the relationship between state power and economic power, who have contemplated and indeed instantiated how different that relationship could be, have used cats to do so. They have theorized using feline metaphors, they have recorded the delights and miseries of writing and organizing with feline companionship, and some of them have discussed their work with cats. I take my introduction's generic title from the specificity of Marxist philosopher Theodor Adorno, who titled his post–World War II essay on the loss of solidary in socialism "Katze aus dem Sack": cat out of the bag.[8]

My project likewise began as a discussion with a cat.

While in graduate school, I had long conversations with my Maine coon, The Mitten, about the range of theoretical approaches to power that I was introduced to daily. We developed a little jingle about poststructuralism, or the philosophical idea that language constitutes one's reality.

I would say to him, "Mitten, Mitten, naughty kitten," as he pushed a glass off a table or used a window screen as his scratching post.

And he would retort:

I'm not naughty, no way
But you tell me that every day
Then the naughtiness doesn't go away
It's just here to stay and stay.

What a performance! He would argue that the words I had used to describe him made him naughty, not that he had acted naughtily and thus warranted my descriptions. Michel Foucault, Jacques Lacan, Luce Irigaray; together he and I tore through these texts—sometimes he did so literally.

In many ways, poststructuralism offers the most natural philosophical setting to host a conversation with and about cats. From Roland Barthes to Jacques Derrida to Guy Debord, this philosophical tradition has celebrated the feline since well before the novel field of animal studies emerged as a site of interdisciplinary academic concern. Indeed, according to some of this nascent field's best-known theorists, animal studies remains in debt to poststructuralism, and to Derrida in particular.[9] And when Derrida presented his field-generating claim, in "The Animal That Therefore I Am (More to Follow)," that humans need nonhuman animals to articulate themselves and to write the biography of their own species, he recruited cats into his efforts: namely his own beast, who appears in his text in medias res and who interrupts his philosophizing. As they stare at each other, a naked (he tells us) Derrida insists "the cat I am talking about is a real cat, truly, believe me, a little cat. It isn't the figure of a cat. It doesn't silently enter the room as an allegory for all the cats on the earth."[10]

Marx would have presented the situation differently. He would not have distinguished between a "real cat" and an "allegory for all cats" but would, rather, have suggested a pairing of an abstract cat and a concrete cat. And, crucially, he would have resisted the temptation to place the concrete cat conceptually prior to the abstract one. "The concrete concept is concrete," he wrote, "because it is a synthesis of many definitions, thus representing the unity of diverse aspects. It appears therefore in reasoning as a summing up, a result, and not as the starting point."[11] To see the concrete cat, we must have already arrived in a certain historical situation. Conversely, "as a rule, the most general abstractions arise only in the midst of the richest possible concrete development, where one thing appears as common to many, to all."[12] As we will see, when Marx introduces cats into his work, it is in the context of explicating what constitutes a true abstraction. With Friedrich Engels, in *The German Ideology*, Marx critiques German idealist abstraction through the example of a cat chasing a mouse.

In this book, I follow cats as they assume both abstract and concrete forms and as those forms change and are changed in certain historical moments. The concrete cats who were executed in eighteenth-century Paris as a symbol of proletarian rage at the bourgeoisie could hardly have been more tangible as they were left dangling from a courtyard gallows. In contrast, the wildcat scalps prized by white settler colonists in the nineteenth-century American Midwest were transformed into bills of currency, representations of an abstract money form that connected petty local transactions to a global network of commodity exchange.

But I, too, have engaged "real cats," and the fact that this book began as a conversation with cats and continues to live in that form at marxforcats.com suggests its own argument. Using the rich trove of feline tropes and references buried deep within the archive of political economy, I began an interspecies pedagogy project in which I attempted to explain Marx to cats through cats. I helped them become acquainted with Marxism, a still-developing theory of how and why capitalism works and for whom. The artists Caroline Woolard and Or Zubalsky and I recorded some of these conversations to share with lovers of

FIGURE INTRO.1. Marx for cats: a discussion of *The Eighteenth Brumaire of Louis Bonaparte.* Courtesy of Leigh Claire La Berge.

cats, readers of Marx, and what we soon learned was the significant overlap between these two groups. To our surprise, artists, teachers, activists, and felines all responded and encouraged further exchanges.

This book is the expanded version of those conversations with an added archival emphasis. Using visual and textual sourcing in Latin, German, French, and English, *Marx for Cats* shares the often secret histories of cats, cat lovers, and cat haters as each of these groups has taught us about labor, money, and class struggle, and as together they have found themselves in a centuries-long conversation about the freedoms and constraints of humans and nonhuman animals in a capitalist world.

Such broad investigations can hardly be left to economics but must be explored in the fields of history, politics, literature and art. Under the Marxist banner we find artists and activists, philosophers and scientists, historians and prognosticators, and all manner of felines: panthers and wildcats, lions and tigers, lynxes and kittens, leopards and domestic shorthairs.

Each of these beasts and areas of study populates the archive of this book, as interspecies work seems to require an interdisciplinary scope.

I present here many little-known feline tales and anecdotes. I was as surprised as readers are likely to be when I learned that American founding father Thomas Paine was accused of cat sodomy and that Paris Communard Louise Michel wrote letters to her cat from her penal exile in the South Pacific. But what *is* known is that humanity's relationships with nonhuman animals are exploitative and unsustainable. It's known, and yet many inhabitants of the Global North, and most Marxists, continue on, as if—as if nonhuman animals warrant exploitation; as if industrial animal agriculture constitutes an acceptable social practice; as if Marxism need not develop to include new populations, including new species.

Sometimes, an argument is not enough.

If there is one approach this book borrows from the feline-focused *philosophes* of France, it is that of "the pleasure of the text": the idea that words and histories are slippery objects full of obscure and shifting messages and the notion that new meanings and possibilities are formed during the reading process. Hopefully, this text is more fun.

I have tried to take my writerly lead from Marx himself, a great lover of literature who consumed multiple styles, languages, and genres. His writings have an artful and literary playfulness that often goes unremarked. Citing his inspiration and antagonist, the great German philosopher G. W. F. Hegel, for example, Marx explains, "Hegel remarks somewhere that all great world-historic facts and personages appear, so to speak, twice. He forgot to add: the first time as tragedy, the second time as farce."[13] *Marx for Cats* should be read as both. I leave it to the reader to determine the proportions of each as I present a history in which class struggle and cat struggle intertwine.

In 1848 Karl Marx and Friedrich Engels penned *The Communist Manifesto*, in which they predicted the abolition of the state and private property as a wave of revolutions swept through Europe. They advocated for a new understanding of history, too: "The history of all hitherto existing society is the history of class struggle," they proclaimed.[14] A year after their famous words circulated, Marx and Engels were exiled from Belgium to London, where they congregated with other communists at London's Red Lion Pub, a location whose name recalls the most imperial animal of all.

Three years later, however, Marx was forced to contend in *The Eighteenth Brumaire of Louis Bonaparte* with the fact that his predictions had failed to materialize, that the revolutions had dissolved. He turned to a cat and claimed that Europe was operating under the spell of a *Katzenjammer*, or cat's wail, which had prevented the overturning of capitalism but from which he believed the continent would ultimately emerge.[15] From Marx's biography to his writing, we begin to see how class struggle and cat struggle articulate each other.

Marx got some of the particulars wrong. But certainly he understood the longer trajectory of how capitalism would develop, and for whom. To listen to Marx today, some one hundred and fifty years after the publication of his major texts, is to be jolted by a sense of immediate recognition. He wrote, "The need of a constantly expanding market for its products chases the bourgeoisie over the entire surface of the globe. It must nestle everywhere, settle everywhere, establish connections everywhere."[16] As Marx saw in the 1850s, for the first time in human history, everything was suddenly for sale, always and in all places. Can we change such a state of affairs? Is another world possible? This sense of a revolutionary horizon continues to be one of the claims for which Marx remains known and it is one to which my book adheres. I attempt only to resituate it and to demonstrate that the revolution has always included and must continue to include nonhuman animals. Marx realized that one can only craft a new world out of the old. He tells us that humans "make their own history, but they do not make it as they please; they do not make it under self-selected circumstances, but under circumstances existing already, given and transmitted from the past."[17] Cats, too, make their own history and seem to be, along with humans, among the few self-domesticated animals. And like that of humans, cats' history has seldom been made under conditions of their own choosing. Rather, they leap into the historical record at surprising and sometimes inopportune moments with little guarantee of how they will be received.

Using the feline in multiple forms, *Marx for Cats* attends to capitalism's tragedies as well as to the farcical moments that punctuate its history. It tells a cat's story of capitalism and delimits the special role that economic history has reserved for cats, from its earliest entreaties of feline feudal glory until our own day of zoos and deforestation, from cat shows to wildcat strikes, from lion hunts to cat cafés. The feline guides us through such tragedies, often becoming part of them; part of the tragedy, for Marxists anyway, has been their failure to appreciate the gravity of this fact. That tendency has recently begun to be amended by critics of what has been called "eco-Marxism," a strand of criticism that seeks a denouement between Marxism and various ecologies, including some adherents to animal liberation. But too much and too often eco-Marxists adhere to Engels's view of humanity's domination and control of nature as a benchmark of its own progress. Or they dismiss Marx as too anthropocentric, as though his concepts do not possess the required elasticity to include animals.[18] Either way, Marxism needs more modesty toward and equality with the many plants and animals that compose that abstraction "nature," and nonhuman animals and Marxists need each other if each is to endure, let alone flourish, in a capitalist world.

Like the great Marxist studies that track historical change over centuries—Perry Anderson's *Passages from Antiquity to Feudalism*, from which I have lifted my epigraph, or his *Lineages of the Absolutist State*; Giovanni Arrighi's *The Long Twentieth Century*; Silvia Federici's *Caliban and the Witch*—*Marx for Cats* assumes a longue durée approach to its subject. That phrase literally means "long duration," and it implies that history is expansive and layered, that history itself accumulates over time, and that even the longest duration can be longer. It was this phrase that the French Annales school historian Fernand Braudel used to refer to the totality of the capitalist world system. Fashion, food, farming—no topic was too small for Braudel, nor none too big, as he also turned his lens toward the history of the Mediterranean Sea. I came to Braudel through Arrighi, who wrote in the mid-1990s of trying to understand the import and novelty of the late twentieth-century global financial expansion. That moment, begun in the early 1970s and still present, saw the value of the world's financial holdings double, triple, and seemingly cease to have much relevance to the value of tangible goods and labor. Had capitalism transformed? Had it entered a new phase of development? Arrighi wondered. "It was in this intellectual atmosphere that I discovered in the second and third volumes of Fernand Braudel's trilogy, *Capitalism and Civilization*," Arrighi writes in the preface to *The Long Twentieth Century*.[19] "In [Braudel's] interpretative scheme," he continues, the soaring value of "finance capital is not a particular stage of world capitalism, let alone its latest and highest stage. Rather, it is a recurrent phenomenon which has marked the capitalist era from its earliest beginnings in late medieval and early modern Europe." Arrighi concludes by asserting that "throughout the capitalist era, financial expansions have signaled the transition from one regime of accumulation on a world scale to another. They are integral aspects of the recurrent destruction of 'old' regimes and the simultaneous creation of 'new' ones."[20]

I have found that replacing "finance capital" with "cat" accomplishes similar work and allows for the articulation of a feline critique in which cats designate an autumnal transition between states and stages of capitalism. *Marx for Cats* uses an interpretative scheme in which cats are not a particular stage of capitalism, let alone its highest stage. Rather, cats are a recurrent phenomenon that has marked the capitalist era from its earliest beginnings in late medieval and early modern Europe. Throughout the capitalist era, cats have signaled the transition from one regime of accumulation on a world scale to another. They are integral aspects of the recurrent destruction of old regimes and the simultaneous creation of new ones.

I have made a few amendments, of course.

Foremost, I have joined the longue durée approach to historical analysis with the bestiary approach to the representation of nonhuman animals. The bestiary genre is a creature of the Latinate Middle Ages, where, in many ways, our story begins. With support from a patron, a learned scholar would assemble a trove of pictures and stories, both real and fictive—the division itself carried little weight—into a "beast book" to document God's creations. Bestiaries followed the guidance offered in the Bible's Book of Job: "ask the animals, and they will teach you."[21] These illuminated books' depiction of beasts revealed crucial truths about the hierarchies that structured the God-made world. I like the bestiary because it connects past and present, allows for a visual logic alongside a verbal one, and, most importantly, takes animals seriously. In the Middle Ages, bestiaries' animal images offered a mnemonic device for those who could not read; here, in the twenty-first century, this text's animal images offer a mnemonic device for those who likely read too much and who, despite looking at animals constantly, require that a connection be made between Marx and animals, cats and class struggle.

Marx for Cats follows many bestiary conventions, including the complementary use of images alongside text, the primary placement of the lion to reflect its noble status, and a focus on the tripartite. Medieval bestiaries used tripartite groupings to accentuate the trinity of Father, Son, and Holy Ghost. For Marx, however, the trinity appeared differently:

[1]   Capital—profit (profit of enterprise plus interest),
[2]   land—ground-rent, [and] labour—and,
[3]   wages;

this is the trinity formula which comprises all the secrets of the social production process.[22]

Marx explicated his version of capitalism's own holy trinity throughout his career, but nowhere in as much depth as in his three volumes of *Capital*.

Each chapter of *Marx for Cats* is named for the feline that guides its local history, from kingly lions to rebellious domestic cats, from revolutionary tigers to divine lynxes, from wildcats to sabotage cats. As they accumulate, these chapters span a longue durée and offer three distinct yet overlapping histories. First, they detail how capitalism became capitalism, an economic system unlike any other in its capacious productive capacity and its rapacious destructive capacity. Second, this bestiary details how Marxism became Marxism, a form of economic and cultural criticism whose unmatched insights into the labor power of the human species have been hindered by its limited imagination of the community of species that labor. Yet in certain moments, Marxists and those similarly aligned have reached out in solidarity with other species, and many fellow travelers, from early proletarians to utopian socialists, Jacobins to abolitionists, October revolutionaries to Paris

Communards, have left archives of the fact of or the potential for interspecies solidarity among their ranks.

Finally, this bestiary offers a tale about how felines became cats, wild and domestic beasts who seem to have been and continue to be among the most represented animals in human culture, particularly where the economy is concerned. That is a far-reaching claim, and because such sweeping historical statements risk weakening their intended force, they should be used sparingly. But cats offer an occasion to do so. The American Marxist critic Fredric Jameson once claimed that the only acceptable transhistorical maxim might well be "always historicize."[23] Cats might very well be our originary transhistorical species, and I track a roughly twelve-hundred-year period from 800 CE to our present to provide a sense of how capitalism has changed cats and how cats have critiqued capitalism.

But for all its similarities, *Marx for Cats* crucially differs from so many bestiaries of yore. Medieval bestiaries contained a Christian moral lesson, but this bestiary imparts a Marxist conceptual one. Capitalism's tragic directions ask us to turn away from animals, to see them as our own, to do with them what we like. We must reject this invitation, and we must criticize it. How many deaths and burnings, factory farms and pandemics, will pass before we embrace a different animal history and thus a different animal future? Finally, mine is a *radical* bestiary. That overused adjective must be situated in its present context. *Radical* derives from the Latin *radic*, for *root*, a botanical etymology Marx identified but whose larger meaning he somehow missed when he argued that "to be radical is to go to the root of the matter. For man, however, the root is man himself."[24] Roots appear radical and tracing their genesis unearths a multiplicity of potentials, some of which lie beyond the scope of "man." Another subterranean past of radical comrades and their cats, and radical cats and their comrades, has existed for centuries; we need only to excavate it.

To understand the economic system of capitalism fully, one starts with its predecessor, feudalism, the economic system of the Christian Middle Ages, whose archive is dominated by multiple felines: empire-seeking Christian kings were called lions, and devils appeared in the form of domestic cats. The lion was not only a symbol of imperialism, however; it was also an imperial conquest. Lions are not indigenous to northern Europe— not for the past twelve thousand years at least. Rather, they were a prized imperial bounty or donation in an empire-making age. Likewise, cats' fantastic shape-shifting abilities allowed them to appear everywhere, as they were said to host the spirits of Jews and witches. Philosophers contended with accusations of possessing catlike intentions, as did vegetarians. The presence of cats guides a historical narrative as they were on the scene for the Christian Crusades, technological invention, and the elimination of the commons of Europe—spaces where peasants shared land and resources collectively and where animals roamed freely. These medieval beasts and their economic resonance are the subjects of chapters 1 and 2.

When the Middle Ages ended with the bubonic plague pandemic and the first iterations of wage labor and merchant capital began to take hold, cats as symbols of economic power and economic disinheritance did not disappear; they were transformed. The ship that delivered the first abducted Africans into Virginia was named *The White Lion*, a claim to both racial and regal power, and this ship introduces into my book the trans-Atlantic slave trade, the largest forced migration in world history. White masters, white indentured servants, and Black slaves arrived on the thriving and diverse continent of First Nations America. The Haudenosaunee traced their lineage back to the Sky Lynx; other Algonquin nations believed that the underwater panther warded off evil and offered them protection. But that feline's power could not stave off successive waves of European colonialism.

As European settler colonists began their continent-wide genocide against indigenous Americans and developed a nascent capitalist economy built on a synthesis of stolen land and racial slavery, their own thoughts turned to freedom. "We hold these truths to be self-evident," declared lion aficionado and founding father Thomas Jefferson, "that all men are created equal."[25] Jefferson's story illustrates just how difficult it can be to distinguish tragedy from farce. Sometimes capitalist history seems "like a cross between a nightmare and a bad joke," in the words of Trinidadian Marxist C. L. R. James; the "L" stands for Lionel.[26] Revolutions were made in this era in France, the United States, and Haiti, and cats did their part in each. Haitian rebel leader Toussaint Louverture ordered his troops to "fight like tigers," while French Jacobin Maximilien Robespierre was described by friends and enemies alike as possessing "a general aspect to that of a cat."[27] Colonization and revolution, as modern nation states come into being and with them fledgling capitalist economies, are the subjects of chapters 3 and 4.

The French and American were the great bourgeois revolutions, and they gave rise to the class for which Marx saves some his most cutting and sometimes most feline words: the bourgeoisie. It is this class that Marx believed had thus far "played the most revolutionary role" in history.[28] The bourgeoisie occupies the role of a transformative class because it spreads capitalism the world over. It is this class that, finally, presents domestic cats in a manner relatable to us today. Quirky, independent, speculative, and — a favorite word of the bourgeoisie — "ours," cats under bourgeois direction are used to sell trinkets and populate cat shows. Yet as the bourgeoisie establishes its legitimacy in the nineteenth century, it likewise confronts its own antagonisms: the American Civil War, various English uprisings, more civil war in France, and the appearance of an in-

FIGURE INTRO.2. Cat meme, 2019. The internet has long been interested in feline ambivalence as a critique of work.

ternationalist commune in Paris, in 1871, led in part by a great cat lover. In these moments of tumult and turmoil, various cats appear on the historical scene. The bourgeoisie and its feline friends and phantoms are detailed in chapters 5 and 6.

Along with the rise of the bourgeoisie occurred that of the leading capitalist empires funded by the first truly global investment banks, the so-called financial houses. With them came decades of financial panic, profit, and plunder. Socialists like John Hobson noted that these banks were a "cat's paw" for imperialism.[29] Cat lover Vladimir Lenin agreed. A domestic feline symbol was drafted by the International Workers of the World, who called for a single laborers' union to fight the forces of global capitalism. In those moments of labor organization and uprising, workers crooned about a cat they called the "sabo-tabby," or sabotage cat. "The fight is tough, and you can't see through it? Shut your traps, and a cat will do it," they sang.[30] From the successful Russian Revolution to the failed German one, cats participated in re-envisioning what a twentieth-century socialist state could be and for whom it could function.

After World War II, communist cats and capitalist cats entered both domestic and international politics. At the height of monopoly capital's Cold War, three years before the famous Stonewall riots, the police raided the Black Cat gay bar in Los Angeles and the CIA launched Operation Acoustic Kitty, in which it used microphone-equipped cats to spy on the Soviets. The FBI trained its own focus on the Black Panthers, whose feline message of armed revolt resounded across the United States and indeed the world. As the Panthers called for replacing capitalism with an economic system of material and racial equality, neoliberal economists including Milton Friedman and Friedrich Hayek used their own feline language to insist capitalism must be bolstered and protected. With the rise of the internet as the medium of communication, whether for work or entertainment, a digital cat emerged, this one an absurd cat, a cat meme. As various digital felines peer out from every computer desktop and phone screen, they ask us: what does it mean to work and why do we do it? The many contours of the long feline twentieth century are detailed in chapters 7 and 8.

We will attend to these moments and many more as felines dart in and out of history, unsure of whether to stay or
go. Each of the four parts of this book is segmented by a condensed dialectic intermezzo. His conception of the dialectic is
perhaps Marx's most important contribution to understanding
how economic contradiction drives history. It is the dialectic
through which Marx asks: How is capitalism both regressive
and progressive? How does the bourgeoisie undermine itself
through its victories? How will communism emerge from
capitalism? And how did capitalism emerge from feudalism? I
have found it necessary to modify some of the great dialectical
propositions of Marxism into feline form. It is here that the
lord-bondsman dialectic becomes the lion-cat dialectic and a
materialist consideration of a signifier-signified pairing takes
feline form. These short dialectic intermezzos allow for some
particularly trenchant problems to be considered in properly
philosophical language as the narrative of the book leaps from
one historical moment to the next.

Marx for Cats is intended for both novice and seasoned
critics of capitalism, for dedicated cat lovers as well as for those
who are allergic. It is for those who have always wondered:
Why do cats continue to endure as symbols, tropes, and memes, century after century? How does the medieval cat so care-
fully stitched into a tapestry relate to the nineteenth-century
satirical cat of French newspapers or the Felix the Cat cartoon
of the 1920s? Why does respect equate to an act of lionizing
and weakness to one of pussying out? Why are cats cherished
and hated so passionately and by so many different constitu-
encies in so many different historical moments?

As we answer these questions, we will follow Argentine
Marxist Che Guevara's haunting observation: "At the risk of
seeming ridiculous, let me say that the true revolutionary is
guided by a great feeling of love."[31] For too long, cats, indeed all
animals, have been excluded from the reach of that loving revo-

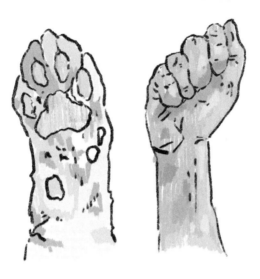

FIGURE INTRO.3. An Contreras Nino, *Interspecies Solidarity*, 2020. Courtesy of Leigh Claire La Berge.

lutionary embrace. The time has come to amend that exclusion. Angela Davis, a Marxist and former Black Panther who came of philosophical age during Che's time and who is still with us today, tells us why such an amendment is important: "The prioritizing of humans also leads to restrictive definitions of who counts as human, and the brutalization of animals is related to the brutalization of human animals."[32] She suggests, too, how to do the amending: "I think that would really be revolutionary: to develop a kind of repertoire, a habit, of imagining the relations, the human relations and the nonhuman relations behind all of the objects that constitute our environment."[33] *Marx for Cats* offers one such imagining.

Menace and Menagerie

THE FEUDAL MODE OF
PRODUCTION AND ITS CATS,
800–1500

PART I

1

Lion Kings

"The Greek word leo *is translated as 'king' in Latin, because he is the ruler of all the beasts."*

—ISIDORE OF SEVILLE, *THE ETYMOLOGIES*

n 799 CE, Alcuin of York penned a letter to Adalard of Corbie, the subject of which was the recently assaulted pope, Leo III. Alcuin, scholar, teacher, and member of Charlemagne's court, inquired of Adalard, Charlemagne's cousin, a count, and a monk turned abbot, as to the goings-on between Charlemagne and the pope, whose assailants had famously sought to cut out his tongue and remove his eyes. Pope Leo III had left Rome and fled to Paderborn, in present-day Germany, to seek Charlemagne's military protection. The pope's turn toward this rising Frankish ruler in 799 would garner more significance in 800, when he crowned Charlemagne Holy Roman Emperor, thus uniting church and state—the pairing for which the Middle Ages remain known.

FIGURE 1.1. Charlemagne's Holy Roman imperial door decoration, date unknown, Aachen, present-day Germany.

Perhaps to disguise his palace intrigue, or maybe simply to have fun, in his letter Alcuin used not the Christian names of those about whom he inquired but animal appellations. Pope Leo III became the "Eagle." Ruler Charlemagne became the "Lion." Alcuin's addressee, Adalard, was now a "Cock," while the letter writer himself was a "Sparrow."[1] The Sparrow wrote that he was waiting for the Cock to crow so he could find out: what of this new alliance between the Eagle and the Lion?

Welcome to the Middle Ages, by which we denote the centuries after the Roman Empire but before the many empires of capitalism. Our first chapter begins where Marx's own history of capitalism does: when the economy and, therefore, society were organized through feudalism, a war-making, agriculture-based economic system a bit more technologically advanced than the Greco-Roman slave mode of production that preceded it, but still stale and stubborn compared to the capitalist system that would follow. Marx starts here, he explains, because "the economic structure of capitalist society has grown out of the economic structure of feudal society. The dissolution of the latter set free the elements of the former."[2]

But we start with Charlemagne not because Marx does but because Charlemagne's rule offers in incipient form the three historical problems that will guide the twelve-century arc of *Marx for Cats:* felines, dialectics, and empires. Charlemagne was called the first (he was a lion), he transformed the second (it was at his court that the return to dialectics began after a Christian-led hiatus that lasted several centuries), and he reinstated the third (after the fall of the Roman Empire in the late fifth century CE, Charlemagne was the first to reconstitute an imperial state anew: namely, his Frankish Christian Empire of the early ninth century).

Who was Charlemagne? On the one hand, who cares? He was an emperor, a pillager, an enslaver, and a hunter, and there is a reason that few Marxists write biographies. On the other hand, he orients us to a different time, a feudal time. No story of capitalism is complete without some mention of its feudal origins, and that is no less true of the feline critique of political economy that this book proposes.

Marx alludes to a certain animality of the period: "The Middle Ages constitutes the animal history of humankind, its zoology," he writes.[3] As the epistle from Alcuin to Adalard demonstrates, we may interpret Marx's claim with some amount of literalness. But there is a theoretical point, too. Marx emphasizes that the period is zoological as part of his attempt to distinguish the nonhuman animal from the human in terms of its abilities to make and inhabit history. Just as an individual grows into maturity, so does the human species. Throughout his oeuvre, Marx returns to this feudal "animal history" to isolate what is truly unique about capitalist history: as humans make history they leave their animal past behind.

Marx claims that these zoological years were "shrouded in darkness." We may remember the now outdated term "the Dark Ages." Of course, no age is defined only by what is obscured. Writing in 1330, at the tail end of the age, the Italian historian Petrarch qualified that these years, "although they were surrounded by darkness and dense gloom," did nonetheless contain certain "men of genius" who "shone forth."[4] The economic historian and progenitor of the longue durée method Fernand Braudel calls these years "carnivorous" due to an increase in meat consumption.[5] The historian of science Lorraine Daston labels them years of wonder because of the many "monsters" and "miracles" that regularly appear in the historical record. She writes that many Europeans of the late Middle Ages believed "that the period in which they lived was both more qualitatively and quantitatively wondrous than earlier times."[6]

Whether they were darker, more carnivorous, or simply more wondrous—and the adjectives we may choose from tell us something—the Middle Ages were a different time: a time without capitalism. According to some, that absence produced more freedom; others claim it produced more constriction.

Marxists have put in hours mapping the precise coordinates of the transition from feudalism to capitalism, today memorialized in the so-called Brenner debate.[7] When did feudalism end and capitalism begin? countless Marxists have inquired. They have considered how peasants labored and for whom, how money circulated and where, and how a commercial society emerged from a Christian one. Yet none have considered the work and lives of felines in their estimation of these ages and the capitalism that sprang forth from them.

The first post-Roman, trans-European imperial rulers were distinguished by their relationships to big cats. Lion statues guarded courts and decorated palaces. The panther's breath was said to be as sweet as Christ's love, and Jesus Christ, the king of kings, was himself described as a lion. Reigning kings, too, were styled as lions. The Middle Ages were an era when god, church, army, and state were often one, and that one was often leonine.

At the lowly other end of hierarchical feudal life dwelled domestic cats, among the most persecuted members of medieval society. They left their mark during the centuries of imperial Christian Crusades, when they were consistently associated with Islam and thus needed to be vanquished, as did Muslims. Cats were persecuted because of their perceived devilish power, and they were regularly imagined as fantastic, war-making creatures in this age of ongoing war. From the great beasts to the diminutive ones, the first centuries of the feudal era revolved around all manner of cats—a fact to which the bestiary, this period's most famous literary genre, attests.

This historical period that opens our investigation remains perhaps the last acceptable site of democratic othering, that cruel practice whereby difference gives rise to dismissal. Look at the natives and how they lived! While that sort of assessment would be rightly considered offensive were it applied to most groups of people, somehow the Middle Ages endure as a site of historical gawking. Marx noted this, too. "It is very convenient to be liberal," he wrote, "at the expense of the middle ages."[8] Indeed, the ongoing application of the term *barbarian* to fifth- to seventh-century northern European groups of what are properly called *foederati* attests to this habit. But whatever one calls them, and whatever one thinks of them, one thing is clear about denizens of this era: they took their cats seriously.

AN EMPIRE OF LIONS

The imperial world of late Rome collapsed much as Ernest Hemingway said people go broke: gradually and then suddenly.

It collapsed through going broke, gradually, as steady access to cheap slave labor dried up, and suddenly, as ever-strengthening *foederati* from northern Europe made their way into a feuding south and finally delivered the coup de grâce in 476 CE.

Between the fall of the Roman empire and the rise of Charlemagne's comparatively small Frankish-Christian one, we can see why these ages were once called dark: urbanization, literacy, trade, and civic institutions were each circumscribed after the demise of Rome. Although the loss of such habits and organizations is often mourned, Rome's fall—which one scholar rightly calls "the cherished nightmare of the West"—brought about a certain freedom for many if not most occupants of this world.[9] Who built the cities, after all? Who undertook the trade routes and fought the wars? Who benefited from Rome's storied cosmopolitanism? What good was literacy and for whom? Indeed, we know from South Asian histories that people have fled literacy and abandoned writing as methods of fleeing surveillance and control by their social superiors.[10]

Guerilla-style wars and marronage communities proliferated with the loss of a single imperial power. Access to land increased for many people, as did the ability to keep more of their crop yields. Conversely, the production of the liberal arts declined and the standardization of coined money essentially ceased. Marx explains of peasants during this era that they "enjoyed the usufruct of the common land, which gave pasture to their cattle, furnished them with timber, fire-wood, turf."[11] Today we call this open land *the commons*, and rarely in history have they not been in a state of vanishing.

In the early centuries of the Middle Ages, Charlemagne and his ilk essentially ended this state of affairs. Marx singles him out for doing so. "The feudal system . . . had its origin . . . in the martial organisation of the army during the actual conquest. . . . Military service . . . was the chief means by which, as in a forcing house, Charlemagne brought about the transformation of free German peasants into serfs and bondsmen."[12] Charlemagne could only achieve this because his father had built a foundation for doing so, having himself vanquished a batch of aspiring imperial overlords. His father, Pepin the Short, the first of the Carolingian rulers, also introduced the first real cat, the lion, into our archive. To consolidate his own power in fractious mid-eighth-century Europe, Pepin staged a *venatio*, an old Roman-style hunting spectacle.

An imported lion was set in an enclosure with a bull, and court spectators were invited to witness the two captives maul each other to death. Unsurprisingly, the lion emerged victorious. Yet when asked to extricate the lion from its bloodied confine,

FIGURE 1.2. Pepin the Short with lion from *Chronique anonyme universelle*, fifteenth century, France.

Pepin's attendants refused. Pepin then did so himself, thereby bolstering his reputation as the kind of fearsome leader who could subdue a lion and, by extension, various roving military foes.

But an empire, even a nascent one, cannot run on cat tricks alone. Pepin the Short began the long road back to some kind of standardized currency, the consolidation of different land holdings, and an alliance with the Catholic church—a project Charlemagne would complete, drawing together lands that today span France, Germany, and parts of Italy. From that unity emerged feudalism, which Marx calls the feudal mode of production. Many peasants and slaves became serfs. Pagans were converted to Christianity. An economic "synthesis developed between donations of land and bonds of service."[13] A ruler would allot a parcel of land to a local chief, who would then pledge his military service to said ruler. That chief would allot smaller plots of land to peasants, who would pledge a certain amount of their yield to the chief, along with a certain amount of their life. It all amounted to "a web of servile obligations" and generations of "hereditary subjection."[14]

Marx explains the basic social structure: "In the earlier epochs of history, we find almost everywhere a complicated arrangement of society into various orders, a manifold gradation of social rank. In ancient Rome we have patricians, knights, plebeians, slaves; in the Middle Ages, feudal lords, vassals, guild-masters, journeymen, apprentices, serfs; in almost all of these classes, again, [we find] subordinate gradations."[15] We can, with some frustration, accept that this is the manner in which history is organized and comes down to us. Why else even mention Pepin the Short? But we must also find a way beyond these hierarchies and give representation to such subordinate gradations. That is the real task of Marxism, and that is what cats offer the Marxist critic.

Charlemagne himself possessed a lion, along with a bear and some monkeys. He was known by his contemporaries as "the lion who reigns over all living creatures and wild beasts."[16] And when, on Christmas Day, 800 CE, Charlemagne was crowned emperor of the newly created Holy Roman Empire, it was another kind of lion, Pope Leo III, who placed the crown on his head.

Non-Marxist historians interested in animals have been partial to Charlemagne's famous elephant, Abul-Abbas, gifted to him by Harun al-Rashid, the leader of the Abbasid caliphate. Charlemagne himself had gifted al-Rashid some "Frankish dogs noted for their nimbleness . . . an anecdote tells of them capturing a lion."[17] Marxists have focused on Charlemagne's economic reforms and policies, almost entirely neglecting his zoological world. We may combine the two approaches, as Charlemagne's imperial appetite hardly excluded the work of animals. He impressed his own elephant into war and in 810 CE marched it and his army north to face a fleet of Viking ships sacking the coast of Frisia, in present-day Netherlands. Perhaps he knew of the Norse divinity Freyja, a goddess of war pulled in a chariot by two domestic cats, and expected an animal confrontation. Abul-Abass died en route.

When not hunting or making war, Charlemagne busied himself with trying to reconstitute some of the trappings of imperial monetary and intellectual life. Marxist historian Perry Anderson notes that during the course of Charlemagne's reign "the coinage system returned and was standardized . . . in close coordination with the church" and "the Carolingian monarchy sponsored a renovation of literature, philosophy, art and education."[18] As new coins began to circulate, so did new styles of argumentation. This connection between money and ideas we introduce now and will note repeatedly throughout our study as capital both demands and produces cosmopolitan cultures. Alcuin—the "Sparrow" with whom this chapter began—was a fixture at Charlemagne's court and the host of and emissary to a number of theological debates, so-called Christological controversies. Was Charlemagne's diktat concerning Christ's

FIGURE 1.3. Freyja, Norse goddess of war, with cat-drawn chariot. Print by Ludwig Pietsch, 1865.

resurrection correct because he said it? Or should the truth be realized through pronouncement or debate?

At the court of the Lion, the Sparrow began to revive the dialectic, or the path to truth through opposition. A method of inquiry well known to philosophers in the ancient world, dialectics had been banished by several centuries of Christian-led thought. To realize truth, the dialectical method insists, one must consider what might not be true—a risky proposition in the ninth century since it meant considering the non-truth of Christ. Alcuin ventured forth, even if he arrived at the expected conclusion that "things have been confirmed through a series of questions and answers so that nothing else remains but to confess that Jesus Christ is truly God."[19]

Now, strangely, we find ourselves in an intellectual lineage that ultimately ends with Marx. True, Marx himself was little interested in the particulars of medieval theology. But, as we will soon see, the dialectics developed therein nonetheless informed his thought through the intermediary of a certain G. W. F. Hegel.

Historians conjecture that Charlemagne never recovered from the loss of his elephant and that the animal's death hastened his own. In departing for heaven, Charlemagne left a world of "increasing subjection" and "generalized serfdom."[20] He bequeathed to his sons a rehabilitated empire, an iconography of lions, and a style of feline accumulation: power through land and land through lions. Once introduced into feudal social and economic organization, the lion would never depart.

In 1066, William the Conqueror left Normandy and invaded Anglo-Saxon England, carrying with him a crest of two lions in repose. We have two records of William's invasion, which effectively brought feudal relations out of continental Europe and into England. In William's own recollection his self-reported savagery takes a feline form:

> I . . . caused the death of thousands by starvation and war, especially in Yorkshire. . . . In a mad fury I descended on the English of the north like a raging lion, and ordered that their homes and crops and all their equipment and furnishings should be burnt at once and their great flocks and herds of sheep and cattle slaughtered everywhere . . . alas! I was the cruel murderer of many thousands, both young and old.[21]

The leonine aspect of William's invasion was memorialized in the famous eleventh-century Bayeux Tapestry, an embroidered history of the conquest eighty panels long.

In one of the tapestry's panels, a lion has its tail wrapped around several other animals, each of whom represent their own localities, thus demonstrating the imperial reach of the lion. The English lion's tail encircles Guernsey (represented by a donkey), Jersey (represented by a toad), and Alderney (represented by a puffin). This feline tail records the present-day Channel Islands becoming an English possession.

After ordering surveys of his newly seized lands and assembling them into the *Domesday Book*, William then allotted parcels of English land to his accompanying Norman lords and nobles, creating a French lineage of English rulers that would last for centuries. One accompanying member of William's army was Ingelram de Lyons, Lord of Lyons, who would be granted English land and soon be joined by his relative, Nicholas de Lyons. Together they would propagate the famous and long-lasting Lyons family, whose coat of arms included, obviously, lions, and whose motto was *Noli irritare leones* (Do not provoke the lions).[22] We will encounter this lineage again.

Marx stresses the land-based nature of feudal power, writing that "the lord *'appears* as king of the estate', even though he actually 'belongs to the land' himself," and that "in feudal times the functions of general and judge were attributes of landed property."[23] Perhaps it was because feudal wealth came from land that rulers styled themselves as territorial and carnivorous animals, especially big cats. We see less anthropomorphizing in this era than we see its opposite, zoomorphism, the applica-

FIGURE 1.4. Detail of the Bayeux Tapestry depicting leonine aggression, 11th century, Normandy, present-day France. Photograph by Jake Woodnut.

FIGURE 1.5. Lion sallet (battle helmet), 11th century, Normandy, present-day France. Photograph by Jake Woodnut. Courtesy of the Metropolitan Museum of Art, New York

tion of animal traits to humans. Charlemagne was called a lion by others. William called himself a lion. Nobles took "Lyons" or "Lyon" as their name. They donned lion emblems on their bodies, their coats of arms, and their battle helmets, too, in later years. Lions symbolized economic power, certainly, but that symbolism has its own materiality. As they represented imperial conquest in feline terms, lions were creatures of another's empire; in becoming creatures of human empire, they were removed from their own.

Peasants, too, were animal-like and tied to the land, but in a different manner. Marx's sometimes coauthor Friedrich Engels noted in his own study of medieval society that the peasant was "everywhere treated as a 'beast of burden.'"[24] In his twelfth-century study of Ireland, Gerald of Wales exemplifies this sentiment: "The Irish people . . . are a people getting their living from animals alone and living like animals; a people who have not abandoned the first mode of living—the pastoral life."[25]

Thomas Paine, an eighteenth-century avant-garde Marxist-lite, to whom we will return in chapter 3, had this to say about the relationship between imperial succession and animality: "Kings succeed each other, not as rationals, but as animals. . . . It requires some talents to be a common mechanic; but to be a King requires only the animal figure of a man."[26] That figure, again and again, was a big cat, a fact that hardly escaped political philosopher Niccolò Machiavelli. "As a prince is obliged to know how to act like a beast," writes Machiavelli, "he should learn from the fox and the lion."[27]

But what would the prince actually learn? How to flourish among fragile alliances and internecine squabbling? How to negotiate interfamily drama, up to and including murderous attacks? The eating of the young of one's enemies? The use of urine as a marker of territory?

In fact, comparisons between the feudal mode of production and social organization within lion prides abound. Machiavelli's advice to the prince might also have applied to lions: Control territory as though one's life depends on it, which it usually does. Make warlike incursions into others' lands. Reproduce often. (The 20 to 30 percent child mortality rate in medieval Europe, while low compared with an 80 percent death rate among lion cubs, is still quite high from our vantage point today.)

Lions need their territory to survive. Feudal princes and kings needed theirs, too. The feudal mode of production offered low crop yields and little agricultural or labor surplus. Goods produced by the peasantry rarely circulated beyond the land from which they came, and distribution was mostly local. And, most importantly, Marx notes that production "served as the immediate source of subsistence for the producers themselves. Most products did not become commodities; they were

FIGURE 1.6. Karl Joseph Simrock, *Henry the Lion*, 1844.

accordingly neither converted into money nor entered at all into the general process of the social metabolism."[28]

Most products did not become commodities. How truly different these ages were from our own.

Without broad commodity circulation, to say nothing of monetary circulation, lords and nobles levied taxes. Peasants were taxed when they married. They were taxed when they died. They were taxed when their children married. They were taxed by the church. They were taxed by their lord. Their animals were taxed. Still, for any ruler to solidify his power, he had to expand his land holdings. Lions don't stray far from their home territories, and their territories are modest, as are, it seems, their ambitions. Not so for lion kings and their nobles, who began to raise their armies and set out on an expansive trail of antisemitic and anti-Islamic violence—the famous Christian Crusades.

Enter the royals Richard the Lionheart, William the Lion, and Henry the Lion. Richard the Lionheart allowed William the Lion to buy himself out of a treaty and used the money to fund his crusade to the holy lands. Henry the Lion also journeyed east, crusading with the Knights Templar (soon to be entangled with cats), whom we'll meet in chapter 2.

Our story now moves out of continental Europe and heads east to the Levant. Feudal adventurism has its own grisly history in which the acknowledged cannibalism of the Christian Crusaders stands out as a particular nadir. Indeed, the whole scene of the Crusades is so gruesome and surreal that we are almost won over by the historical narrative that these men went on their spree of raping, torturing, and killing out of a sense of religious determination.

That may be partially true, but we need an economic answer, too. In Marxism, we always need an economic answer. No doubt Richard the Lionheart descended on the Levant for Christendom, but he also went for money. No doubt he carried Christ in his brave heart, but he also scouted and sought to secure new trade routes. As Marxist political theorist Benno Teschke explains, "the Crusades were a feudal land grab."[29] They were a feudal land grab because Henry the Lion and Richard the Lionheart needed more land. Yet they have a religious appearance because, as Engels explains, "class struggles of that time appear to bear religious earmarks."[30]

They also bear feline earmarks.

Part of the crusaders' ideological degradation of their Islamic enemies was based on Muslim appreciation of cats. The prophet Muhammad so cared for his cat, Meuzza, that he once cut around the prayer robe the cat was sleeping on rather than disturb the feline as he heeded the call to pray. Muhammad's fondness for cats is conveyed in his famous hadith, "Affection for cats is part of faith." One of the prophet's companions, Abu Hurairah was a prolific generator of such hadiths and known for his own associations with cats. Indeed, his name was derived from the beasts. "I was called Abu Hurairah because I would tend to the goats of my family, and one day I found a stray kitten which I placed in my sleeve. When I returned to my people they heard the kitten purr in my sleeve and they asked, 'What is that, O 'Abd Shams?' I replied, 'A kitten I found.' 'So you are Abu Hurairah (Father of cats),' they responded and the name stuck thereafter."[31]

Muslims, for their part, saw these invading Christians as fierce but also as little more than "beasts" and "dogs" (no doubt their cannibalism didn't help matters). The assessment of Christians as canine by Muslims was likewise a moral one, as they considered cats hygienic and dogs filthy. In Christian medieval depictions of previous wars in the holy land, the cat was associated with cowardice and degradation. Describing an image in a certain medieval text, one scholar notes, "The illustration of the great army of the Syrians is paralleled in the commentary foundel [picture] by the depiction of a ragged figure kneeling before a cat on the altar and kissing it below the tail."[32]

Cats in multiple forms enter into some of the most dramatic

moments and techniques of the Crusades. The great battle of Richard's Third Crusade was, like the first two crusades, a loss for the Christians. The Lionheart wanted Jerusalem under Christian control; according to one historian he "all but emptied the kitty in pursuit of his aim."[33] The Christians used a weapon simply called the Cat. The Cat was "a wooden structure built (or moved) up to a defensive wall.... [The Cat's mechanical] arm could be manipulated to claw away at the castle wall—hence the name."[34] Cats were also imagined as fantastic creatures of war making. Yet in the decisive Battle of Hattin, Muslims prevailed. They surrounded the crusaders' camp so closely that "a cat could not have escaped," according to witness of record Ibn-al-Athir.[35]

It was supposedly during Richard's failure-laden journey home that he earned his leonine appellation. Captured by King Modard of Almayn, he was imprisoned, and a lion was sent to devour him in his cell. Richard, like Pepin the Short, overcame the lion. He did so by removing and ultimately eating its heart—thus he became Lionheart. He did not capture Jerusalem, but he did return home with a new sobriquet, and, serendipitously, kings could levy a tax if they were captured and had to pay a ransom. So, having escaped from lions and Muslims, one of Richard's own guards accidentally shot him with an arrow and he died, likely of gangrene, in 1199. Today he is perhaps best remembered in popular culture as a Disney character, in *Robinhood*, where he is a lion king. It's a perfect image, really: king, Christ, and lion are one. When Richard the Lionheart died, his death announcement contained a coat of arms bearing three lions. The basic composition remains today and is used by the British royal family as well as by the English national soccer team.

By 1235 lions had been installed in the royal menagerie at the Tower of London, which colloquially became known as Lion Tower. Heraldry, the canon of icons that organize coats of arms, had become more developed and diverse. It began to include multiple variations on the presentation of lions and their corresponding significance: the color, number, and bodily posture of lions were transformed into chains of noble meaning. Likewise, the definition of the word *lion* itself expanded. By the late Middle Ages the term referred to both the giant cat and a desirable person.

Unsurprisingly, when the city of London recently decided to memorialize the terrors and torments that animals of so many menageries had endured, century after century, at the Lion Tower, lions featured prominently. Medieval animal images often have distinctive human-like facial characteristics, said to emphasize the pedagogical relatability between human and beast. In contrast, the memorial lions have a realistic hollowness and sadness that no doubt accompanied them on their journeys from the East to northern Europe and that renders them distinct from the period they represent.

BESTIARUM VOCABULUM: A BOOK OF BEASTS

While heraldry remains the most popular and best-known category of medieval design—no doubt because of its ongoing use today—the visual logic of armorial animals derived from the most famous literary genre of the Middle Ages, the *bestiarum vocabulum*, or book of beasts. Now called bestiaries, these texts emerged in the twelfth and thirteenth centuries, at the high point of medieval cultural production, along with universities and cathedrals. And of this genre, the lion was undoubtedly the star. Scholars and scholastics wrote of lions, and lions graced the stained glass windows of Europe's most vaunted buildings.

Like so many things medieval, the bestiary is a Christianized version of a Greco-Roman form. Whereas the ancient book had been a compendium of animal descriptions, the medieval form added illustrious, or "illuminated," images as well as a moral element. Animals were presented with their habits and traits, both of which were construed as biblical lessons.

Ein Schloß mit Ainer Katzen an Zue Zündten.

Kugelen hinrachen die
da Lauffenr vnnd frer
renr.

Nimb fünff haill Salitter, Zway thil

Cattus grandis esset fiat quemadmodum affat

scores quadratie si vndiquas bn (mmitus

hunc voluant homines abint quatuor rotis

d op singua lambit, morsu venenoso disrumpit

turres propugnacula, domos muros cantalum̄

FIGURE 1.7 (*opposite*). Feline flight as medieval military craft. Franz Helm, Manuscript Codex 109, 1584. Source: Kislak Center for Special Collections, Rare Books and Manuscripts, University of Pennsylvania.

FIGURE 1.8 (*above*). "Cattis Grandis," Manuscript Codex 63. Source: Staatsbibliothek Göttingen.

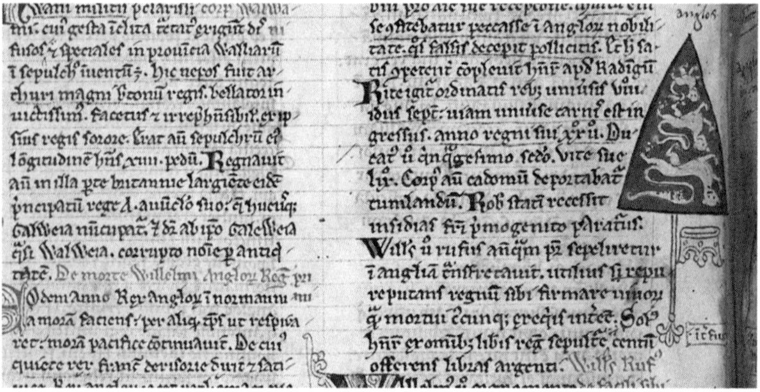

FIGURE 1.9. Richard the Lionheart's coat of arms (inverted). Matthew Paris, *Chronica majora*, thirteenth century, St. Albans, England. Source: The British Library.

FIGURE 1.10. Contemporary memorial to menagerie animals at the Tower of London. Sculptor: Kendra Haste, 2010. Photograph by Julian Mason, Matt Brown, James Burke, and Tammy Young Heck.

FIGURE 1.11. Detail of medieval bestiary: resurrection of lion cubs.
From *Two Lions*, about 1270. Tempera colors, gold leaf, and ink on
parchment. The J. Paul Getty Museum, Los Angeles, Manuscript
Ludwig XV 3 (83.MR.173), fol. 68.

Ancient bestiaries had contained lions, too, and no lesser authority than Aristotle had offered consideration of them in his study the *History of Animals*. But the medieval bestiary was distinguished by the lion's placement in the text: the lion always appeared as the first entry. He did so because he was king. And because Christ, himself a king, was a lion. Lion kings, meanwhile, were earthly representatives of Christ.

Guillaume le Clerc's 1210 bestiary, *Bestiaire divin*, notes:

> It is proper that we should first speak of the nature of the lion, which is a fierce and proud beast and very bold. It has three especially peculiar characteristics. In the first place it always dwells upon a high mountain. From afar off it can scent the hunter who is pursuing it. . . . Another wonderful peculiarity of the lion is that when it sleeps its eyes are wide open, and clear and bright. The third characteristic is likewise very strange. For when the lioness brings forth her young, it falls to the ground, and gives no sign of life until the third day, when the lion breathes upon it and in this way brings it back to life again.[36]

Three peculiar features; three days of stillborn cub lifelessness before resurrection; father, son, and holy ghost—the Christian trinity—may also be rendered lion, king, and Christ. Thus, there appear three lions on the Lionheart's coat of arms. Everything about the lion comes in three to reflect its Christlike character.

Domestic cats, too, appear in bestiaries, where they may be seen attending to their genitals or chasing mice out of a page's bounded text and into its marginalia—a kind of medieval postmodernism. Oxford-educated Bartholomaeus Anglicus, for example, notes in his late thirteenth-century bestiary, *De proprietatibus rerum*, that the cat is "a full lecherous beast in youth, swift, pliant, and merry, and leapeth and reseth on everything that is to fore him." The language moves from moralizing to descriptive, and the latter section includes a physical

locis quibz ille uersantur. quo rapiente uisu simules generent
Inde. E quod quidam gignelas mulieres uiderit nullos intue-
ri tpissimos animalium uultus. ut scenophalos et simias.
ne uisibz occurrentes simules fetus pariant; Han enim femi-
narum. cc. nascam. ut qles psyexerirt. siue ste conteperirt
in extremo uoluptatis estu dum coiciprurt talem isobolem
parerent; rerum animalia uisu uenerio formas extrinsec
transmitturt intr. eorumq; saciata typis. rapit species eorum
ippam qualitatem; In animantibz bigenia dicunt q; ex did-
sis nascuntr. ut mulus. ex eq rasino. burdo ex equo rasina.
ybride ex apis iportis. tpri ex oue ihyrco. musino ex capra rarie-
te. est autem dux gregis; De musi

O H E.
usio apellatus
qd muribz infest sit.
hunc uulgus catum
a captura uocant. Alii
dicunt quod captat
i. uidet; Bsam tanto
acute cernit; ut ful-
gore luminis noctis
tenebras superet; Vn-
de a greco uenit catus idest ingeniosus; De mure.

Vs pusillum animal grecum no-
men. E. quidqd u ex eo trahit. lati-
num sit; Alii dicunt mures qd ex umore
tre nascant; Bsam huiuis cia i muis. i. he-
inplenilunio iecur crescit.
sicut quedam marittima augentur. que rur-
sul minuente luna deficiunt;

De mvstela

FIGURE 1.12. Page from the medieval Ashmole Bestiary: cats and mice framing the margins.

attribute that becomes in *Marx for Cats* a concept: the feline leap. Indeed, one of the earliest recorded English-language usages of the term is itself feline; a *leap* as a group of leopards circulates in thirteenth- and fourteenth-century English.

Bestiaries record a domestic cat both appreciated for its physical attributes and joie de vivre and seen with suspicion as a result of the same attributes. Thus, another element of Christian zoology was to cast modest aspersions on cats and offer some equivocation as to their character and holiness. This cat entry continues:

> and when he taketh a mouse, he playeth therewith, and eateth him after the play.... And he maketh a ruthful noise and ghastful, when one proffereth to fight with another: and unneth is hurt when he is thrown down off an high place. And when he hath a fair skin, he is as it were proud thereof, and goeth fast about: and when his skin is burnt, then he bideth at home; and is oft for his fair skin taken of the skinner, and slain and flayed.[37]

Lecherous. Ashamed and less useful if it had dark fur. (People indeed wore catskins.) The cat lands on its feet, not when it springs but when "he is thrown down." Such descriptions alert us to the fact that the cat was far from the lion, perhaps closer to the leopard, which was understood in bestiaries to be the offspring of the illicit sexual liaison between the lion (leo) and a cat called the *pard* and was associated with the leap.

The lion was the only noble cat. One historian today notes that "felines such as the ocelot, the leopard, [and] the panther were [understood to be the] reincarnated souls of sinners that bore the signs of their sins."[38] Each feline's coat contained blackness and that was enough to signify its fallen nature, as cats began to be participants in the development of medieval racial codes.[39]

The Aberdeen Bestiary connects the etymology of the word *cat* with another of the animal's physical attributes. "It is commonly called catus, cat, from captura, the act of catching. Others say it gets the name from capto, because it catches mice with its sharp eyes. For it has such piercing sight that it overcomes the dark of night with the gleam of light from its eyes. As a result, the Greek word catus means sharp, or cunning."[40] This particular attribute, feline vision, will migrate from domestic cat to lynx with the initiation of imperial voyages from Europe to the Americas.

While the bestiaries represented the lion as beyond reproach, the domestic cat began to assume the opposite role. We cannot fully appreciate this literary history until we witness how Christians began to hunt, torture, and terrorize cats in subsequent centuries. As feudalism took the lion as its medium and message, it began extinguishing the domestic cat. That is the subject of our next chapter, but for now we must note that, like the organization of land, nobility, and war, bestiaries were part of the feudal mode of production. They appear Christian in meaning and method, but so do the Crusades, and those were for Christ *and* land. Naturally, the lion has the starring role in these beast books; kings were lions, and lions, kings. Lions rule over and extract from the poor, or the beasts of burden. Of course, those poor beasts were not reading bestiaries. Slathered in gold, bestiaries had patrons and were composed by and for nobles and clergy. They were mostly written in the holy language, Latin, which was becoming more rarefied with each passing year. Bestiaries reflect their own conditions of emergence. Feudalism as a mode of production was becoming more disconnected from and threatened by the social world from which it emerged and over which it governed.

In their disparate cat assessments bestiaries offer a foretelling of class conflict, which the few Marxists who have considered them have tended to overlook. Literary critic Fredric Jameson, for example, sees in the bestiary: "The medieval conception of the world as God's book, in which for example the beasts are so many sentences in a bestiary.... [They are] still close enough to [a] naive coding to convey [their] atmosphere to us."[41] His is an oversimplification, a surprising one from a critic who should know better but for whom any truly complex history begins with modernity. Only Marxist philosopher Louis Althusser could see in the genre both a past and a future, if in an incomprehensible manner:

> Just as at the dawn of Human History the first stammerings of the Oriental Spirit—joyous captive of the giants of the sky, the sea and the desert and then of its stone bestiary— already betrayed the unconscious presage of the future achievements of the Absolute spirit, so in each instant of Time the past survives in the form of a memory of what it has been; that is, as the whispered promise of the present.[42]

For Jameson, the bestiary represents a stalled history of a long-vanished past whose relationship between image and meaning is too literal. Using the example of the bestiary, Althusser explains cultural artifacts both record the past and offer a sense of a then-future in our present. And that we can certainly sense in medieval bestiaries. Neither really offers a site for Marxist interpretation of the bestiary tales, yet one can be located.

As the nobility and the church sought to control peasants and extract their labor, peasants sought to live independent of such control. The domestic cat began as a worker with good eyesight and a quick pounce, but century after century it was transformed into something sinister. Peasants, we will see, along with the disenfranchised in a variety of times and places, were consigned to and eventually came to embrace the domestic cat. The lion, so saintly and valiant, can win a battle with any man or beast, but somehow begins to feel threatened by domestic shorthairs. The history of all hitherto existing society is—as Marx and Engels famously claimed—the history of class struggle, which, in the Middle Ages, was both a Christian struggle and a cat struggle. It was then that class history and cat history began to take dialectical form.

THE LION-CAT
DIALECTIC

Before we leave this particular medieval moment, what can we conclude about all of these lion kings? Charlemagne, a lion. William the Lion, king of Scotland. Richard the Lionheart, king of England. William, the Norman conqueror of England, a king who calls himself a lion? Henry the Lion, Duke of Saxony?

We can say this: as lions become symbols of heraldry, as rulers fashion themselves as lions, as both king and Christ are signified by but also *are* lions, domestic cats begin to appear as elements of social disorder. We noticed an outline of this dynamic during the anti-Muslim crusades and glimpsed it in the bestiaries.

And yet no sooner is that truth stated than we are presented with an irony: lions *are* cats. Lions and domestic cats are of the same kingdom, phylum, class, order and family. They are both *Felidae*. Not of the same genus and species, true. But there is more similarity here than difference. What then constitutes similarity and difference? How can one be a lion and not a cat?

To understand this strange feline contradiction that emerges in the Middle Ages and will continue into the development of capitalism and throughout this book, we must turn toward not only Marx's words but toward Marxist method, the dialectic, a philosophical form that precedes him and that was made modern in the Middle Ages. Only the dialectic offers a way to think sameness and difference together, a way to comprehend how one thing might transform into another. Marx will use the dialectic to understand how capitalism could come out of feudalism and how communism can arise out of capitalism.

It may have been at Charlemagne's court where the dialectic was revived, but it was G. W. F. Hegel who refashioned the dialectic as a form of thought and enabled it to be appropriated by Marx. Hegel was nothing if not a medieval scholar. Just as capitalism begins with feudalism, Marx begins with Hegel, who said, "There is no good in calling the Middle Ages a barbarous period."[1] Just how medieval was the nineteenth-century Hegel? He may be dated with this comment, "The lion is indeed lord and king."[2]

Hegel intercepted and transformed a problem that might be our most basic philosophical question: Why does some particular entity exist as itself and not as something different? He notes that "in all cases of distinguishing we are always also dealing with something common, which embraces the things that are not distinguished."[3]

To distinguish the lion and the domestic cat is to distinguish among felineness, which both animals share. Only in their mutual felineness may they be both related and separated. Thus, Hegel stresses, "unity, difference, and relation are categories each of which is nothing in and for itself, but only in relation to its opposite, and they cannot therefore be separated from one another."[4] Lion, cat, panther, tiger, lynx—all important cats in our archive—may only be identified through their "otherness," yet without the other there would be no otherness with which to distinguish them. And how do we actually register the movement from one to another? With feline language, it seems. "The transition is a leap," writes Hegel in *The Science of Logic*.[5]

As the kings and nobles who rule in the feudal mode of production become signified by the lion, that other feline, the domestic cat, appears as a threat precisely because it is so similar. For the lion to maintain its holiness it must be distinguished from the unholiness of the domestic cat. For lions to continue their feudal rule, domestic cats must be first distinguished and then extinguished. To understand how this distinction transpired, and why it did so through violence, we must grasp a lion-cat dialectic.

The path that Hegel laid out for doing so is one that continues to inform Marxism today. We are now in the realm of what Hegel calls, using medieval terminology, the lord-bondsman dialectic. The lord is the "ruler of social life and production."[6] Who is the bondsman? He is bound to the land and bound to the lord. In this scene of subjection the lord possesses power, but his power derives from the person over whom he rules; without someone to rule he would not be a ruler. His power cannot be separated from the power of the bondsman. So the bondsman, too, possesses power. The lord's power is predicated on not realizing this interdependency; the bondsman's power is predicated on the fact that his life consists of realizing nothing else. The power that results from the lord and his bondsman cannot "therefore be separated from one another."[7]

In a passage that generations of Marxists have read as possessing a logic of liberation but that none has applied to cats,

Hegel concludes in *The Phenomenology of Spirit*, "On approaching the other it has lost its own self, since it finds itself as another being; secondly, it has thereby sublated that other, for this primitive consciousness does not regard the other as essentially real but sees its own self in the other."[8] A wonderful German word whose English equivalent is not exact, *aufheben* (to sublate) means to cancel and preserve at the same time. The lord and the bondsman are entangled; they cannot not approach each other; they cannot not want the recognition of the other.

In appropriately dialectic terminology, but exclusive to felines, we may rewrite Hegel's famous passage. "The lion approaching the cat has lost its own self, since in the cat it finds itself as another feline; secondly, the cat has thereby overcome the lion, for the cat does not regard the lion as essentially real, but sees in the lion its own self." As the lord and bondsman are entangled, so are the lion and the cat.

The lion is something no king or noble ever truly possesses, even as such large cats might languish in their palaces and adorn their bloodred flags. To have a lion, to place it in a private collection, is to begin the process of killing it. And to attempt to possess a lion's power is to empty it of that power. The domestic feline, wily and diminutive, emerges from the lion's powerful aura as an actually existing site of subterfuge and possibility. The lion, from the heights of its reign, glimpses another, related to itself, but seemingly smaller, weaker, devilish. These two felines confront each other in their radical difference and interdependent sameness. They must fight to win recognition from the other. Which animal is stronger, more powerful, statelier? Which one will drive history forward? The domestic cat has a crucial advantage: she may see in herself the lion, as a well-known image captures (see figure 11.1), but the lion refuses to see himself in the domestic cat.

FIGURE 11.1. *The Lion Within*. Photograph courtesy of Mary-Ella Bowles.

Lions inspire awe while domestic cats are creatures present at hand. It is they who are poised to transform history. But not yet. Like the structure of capitalism, and of this book, the kernel whose final form is not completed until the end is planted and appears as yet another unmarked seed at the beginning.

2

The Devil's Cats

"If any beast has the devil's spirit in him without doubt it is the cat, both the wild and the tame."

—EDWARD, DUKE OF YORK, *MASTER OF THE GAME*

 hen Pope Gregory IX published his papal bull concerning the increasing number of heretics in thirteenth-century northern Europe, animals were a locus of his concern. Frogs and toads introduce the edict and are identified by the pontiff as accomplices of heresy. Yet it is the black cat who is presented as the most worrisome creature in Lucifer's growing menagerie. The 1228 *Vox in Rama* describes a series of heretical rituals about which church authorities had collected precise information. The pope paints a lurid scene:

> Then [the heretics] sit down to a banquet and when they rise after it is finished, a black cat emerges from a kind

of statue which normally stands in the place where these meetings are held. It is as large as a fair-sized dog and enters backwards with its tail erect. First the novice kisses its hind parts, then the Master of Ceremonies proceeds to do the same and finally all the others in turn; or rather all those who deserve the honor. The rest, that is those who are not thought worthy of this favor, kiss the Master of Ceremonies. When they have returned to their places they stand in silence for a few minutes with heads turned towards the cat. Then the Master says: "Forgive us."[1]

Gregory IX's papal bull was one of many anti-cat screeds issued by the Catholic church in the later era of the feudal mode of production. As medieval society began to become commercialized—as money independent of land began to circulate more broadly and with more velocity as the labor market tightened as a result of between one-third and one-half of the continent's laborers dying during the century-long bubonic plague pandemic—feudal lords and nobles began to feel threatened by an increasing number of "witches," "millenarians," and other "heretics," many of whom were identified by their relationships with domestic cats.

The feudal ruling class had reasons to be concerned: peasant uprisings and rebellions, for one example; social chaos if not breakdown from the pandemic, for another. Yet there also emerged a historical problem that every mode of production faces when it reaches its full capacity and can expand no more. In such moments occurrences like plagues and rebellions become truly critical and perhaps augur genuine historical transition.

According to Marx, every mode of production has its limits. The Greco-Roman slave mode of production did, as did feudalism, and capitalism will reach its limits at some point as well. The older limits are only easier to see, so clear are they in

FIGURE 2.1. Cat hunting in the fifteenth century. Artist unknown. Source: Getty Collection.

retrospect. For feudalism, a land-based mode of production that always needed more land, the failure of the colonizing crusades was an ominous portent. Low production yields on crops and limited technology did not help matters. Indeed, the instrument that needed to be invented to overcome feudal barriers wasn't a mechanical technology at all; it was a form of financing that today we call *national debt*. With national debt, a government can materialize predicted future wealth in the present in the form of state-backed loans. It is this debt financing that would fund the world-changing imperial voyages to the Americas and that would, finally, unfurl a new economic form: merchant capitalism.

Some of those voyages left from the Republic of Venice, a city-state well acquainted with images of marvelous felines. Venetian Marco Polo had returned from his travels in the thirteenth century and described the Indian kingdom of Quilon as possessing a "diversity of beasts different from all those of the rest of the world" and noted "there are black lions with no other visible colour or mark."[2] But tales of adventure and the presentation of magnificent beasts were secondary to the real goal of these travelers: they sought gold and precious metals to be accumulated and turned into circulating currency.

Venice, city of money, city of cats, was one of the first republics to develop such debt financing, and thus it has long been important to Marxists and historians of money. The city has an unappreciated importance for Karl Marx, too. In the intermezzo we became acquainted with the theoretical genealogy of Marx through Hegel. In this chapter we will become acquainted with a more literal genealogy of Marx. We will meet his ninth great-grandfather, a man who bears a feline surname and who, like Marx several centuries later, was forced to flee his homeland. In the fifteenth century, at the behest of the Inquisition, in which both Jews and cats were judged to be guilty parties, Marx's familial forebearer left the Rhineland, in present-day Germany, for Venice.

In this chapter we will observe the historical unfolding of the second half of the lion-cat dialectic. The lions who herded their beasts of burden to the heights of feudal glory find their power waning and their economies contracting while domestic cats emerge from history's shadows to challenge their leonine lords and rulers. As lions functioned as symbols of king and Christ, cats became symbols of Satan and serfdom, of rebellion and dissent. Now, as Hegel's lord-bondsman dialectic instructs us, the strong and the weak of history must confront each other in a battle for social recognition. Such contests drive history. Those in bondage and all of history's cats score important victories in the waning years of the Middle Ages. In London, in Flanders, in Paris, Bohemia, and Catalonia, peasants rise up and demand to keep more of their surplus, and serfs demand freedom from bondage. Many of these rebels were branded as cat associates. Some fought for animals, too, and demanded their freedom as well. Following domestic cats through the Middle Ages allows us to glimpse a history parallel to that of the lion.

Today one often hears discouraged Marxists quip, "It is easier to imagine the end of the world than the end of capitalism."[3] In the Middle Ages, however, it was easier to imagine the end of the world than the beginning of capitalism. Cats were present for both scenarios. In this chapter, we begin before capitalism and end during its ascension.

ECONOMIES SEEN AND UNSEEN

"Let us now transport ourselves . . . to the European middle ages," writes Marx in *Capital*. When Marx and his invited readers arrive in that long-gone time and place they "find everyone dependent, serfs and lords, vassals and suzerains, laymen and clergy. Personal dependence here characterises the social relations of production."[4] It might seem an odd way to describe this era, but for Marx such interpersonal entanglements reveal an economic truth. "For the very reason that personal dependence forms the ground-work of society, there is no necessity for labour and its products to assume a fantastic form different from their reality."[5]

This famous passage describes the way economic and thus social power appeared and was experienced in the Middle Ages: the economy was fully visible and well understood. There was little economic obfuscation of the kind we experience so often today. There were no derivative contracts, complex financial instruments, hidden fees, or surprise bills. A lord commanded that he needed a bondsman for his labor and the bondsman understood he needed access to the lord's land to live and eat.

As a result, people knew the value of a day's work, and none more so than the peasants and serfs whose daily toil underpinned the feudal world. Marx contrasts feudal economic transparency with capitalism, in which people don't know, for example, what their own labor is worth. It's not just that one doesn't know; one cannot know. Delivery drivers for Amazon do not understand themselves to be in personal relationships of dependence with Jeff Bezos.

Some of our English financial terms derived from the period bear out this personal, dominating quality of the medieval economy. *Mortgage*, or *mort gage*, for example, means *death measure*—it represented what could be extracted from a subject before he died. *Finance* breaks down etymologically as *to the end*—think of the Romance language words *fin* or *finir*.[6] It was likewise a term with fatal resonance. "There is no more, but death is my finance," goes one of the first English-language uses of the term.

Under feudalism everything economic was mostly what it seemed, yet Europe was beset by regular appearances of the devil, witches, and monstrous forms. In 1496, in present-day Germany, "the humanist and imperial publicist Sebastian Brant refused to comment publicly on the birth in June of a child with two heads: 'Some people have pressed me to write,' he noted, '[and I would do so,] except for the fact that monsters have become so frequent. Rather than a wonder [*miraculum*], they appear to me to represent the common course of nature in our time.'"[7]

Marx was attentive to this difference. In his explanation of how work time should be valued in capitalism he makes a joking reference to sorcery. "Therefore since his wages are produced in 5¾ hours, and the yarn produced in one hour also contains 5¾ hours' work, there is no witchcraft in the result, that the value created by his 5¾ hours' spinning, is equal to the value of the product spun in one hour."[8] The humor is found in mixing the lingua franca from two different modes of production. Dwellers in a capitalist age know well that witches and monsters do not exist, but they don't know the value of labor. Members of feudal society know full well the value of work, but they live in a world dominated by heretics and sorcery, overseen by kings who were earthly representatives of Christ.

Even the economic aspects of Catholicism were fully visible. "The tithe to be rendered to the priest is more matter of fact than his blessing," Marx comments of the tax required by the church. Again, a contrast with our present is helpful. Today one cannot literally pay to be absolved of one's sins. An important patron of a given church might be absolved of his sins, but not for a discrete amount of money. Not so in the Middle Ages, a fact captured by the wonderful verb *amerce*. To be *amerced* is to be forced to pay a given amount for one's mercy.

To understand how and why cats must be seen as both economic agents and companions of political radicals and heretics we must keep in mind the claim of Marx's coauthor, Friedrich Engels: "All general and overt attacks on feudalism, in the first place [are] attacks on the church . . . [and] all revolutionary, social and political doctrines necessarily became theological heresies."[9] In his study of medieval peasant rebellions, Marxist historian Rodney Hilton adds specificity to this claim when describing a certain Italian heretic: "In the only way possible for a leader of that period—in other words, in religious terms—he was a revolutionary."[10]

Rulers understood their rule as religious. Peasants understood their revolts as religious. Bestiaries presented animals as religious. And cats, too, were understood in religious terms. But religion itself reflected economic organization. "This much, however, is clear," Marx quips; "the Middle Ages could not live on Catholicism."[11]Groups that questioned the doctrines of Catholicism offered different conceptions of social power and were rightly seen as assaulting the economic structures of feudalism. Whether their departure from orthodoxy was in their understanding of the role of women, the appropriate relationship to the material world, forms of diet, or the dimensions of the relationship between Christ and his believers, such challenges would necessarily have ramifications for power in daily medieval life. Regardless of the scale and scope of these groups or their messages to followers, many were consigned by authorities to the world of the domestic cat, who represented the devil and was vested with an appreciable amount of power.

Eventually, groupings of Jews, philosophers, women, and vegetarians all fell into feline disgrace. The consequences of such a fall were hardly a wearing of the scarlet letter *C*; rather, they often included a public execution. We can broadly group these subjects of feudal scorn under the rubric of heretic, but, as different as the Middle Ages were in terms of their economy, we will notice a remarkable continuity in terms of their choice of whom to persecute. Who, exactly, was burned at the medieval stake?

> peasant women
> witches (mostly women)
> cats
> sodomites (broadly defined)
> Jews
> vegetarians
> sex workers

Heretical categories often overlapped. Peasant women loved cats. Jews conjured magic with cats. Sodomites had sexual relationships with cats; sometimes so did witches. Vegetarians were too deferential to animals in general, but so were people who engaged in bestiality. Jews used cats to mock Christianity.

Witchcraft was similarly mocking. Sex with a Jew was sometimes considered bestiality, as Jews were sometimes considered
animals. "The Church insisted that since animals had no soul
and were simply a reflection of the power of God, studying
them was neither useful nor desirable for salvation. Too much
interest in them was close to idolatry," one scholar has noted.[12]
A monastic guide from the period advises, "Take neither a cat
nor birds nor a small animal or any other senseless creature as
pet to be with you. Be withdrawn and alone with God."[13] We
might say—if awkwardly in historical terms—that these categories reflected a cat-themed criminalization. By the 1700s female prisoners were called "hell-cats" in England.

Vox in Rama was not the first document to condemn felines, nor was Pope Gregory IX the only pontiff to do so.
Indeed, he had collated a growing literature and used it to
buttress his claims. In 1185 Welsh geographer and chronicler
Walter Map documented a heretical feline ritual in *De nug-
lis curialium*. "There is, too, another old heresy which has recently increased beyond all measure. There are called Publicans
or Patarenes . . . about the first watch of the night each group
of these, closing all gates and floors and windows sitteth in
expectant silence in their synagogues. Then cometh down by
a rope a black cat of marvelous size. [The heretics] approach,
feeling their way, to the spot where they have seen their lord
and . . . they kiss him . . . some his feet, many under the tail, and
very many his private parts."[14] Then there were the more ca-
sual musings of Edward, Duke of York: "Of common wild cats
I need not speak much, for every hunter in England knows
them, and their falseness and malice are well known. But one
thing I dare well say that if any beast has the devil's spirit in
him without doubt it is the cat, both the wild and the tame."[15]

Even the ostensibly benign descriptions of cats in the bestiaries, such as their proclivity for chasing mice, seemed more
worrisome as religious leaders understood many feline actions

que le corps auoit qui auoit peine de
son pechie fu apres fait remede z garde
a la plente de ses merites

Du deable quil demonstra et enchaca
en forme d'un chat au guerissent. De .xv. femes
Sicomme il estoit vne fois en pre dico-
cation en vn chastel qui est-
oit le temple de souis en ap
prouuant vne seule foy catholique z
en approuuant la mauuaistie des here-
ges Et sicomme il auoit acoustume il
demoura en leglise apres sa predication
pour orez Et .v. nobles dames de

FIGURE 2.2. The devil appears in feline form to St. Dominico
of Caleruega. Miroir Historiale, ca. 1400–1410, Bruges, present-day
Belgium.

as indicative of some sort of devilish intention. William Caxton presented a cat-devil parallelism in his *Royal Book* and noted, "The devyl playeth ofte with the synnar lyke as the catte doth with the mous."[16] There exist more examples of cats as devils than can be recounted here. In the late medieval genre of *exempla* (examples), the cat began to appear suspect. Authors of all genres note not only the appearance of heretics associated with cats but their increasing frequency—always a sign of moral panic.

Why the cat? Many an animal historian has pondered that question. Their lingering pagan associations? Perhaps. Their refusal to work, or really do anything, according to schedule? Possibly. The question itself requires an economic answer, which Marxists would seem to be inclined to provide. Yet in the great Marxist studies of the breaking of the bonds of feudalism (Rodney Hilton's *Bond Men Made Free*, for example), or in studies of the violent and misogynistic transition from feudalism to capitalism (Silvia Federici's *Caliban and the Witch*, for another), cats remain in absentia. Where they abound is in textual and literary histories in and of the period—not only in bestiaries and *exempla* but in illustrated bibles, too, where they were omnipresent on the page. "It seems that the adoption of [the cat] to represent heresy must be considered one of the important and influential innovations of the redactors of the *Bible moralisée*," writes one scholar of these newly illustrated twelfth- and thirteenth-century anti-cat bibles.[17] Yet this study too fails to proffer an explanation as to why that is the case.

It is time that these two histories, the first by Marxists who neglect cats (and animals more broadly), and the second by cat aficionados (it seems) who neglect economic interpretation, are read together. Doing so will offer both economically oriented scholars and cat lovers a new appreciation for the role of cats in this contested history of the transition from one mode of production to another.

Marx claims that the feudal order must everywhere be destroyed for capitalism to emerge. He argues that it was necessary that a slowly emerging capitalist class "put an end to all feudal, patriarchal, idyllic relations."[18] Just as a nascent merchant capital class had to "pitilessly [tear] asunder the motley feudal ties that bound man to his 'natural superiors,' and ... [leave] remaining no other nexus between man and man than naked self-interest, than callous 'cash payment.'"[19] Finally, Marx comments that capitalism had to "drown the most heavenly ecstasies of religious fervour, of chivalrous enthusiasm, of philistine sentimentalism, in the icy water of egotistical calculation." He forgot to add that cats must be drowned, too, sometimes literally. Under the guidance of the Catholic church, the domestic cat would be burned, buried, and terrorized. And once so condemned by the church, cat persecution became secularized and cat torture made an object of public spectacle and communal joy. Yearly cat massacres as a part of communal festivals took place in Ypres, Belgium, for example, until 1802. (The town now hosts a yearly pro-cat festival, the *Kattenstoet*, in which they ask for historical forgiveness through cat celebration.)[20]

Marxists have rightly understood that the prosecution of heretics was a class-based phenomenon. Not only Engels and Hilton but Federici notes of such heretical groups as "the Cathars, Waldenses, The Poor of Lyon, Spirituals, [and the] Apostolics" that "for more than three centuries [they] flourished among the 'lower classes' in Italy, France, the Flanders, and Germany in what undoubtedly was the most important opposition movement of the Middle Ages."[21] I note that Federici omits a key fact that Charles Lea, one of Federici's nineteenth-century sources, had included: many if not most of these heretical sects were associated with domestic cats. Indeed, one of Federici's images includes a witch with her accompanying cat, often called a familiar.[22] Federici catalogues which animals took the "familiar" role, and cats receive their only mention from her in that list. Because of the brutality with which witches and their familiars were treated, she then notes, "Such was the presence of animals in the witches' world that one must presume that they too were being put on trial."[23] Animals, in fact, *were* put on trial in these latter medieval years, and we will consider that history in chapter 4. For now, however, we note that Marx's point is that feudal ideology had to be destroyed for capitalism to emerge. Federici's point is that heretics, many of whom were witches, most of whom were women, had to be destroyed for capitalism to emerge. My point is that cats had to be destroyed for capitalism to emerge.

We begin with the Cathars, an ascetic community in southern France in the twelfth and thirteenth centuries. They are described by Federici as

> the most influential among the heretical sects.... [They] stand out as unique in the history of European social movements because of their abhorrence for war (including the Crusades), their condemnation of capital punishment (which provoked the Church's first explicit pronouncement in support of the death penalty) and their tolerance for other religions. The Cathars also rejected marriage and procreation and were strict vegetarians, both because they refused to kill animals and because they wished to avoid any food, like eggs and meats, resulting from sexual generation.[24]

The Cathars were radical dissidents from the feudal order's insistence on the unity of the state-religion-war economy as well as its celebration of carnivorousness, of which the lion was part and parcel, and for these reasons they were labeled heretics.

We note, of course, the first three letters of their name: C-A-T. Scholar Alan of Lille noted this, too, in the thirteenth century. In his treatise, *Contra haereticos*, he linked the etymol-

FIGURE 2.3. Witches with animals, cat unremarked. Source: Federici, *Caliban and the Witch*, 172.

ogy of the name Cathar to the word *cat*. Cathars are named after the cat, he argued, "because they kiss the posterior of a cat in whose shape, it is said, Lucifer appears to them."[25] His theory is not as odd as it sounds, actually, as he also offered analogies between the "rules of grammar and the prescriptions of nature regarding human copulation in his *De planctu naturae*."[26] Nor are those claims so idiosyncratic, relatively speaking: in ancient Greek, the sound of particular words was thought to reflect the properties attached to the things to which the word referred. Still, the Cathars themselves traced their name to the Greek word *cathario*, meaning *pure*—the root for our own word *catharsis*.

The cat-cathar-heretic transposition is found in German as well. The Cathars were known in Germany as Katters and in the north of France as Katiers. In Germany heretics simply became known as *ketzer*, from the German *katze* (cat).[27] *Ketzer* traced back to *Kater* (tomcat), and those committing heresy—*Ketzerei* in German—became conflated with those committing unspeakable acts with *Kater*. German also offered the more direct neologism of *Katzenküsser* (cat kisser) for *heretic*. In Latin, language of scholars and the church throughout the Middle Ages, the act generating the most abhorrence was known as *bacium sub cauda*, the kiss under the tail of the cat. However one derives or associates their name, the Cathars were charged with devil worship and cat idolatry and ordered burned.

Then there were the Poor of Lyon, as the Waldenses, led by Peter Waldo, were known. Itinerant preachers in Northern Italy, they believed that Christ was poor and argued that practicing Christians should take a vow of poverty. They also suggested the coming of a female messiah. The Poor of Lyon were condemned on both feline and economic counts. In response to their declarations, Pope John XXII argued that "the assertion of the poverty of Christ was itself heretical."[28] Medieval historian Irina Metzler recounts, "In 1236 Stephen of Bourbon, acting as inquisitor, was called to Clermont by Bishop Hugues de la Tour to judge a group of heretics, probably Waldensians. Among them was a woman who participated in secret gatherings where Lucifer was called upon and a dreadful cat appeared, descending down a lance that had been rammed in the ground. The cat sprayed those present with water, using its tail to flick the water in a mockery of the actions of a priest blessing with holy water."[29]

The composition of the heretical groups must be noted. The majority of heretics and their supporters were "artisans, workers and peasants . . . and amongst these, as in other heretical sects, [was] a high proportion of women . . . there were also representatives of what we should now call the intelligentsia."[30] Yet also represented as cat associates were those who desired wealth, including members of the church. In one depiction, a priest too concerned with earthly riches, his greed symbolized by spotted cats, attends to a dying man while angels attend to the death of a poor person in the contra-feline scene at the bottom of the frame (see figure 2.4).

Jews, too, were included in variety of anti-cat propositions as they were ostracized, attacked, and executed. They were said to worship the cat and be able to transform themselves into cats to sneak into Christian homes to practice mischief and cast spells, a trait also attributed to witches. Jews were also believed to crucify cats in order to mock Christ's death on the cross.[31] The persecution of Jews under the sign of their cat worship alerts us to a dynamic that will shape our story toward this chapter's end: Jews begin leaving central and northern Europe under the growing Inquisition, which Federici calls "one

FIGURE 2.4. Avarice at the deathbed, represented by multiple cats. Artist unknown, fourteenth century, France.

of the most perverse inventions ever recorded in the history of state repression."[32] Marx's ancestors were among those so exiled. Jews were regularly depicted in medieval manuscripts with beards and yarmulke-like hats, often accompanied by cats. Metzler notes of one image that "the miscreants seem to be identified by their beards and hats as Jews; the cat is now depicted in a new position: it sits, still and upright, on a table lined with gold coins. The cat is thus accorded a dual role: it may be seen as both a living animal perched on the equipment of its (moneylending?) confederates *and* as a metaphoric equivalent: an idol on an altar."[33]

It wasn't just the usual suspects (women, workers, sodomites, Jews) who received this kind of disapprobation. Two rather surprising groups were targeted as feline associates: philosophers, particularly those who engaged in dialectics, and the religious order of the Knights Templar. An image from the Viennese *Bible moralisée* includes the text "The women who went offering to the Temple and were deceived signify certain people who came before bad philosophers. And these philosophers deceive them through their perverse proofs."[34] The philosopher was presented as kissing a cat. A contemporary of these bibles in the thirteenth century warned of "presumptuous people who too subtly seek into divine things and thus enter heresy," another condemnation of philosophy in its dialectic variant.[35] In addition to heretics being executed, the work of Aristotle (too dialectic, translated by Muslims and Jews) was soon banned. Philosophy itself was characterized through reference to two other pro-cat groups, women and sex workers, when Garnier de Rochefort preached in the thirteenth century that "philosophy was a 'prostitute, strange woman, concubine.'"[36]

Finally, we note the fate of the Knights Templar, a centuries-old religious order founded to protect Christian pilgrims during their crusades to the Holy Land and perhaps the most surprising of the supposed cat associates. Henry the Lion had traveled with the Knights Templar to the Levant, we recall from chapter 1. As the Crusades continued, the order assumed greater military duties. But their reputation and growing wealth provoked resentment. In 1307, Philip IV of France arrested the knights and accused them of crimes including cat worship and feline sodomy. One charge stated that the Templars worshipped idols, specifically made of a cat and a head, the latter having three faces. In this particular case, the accuser, Phillip IV, stood to be absolved of some amount of debt owed to the Knights. The affair is a reminder that we must be suspicious of the class interests of those who persecute cats and cat lovers.

The cat came to represent everything disorderly and discordant to church and state authorities: poverty, which itself was suspect; Jews, quite suspect; women and the devil, obviously a worrisome pairing; even the dialectic itself came to be signified by the cat. Then there were the witches, that broad sect of sometimes Jews, sometimes Cathars, sometimes vegetarians, but almost always women, who received the lion's share of late feudal persecution and torture for century after century. Pope Innocent VIII declared in 1484 that "the cat was the devil's favorite animal and idol of all witches."[37]

Cat-loving witches were said to engage in a second anal practice, the *infamous osculum*, in which they replicated the cat anus act with the anus of the devil himself. As women were attacked for displays of sexuality in relation to cats, we are unsurprised to learn that this is the period in which women's sex work becomes associated with cats. "Prostitutes have been called 'Cats' since 1400 and sexualized girls have been referred to as 'pussy' from the 1500 onwards," writes cat-focused historian Katharine M. Rogers in her wonderful study, *Cat*.[38] (The

FIGURE 2.5. Witches before a cauldron, with cat. Woodcut, sixteenth century.

later term *pussy* does not come into use as a descriptor of female genitalia until the early 1900s.) Cats and women together began to represent an attack on the feudal phallus. Often seen in bestiaries attending to their own genitals, cats can also be seen absconding with the genitals of others.

Many of the long historical connections we can make between this era and Marx—Jew, philosopher, refugee, heretic— can be traced through the sign of the cat.

To add a different species to our bestiary, to which animal did the authorities turn to bolster their anti-cat sentiment? Incredibly, some medieval inquisitors turned to the dog. It was in the waning years of the Middle Ages that the cat-dog controversy, still so ripe and divisive today, seems to have been birthed in its current form in Western culture. The Dominicans, investigators of heretics, became known as "Dogs of the Lord" in a play on their Latin name: "Dominican" = *domini canes*. Under the sign of the loyal, obedient dog, these inquisitors aimed to ferret out the devil's cats.

By the mid-thirteenth century, a time of cereal production increase through technological know-how, English nobles began demanding more, not less, from their peasants and serfs.
Multiple taxes were still required (paid in kind, or with goods,
because of the ongoing shortage of hard currency), and additional labor was now demanded from peasants by lords in exchange for the use of their land. Not that there was much other
land that peasants could have accessed. A population explosion
had caused expansion into marshes, more mountainous ter-
rains, and other previously uncultivated places. Peasants who
had acted in accord with customary rights to common land
began to clash with nobles who argued that the land had been

FIGURE 2.6. *Flaisch macht Flaisch*, 1555. The title refers
to a proverb: "Flesh gives flesh, fish gives nothing." Source:
Rijksmuseum Amsterdam.

granted to them by various, sometimes centuries-old, royal decrees. Serfs, lacking many of the meager freedoms of peasants, became even more desperate. Their lords viewed them, according to one abbot, as "a miserable race which owns nothing that it does not get by its own labour," a definition to which the serfs themselves seemed not to have subscribed.[39] As far back as 800 CE, in the days of Charlemagne, the historical record is dotted with cases of serfs who "claimed to be free," ran off to the forests (those not already turned into the private hunting grounds of nobles, anyway), and declared, "We will have our will in the woods."[40] Now, as the population rose, access to land declined, and demands on them increased, peasants and serfs began to agitate, to organize, and to imagine, in heretical fashion, a different social world.

During these long years of cat persecution, the feudal order was reaching its breaking point. That's when the black plague descended into northern Europe, home to most of what we recognize as properly feudal accoutrement, from the bestiaries to the knights errant. Moving from the east over land and sea, the plague had already encircled Constantinople, Sicily, and southern France. Infected rodents traveling on merchant ships throughout the Mediterranean and the East were bitten by fleas, which then spread the disease to humans. Ultimately, the plague achieved person-to-person transmission via respiratory droplets of the kind that we have become so familiar with as a result of the COVID-19 pandemic.

Over the course of the fourteenth century successive waves of the illness decimated towns, emergent urban centers, and rural hamlets. All the while cat massacres continued, ridding Europe of some of the few community members who might have reasonably been described as efficacious plague fighters. Other helpful community members, traveling Jewish doctors with knowledge of Arabic medicine, were likewise rendered outcasts and persecuted, in part due to their association with cats.

How did witnesses on the scene understand what befell Europe during the worst of the plague years? "This is the end of the world," wrote one Italian chronicler.[41] Those who lived through the black death did not imagine the end of the world (as today's saying goes); they believed they had witnessed it. And yet we must note the economic dimensions of the pandemic. Even as the world ends, we turn to Marx: "The history of all hitherto existing society is the history of class struggles"—a statement as true in times of calamity as in prosperity.[42] Some peasants and rebels used their own suppurating bodies or the bulbous, infected corpses of their comrades as weapons and sought to infect lords and nobles. As serfs, peasants, and nobles died in Europe and England, the labor market changed and many estates were vacated.

One effect of the pandemic was that peasants and serfs were emboldened to make demands. In England, after the plague, peasants and serfs rose up in towns and villages across the country in what is now known as the Peasants' Revolt of 1381. In their own religious words, the peasant rebels offered, "We pray that all bonde men may be made ffre for god made all ffre wt [with] his precious blode sheddyng."[43] These rebels attempted to translate their understanding of Christ's life into their own political reality. Marx saw the situation differently, several hundred years later: "Christians are equal in heaven yet unequal on earth," he quipped.[44] Supposedly led by peasant rebels Wat Tyler, Jack Straw, and John Balle (their identities cannot be confirmed and the names seem generic enough as to be fictitious—Jack Straw?!), the uprisings made demands larger than those of any individual or local community. They articulated "a radical political agenda which, if it had been implemented, would fundamentally have transformed English society: the abolition of serfdom and the dues and services owed by tenants to their lord of the manor; freedom from tolls and customs on buying and selling goods throughout the country; the recognition of a man's right to work for whom he chose at the wages he chose; the state's seizure of the Church's wealth and property."[45]

Their violent rebellion targeted those who daily enforced their poverty and unfreedom, from the local tax collector to the town clergy. They did not seek out kings, princes, or wealthy nobility, as we might have expected, although in the English case there was one exception. The rebels killed a lion—Richard Lyons, that is. Described by historian Juliet Barker as a "notorious financier," Lyons "might not have been an aristocrat but he lived like one; his hall was hung with tapestries from Arras, leopard skins and ermine decorated his chamber, and his bed curtains, fashioned from the finest red and blue worsted cloth, were embroidered with lions (a playful allusion to his name)."[46] Richard Lyons was a descendent—albeit an illegitimate one—of the great Lyons family, which we first met during the Norman Conquest and which will be present in English finance and politics for hundreds of years still to come. The attack on Lyons was an attack on the lion itself, on the image of an animal who represented feudal power. Of course, the Lyons family did not perish with the assassination of one of its members. But the end was coming, not just for this Lyons but for many others. In England, the rebel leaders met the same fate as Lyons, but their actions succeeded in temporarily abolishing serfdom and hastening its final demise.

Lyons was a contemporary and associate of Geoffrey Chaucer and John of Gaunt, both important historical figures with their own feline associations, both of whom fared better in the Peasants' Revolt than did Lyons. In these years after the plague, Chaucer memorialized cats' mousing work in *The Canterbury Tales*, in which "The Manciple's Tale" is given the subtitle "an example of pleasing a cat." Chaucer writes:

> Or take a cat, and feed him well with milk
> And tender flesh, and make his bed of silk,

And let him see a mouse go by the wall;
At once he leaves the milk and flesh and all
And every dainty that is in that house,
Such appetite has he to eat a mouse.
Desire has here its mighty power shown,
And inborn appetite reclaims its own.[47]

John of Gaunt, meanwhile, was memorialized as a cat in William Langland's poem *Piers the Plowman*, written around the same time (the exact date is unknown). The son of King Edward III and the duke and ruler of multiple English and continental jurisdictions through the usual combination of marriage and war, John of Gaunt is presented in the popular poem as a cat ruling over a land of rats and mice. We need not attend to the particulars of Lyons, Chaucer, or John of Gaunt. It's enough to note that the seeming invincibility of the lion and the satanic lore of the domestic cat had become somewhat destabilized by the penultimate century of this era.

So persecuted for so long, the domestic cat in one instance became a symbol of resistance. In London a tale emerged of a Richard "Dick" Whittington, a man who was made wealthy by his cat. Whittington, a mayor of London thrice in the fourteenth century, both before and after the uprisings, supposedly rose from a poverty-stricken childhood to make a small fortune through the sale of his cat to a rat-infested county during the plague years.

The legend seems to be apocryphal. There certainly existed a Richard Whittington and he was mayor of London not thrice but four times. But there is scant evidence of a cat-based transaction of this magnitude. Nonetheless, stories, ballads, puppetry shows, and poems memorialize this feline and the fortune its sale bequeathed. Whittington died in March 1423 and was supposedly buried in the church of St. Michael Paternoster Royal, of which he had been a patron. His tomb

FIGURE 2.7. Filippo Pistrucci, *Whittington and His Cat and the Old Cook*, 1829. Courtesy of the National Portrait Gallery of the Smithsonian Institution, Washington, DC.

has been lost to history but, in 1949, during an excavation, a mummified cat was found in its supposed location.

Today a steel cat sits crouched above Whittington's gravestone in Hampstead Heath, near Highgate Cemetery, where Karl Marx is buried. Whittington's cat may be fictitious, but it is not without its own ambivalence in the historical ar-

FIGURE 2.8.
Richard ("Dick")
Whittington's
gravestone in
London, with cat.

chive. On the European continent witches and heretics continued to be burned at the stake for their crimes against the
church. But in England, a new crime was emerging: crimes
not against Christ or with cats but against capital. As historian Peter Linebaugh has detailed, in England those who refused to participate in an emerging money economy were sent
off to the feared Newgate Prison, where they reportedly could
view a statue of Whittington's cat from the entrance.[48] Was
their view from Newgate received as a symbol of defiance or
a hope for survival? We cannot be sure, as the prison burned
to the ground in 1666 during the Great Fire of London. We
can, however, be sure that the economy of cats was slowly
changing.[49]

The Devil's Cats - 83

In Germany, peasant wars ensued two centuries after they had in England. German preacher and radical Thomas Müntzer, who participated in and sometimes led armed peasant revolts, declared his hope that freedom be realized for more than peasants. In a report from 1524 Müntzer pleaded, "All creatures have been turned into property, the fishes in the water, the birds in the air, the plants on the earth; the creatures too must become free."[50] No less a Marxist than Friedrich Engels conducted a study of the German peasant revolts. Engels discusses Müntzer in his classic work *The Peasant Wars in Germany*. But he overlooks Müntzer's calls for animal freedom, an oversight common to Marxists, as we will see throughout *Marx for Cats*. As Müntzer could imagine freedom for both peasants and other species, he knew, too, to avoid the always present lion. Peasants and their comrades understood precisely what the lion signified. In a letter to Martin Luther, leader of the Protestant Reformation, Müntzer offered an ominous leonine prognostication:

> I am most confident, given my previous dangerous experience that I am being singled out for other battles in the world. He who saved me from the most pernicious swamp will save me from the hand of the beast, the lion and the dragon, so that I shall have no fear as I wander in the midst of the shadow of death.[51]

Like so many cat associates and peasant revolutionaries, Müntzer met a violent end. He was executed in Frakenhausen in 1525.

KARL MARX'S FELINE LINEAGE

We now localize our story to the late fifteenth century, to a particular town in the Rhineland, in present-day Germany, named Katzenelnbogen. Note the resonant name of this municipality, still in existence today: *Katzen* (cats) *ellenbogen* (elbow), a name that seems to have two genealogies. Some claim it refers to a hindquarters-like crook in a local creek, the Dörsbach. Others think it more likely that Katzenelnbogen is a Germanized version of the Latin Cattimelibocus, which may refer to the people of Catti, who inhabited the land in Roman times.

FIGURE 2.9. Town of Katzenelnbogen, Rhineland-Palatinate. Steel engraving, 1877, Germany.

KATZENELLENBOGEN.

Either way, we will not be surprised to learn that Katzenelnbogen has a red lion rampant on its coat of arms.

There, in fifteenth-century Katzenelnbogen, a young Jewish scholar prepares to flee his homeland. Here we encounter Karl Marx's ninth-great-grandfather, a man who takes, like so many Jews did, his locality as his surname upon his emigration. We now meet Meir Ben Isaac Katzenellenbogen, progenitor of the famous Katzenellenbogen line of Ashkenazi Jews. Classist and racist though they are, family trees do offer a sense of how propriety and property merge to produce a historical record. Martin Buber, Felix Mendelssohn, Marcel Proust, Helena Rubinstein, and Karl Marx all descend from Katzenellenbogen. Just as the famous Lyons family provides one lineage of our story, the Katzenellenbogen family provides another, continuing the contrast and contradiction of the lion-cat dialectic.

Nothing in the historical record indicates that a direct association with cats prompted Katzenellenbogen's emigration. No doubt Katzenellenbogen left Katzenelnbogen because of the always present and, by the mid-fifteenth century, intensifying antisemitic persecution. Of course, antisemitism itself has long feline heritage, which, as we have seen, tied in with philosophy in its dialectic variant, a tradition in which Katzenellenbogen also participated.

Katzenellenbogen arrived via Prague in cosmopolitan northern Italy, which, at the time, had the largest population of Jews remaining in Europe. Venice was (and remains) a city of cats. A famous winged lion still stands watch over its harbor from a prominent place in the Piazza San Marco. For centuries Venetians credited local cats with assisting them in lessening the impact of the plague by exterminating rodents. (No doubt these felines helped, but so did Venice's policy of *quaranta giorni*, the forty days of waiting before disembarkation that Venetians required of arriving ships.) The famous *gatto* cat mask is one reminder of Venetians' appreciation of cats. William

Shakespeare offered another. He left it to a Jew to recognize cats' work in *The Merchant of Venice*, in which Shylock notes that cats are both "harmless" and "necessary" to the republic.

The Republic of Venice possessed several other important distinctions, all of which indicate that, for our purposes, the Middle Ages, and with them feudalism, were receding into history. Radical new technologies were beginning to emerge after centuries of slothful technical progress. Printing was brought to Italy soon after Gutenberg's invention of movable type, and by 1480 Venice had come to dominate the Italian printing industry—indeed, it had become the "capital of printing of all Europe."[52]

Katzenellenbogen served the semiautonomous Jewish community of the Republic of Venice as spiritual leader, judge, legislator, professor, and dean. He presided over the Jewish community court of Venice, the Venetian regional council of rabbis, and the Academy of Padua. He was a scholar whose magnum opus was a printed edition of *Mishneh Torah*. In that new interpretation of the Talmud, Katzenellenbogen weighed in on a millennium-long (and still ongoing) debate: he argued that law could be both codified and open to interpretation, that one need not dichotomize too rigidly between the spirit and letter of law.

But as a Jew, Katzenellenbogen was barred from publishing texts himself. The Christian publisher Alvise Bragadini was engaged to publish his work. Soon enough, though, unauthorized copies of *Mishneh Torah* were circulating around Venice at the behest of one Marc Antonio Giustiniani, another Venetian printer. Giustiniani had removed some of Katzenellenbogen's editorial marginalia and errata and cast aspersions on others, but fundamentally copied and sold Katzenellenbogen's text at a price significantly lower than Bragadini's. Rightly furious, Katzenellenbogen issued an appeal to Moses Isserles, the rabbi of Kracow. From that rabbi he won a Jewish law ruling permitting him to continue to sell his version of his own texts before others could sell their copied versions. Certainly, Isserles's was not a very strong judgment and was no doubt made weaker by the fact that Katzenellenbogen's legal antagonist was not Jewish and probably cared very little about the nonbinding opinions of the rabbi of Kracow.[53]

Yet one can glimpse some of Marx's spirit in his paterfamilias: the devotion to the history of the interpretation of texts, the dogged and far-reaching correspondence, and an intrepid sense of his own righteousness and place in history along with a certain resigned sense of futility about the strictures that history imposes. Katzenellenbogen died in 1565 and was buried in Padua's Jewish cemetery, where his grave remains today. His tombstone is marked by a small stone engraving of a crouching domestic cat—the family's crest—as is that of his son. A rejection of the lion, but also perhaps a rejection of the various states that had so persecuted him. Katzenellenbogen's cat appears delicate and diminutive, crouching without an arched back.

Katzenellenbogen's Talmudic scholarship wasn't the only thing being doubled and discounted in sixteenth-century Venice. The most important copying was happening in the Venetian banks and money houses. There, a new technology called double-entry bookkeeping was being introduced, a reflection of novel state-backed loans that transformed institutional forms of credit and debt. It is for that reason that Marx presents Venice, land of his cat-named forefather, as one of the key progenitors of capitalism. "As with the stroke of an enchanter's wand, [republics like Venice] endowed barren money with the power of breeding and thus turned it into capital," Marx writes.[54]

From the late Middle Ages to our own time, national debt predominates as one of the key buttresses of capital accumulation. Its mechanism is that the state essentially receives an ad-

FIGURE 2.10. Katzenellenbogen tombstone in Jewish cemetery, Padua, Italy. Courtesy of Leigh Claire La Berge.

vance against future taxation through the sale of bonds. Marx continues, "The system of public credit, i.e., of national debts, whose origin we discover in Genoa and Venice as early as the Middle Ages, took possession of . . . Europe. Public credit became the *credo* of capital. And with the rise of national debt-making, want of faith in the national debt takes the place of the blasphemy against the Holy Ghost, which may not be forgiven."[55]

Humorous as usual, Marx's language moves between church and state to capture an important historical transition whereby the economic power of the church was gradually replaced by that of merchants and bankers. The effects were dramatic. Foremost, Italian city-states such as Venice became rich. The circulation of their credit and debt instruments produced a new wealthy class now independent of their landholding that we might even call a class of nascent capitalists. Marx labels them a "class of lazy annuitants." He notes "the improvised wealth of financiers, middleman . . . tax-farmers [and] merchants to whom a good part of every national loan renders the service of capital [like a gift] fallen from heaven."[56]

Soon Venice, like other Italian city-states, had become what Marx calls "a modern bankocracy," full of "financial swindling [and] celebrated cosmopolitan orgies."[57] We have to note that in the city most generative of capitalism we find intellectual character, freedom, and cosmopolitanism. We cannot dismiss this as coincidence, and neither does Marx. That, in part, is why Katzenellenbogen selected Venice for his immigration and why Jews, even barred from printing and consigned to the ghetto, sought out Venice. Whatever else it generates, capitalism produces cosmopolitanism.

In Italy so much wealth soon flowed from this new system of banking and credit that it ushered in a renaissance. Painters used gold on the ceilings of Florentine chapels just as Northern European scholars had painted it into their bestiaries. The flat perspective of the human-faced cats that populate medieval paintings and books was slowly replaced with more nuanced and realistic ones, for example, in the remarkable cat sketches of vegetarian Leonardo da Vinci.

It was this money, this capital, that transformed art, literature, and philosophy. It funded the various imperial voyages that soon set sail from Europe. The Italian merchant Christopher Columbus journeyed across the Atlantic—likely with a cat on board—and began a genocide in the present-day Caribbean. He left Spain on a search for spices and returned a slave trader.

What Marx calls "primitive accumulation," the non-market-based acts of violence and seizure that form the necessary conditions for capitalism's emergence, were well underway by the

FIGURE 2.11. Ashley Lyon, *self-same*, 2014. Image courtesy of the artist. Photograph by Mike Flemming.

mid-sixteenth century, and the stage was then set for the capitalist mode of production to emerge. Marx emphasized that "force is the midwife of every old society pregnant with a new one. It is itself an economic power."[58] Ultimately, we cannot say when capitalism starts. We can say only that capitalism starts. We know it has begun from a compendium of observations and convergences. We know wage labor and finance capital will emerge as new forms of value generation. We know that domestic cats will be reevaluated; the first cat competition to assess their mousing and ratting skills was held in 1598 in England.[59] We know that the remaining commons of the feudal era will be gone. And we know these changes will affect all species, not only humans and cats. But we close this first part of our bestiary with a quote not from Marx but from Hegel, who uses a feline vocabulary to represent the magnitude of any true historical transition: "We stand at the gates of an important epoch, a time of ferment, when spirit moves forward in a leap, transcends its previous shape and takes on a new one."[60] We now prepare for the dawn of capitalism.

The Feline
Call to Freedom

SLAVERY AND REVOLUTION IN AN AGE
OF EMPIRE, 1500–1800

PART II

3

Divine Lynxes

"The Lynx lives now as Our Mother, the Earth."

—HAUDENOSAUNEE MYTH, "SKY EPOCH"

 ome time on August 25, 1619, a privateer docked off the coast of the newly settled English colony Virginia. Named the *White Lion*, this ship had recently been involved in a raid on a Portuguese slaver, the *São João Bautista*, which carried some 350 Africans who had been abducted from what is present-day Angola. That ship was bound for Veracruz, in what is today Mexico, where Spain was building its new world empire through conquest, genocide, and, increasingly, African slave labor.

During their raid on the slaver, the *White Lion* and its companion ship, the *Treasurer,* managed to seize sixty or so black captives. Reversing course, the privateers headed for the closest English port, at Point Comfort, in Virginia; the *White Lion* arrived several days before its companion. John Rolfe, husband

of Pocahontas, nascent tobacconist, and colonial secretary, recorded the disembarkation of the *White Lion* in a letter and
noted that "some 20 and odd Negroes" had landed in Virginia.[1]
These captives were sold for "victuals" and joined a burgeoning population of those consigned to make their lives anew in
a New World that also included impoverished English, who
were indentured or in debt bondage; indigenous Americans,
who would now experience an apocalypse similar to the one
medieval Europeans had endured during the plague; and other
enslaved Africans.

Marx for Cats now enters what historians have long called
the age of democracy, and what an entrance it is. In this chapter
we will witness how capitalist democracy arrived in the Americas, how imperial conquests began to remake the world, and
how the lion and the domestic cat were transformed from feudal felines into early capitalist ones. It was a lion that delivered
the first slaves into what would become the United States. And
that lion was *white*, alerting us to a new category of domination and profit that we now know as race. During the age of
democracy, some twelve million Africans would be abducted
and sold into slavery, producing a racist social order whose effects still resonate today.

White masters and black slaves arrived in a thriving First
Nations continent where many eastern seaboard and midwest-
ern nations traced their lineages to that of cats—the lynx in
the case of the Haudenosaunee, or Iroquois, for example—and
other Algonquin nations revered or sought protection from the
Mishipeshu, a mythical underwater panther. Just as Europeans
introduced novel animals into the Americas, these two felines
now enter our bestiary. In 1620 domestic cats, cattle, dogs, and
horses arrived in so-called New England, where each would
serve its own colonizing function.[2] A domestic cat's presence
aboard the Mayflower is confirmed by that ship's Bible. Yet
colonization set off such destruction that the true measure of

cats' presence in First Nations America may never be known. In 2020, for example, a mountainside cat etching was discovered in the Peruvian desert and estimated by archeologists to be over two thousand years old (see figure 3.1). In the verdant South American lowlands the jaguar roamed through jungles and cultures.

British settler colonists and their cats had left an England that was no longer ruled by lion kings but was undergoing its own transformation into an absolutist state. No more a string of motley fiefdoms organized by competing lords and kings, Europe was beginning to be composed of vertical state organizations proper, each with one ruler whose power and authority was absolute, divine, and hereditary. Yet even as they ceased to be ruled by lion kings, these new nations—and their rulers— still imagined their kingdoms as lions, as a Dutch map indicates (see figure 3.2). It was the Dutch who, in the seventeenth century, pioneered the relationships between finance and geography, and money and imperialism, in the form of the joint

FIGURE 3.1. Present-day Nazca, Peru, estimated to be two thousand years old.

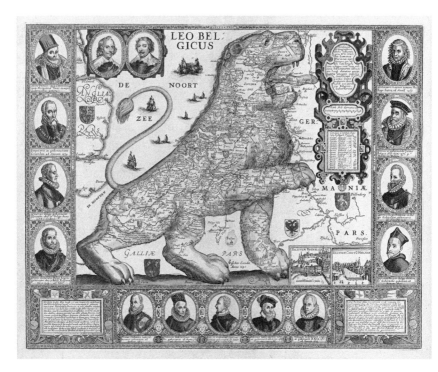

FIGURE 3.2. Dutch imperial cartography, ca. 1650. Source: https://
www.cartahistorica.com/our-catalogue/europe/benelux/xvii
-provinces/leo-belgicus-a-unique-and-unrecorded-map-anno-1641/.

stock company, an innovation that introduces into history
what we can now recognize as a capitalist enterprise. But it
was the British and French who excelled at the synthesis of
money, land, and slavery; and it is they who will be the subjects
of chapters 3 and 4, respectively.

The English Virginia Company set up colonial camp in
1607 and the English Massachusetts Bay Company some years
later. With charters to claim land and to self-govern offered by
King James, these colonies existed in a crucible of peonage, indigenous genocide, and racial slavery, some of which was imported from the Old World but most of which developed out

of the sinews of the new. It was here that a novel political project was born, capitalist democracy, one that would bequeath to history what became the United States.

That capitalist democracy was born in bondage is a fact that has led to some uncomfortable discussions for its proponents. How could the freedoms announced by the democratic project be realized in such a scene of domination? How could equality come out of slavery? How, to quote one of the protagonists of this chapter, lion aficionado and slaveholder Thomas Jefferson, could there be "empire for liberty?" One influential American historian has called this enduring idea of the comingling of freedom and slavery "the American paradox," which he claims defines the very spirit of the nation.[3] His is an interesting theory. A paradox is something quizzical, something that eludes explanation. Recall one of philosophy's most enduring paradoxes, that of the liar. "Everything I say is a lie," this riddle begins. But is *that* statement true? Or is it yet another lie?

Perhaps more apt for us is the Schrödinger's cat paradox,

FIGURE 3.3. Schrödinger's cat: feline philosophical paradoxes in philosophy. Illustration by Kathleen Kimball, 2018.

a gruesome little thought experiment involving a cat, a radio-active atom, and a sealed box. It states that a scientific theory cannot be fully proven and thus remains in paradoxical limbo, until realized in material form.

Once the "American paradox" of democracy has been given material form it begins to look less paradoxical and more contradictory. In Marxism, a contradiction pulls together competing forces whose necessary clash becomes the very stuff of history. And for Marx, the notion that eighteenth-century Euro-American democracy was generated out of empire and slavery was hardly a paradox. Rather, it was a case of cause — slavery produced more wealth distributed among more people — and effect — those newly wealthy people desired a new system of government. History's newly wealthy, newly self-governing people have a new name, too: they become the bourgeoisie. Those not so lucky in the nascent historical formation: the proletariat. "Society as a whole is more and more splitting up into two great hostile camps, into two great classes directly facing each other — Bourgeoisie and Proletariat," Marx tells us.[4] The process of the long divorce between these two classes was in its infancy in colonial America, so this chapter begins there.

We will trace the path of early modernity and capitalist democracy through the American Revolution and the formation of the United States. "Revolutions are the locomotives of history," Marx writes, and in the next two chapters we will see revolutions everywhere as they begin in the 1770s and continue for a hundred years.[5] Of what Marxists call the bourgeois revolutions, the United States remains unique both for its conservative scope and the fact that it emerged from a land that knew no feudalism. Marxists have made much of this; the capitalist mode of production is supposed to emerge from and in conflict with the feudal mode of production. But history rarely follows models so neatly, which Marx knew as well as anyone. In the United States Marx saw both the rapaciousness of the beginnings of capitalism as well as the freedom from that order to be found in indigenous nations and their cats. He understood the bourgeoisie as a class of genuine contradictions: progressive and regressive, provincial and cosmopolitan. Those contradictory relationships applied to cats as well, and indeed there is no better way to assess the fundamentally ambivalent nature of the American Revolution than to look at the distribution of felines within it. In the American case, cats and capitalism track and are transformed by each other.

THE FAT-FACED LYNX

The European colonization of the Americas, and the world, is one of the defining acts of the modern era and of the class that will come to dominate that era, the bourgeoisie. Marx explains, "The discovery of America, the rounding of the Cape, opened up fresh ground for the rising bourgeoisie."[6] We remember that medieval Europe continually confronted two barriers to stabilizing and expanding its feudal mode of production: the need for more land and the need for some form of debt financing. The Italian city-states had begun to amend the second problem; the conquest of the Americas amended the first.

When British colonists arrived in the New World of the Atlantic Americas they found virgin land, unmanicured and undisturbed. These perceptions were quite wrong, of course; the land had been cultivated for centuries by the many First Nations of the continent.[7] Yet these settler colonists' misapprehensions function as a helpful historical reminder: to survive they needed others' skills and knowledge, and then to prosper as capitalists they needed to degrade if not destroy those from whom they had learned. A catalytic mix of English industry and credit, indigenous knowledge, and forms of indentured and enslaved labor began to grow the colony in its capitalist prehistory.

For capitalism to begin to thrive and for a democratic revolution to spring from it, the land had to be made free, as in free of its previous occupants. Workers, too, had to be made free, as in free from their feudal obligations to particular lords and nobles. The process took almost two hundred years, none of which passed seamlessly or peacefully. This primitive accumulation was composed of violence and submission, seizure and terror, all of which prepared the world for the arrival of an unequal (in terms of money) equality (in terms of political rights) that we now recognize as democracy. Braudel offers a more poetic explanation of the foundation necessary for a market economy to emerge. The market is a place where contracts are respected and sales and purchases always seem to align. For Braudel, such a market economy requires a space of its opposite. He writes of "the zone of the anti-market, where the great predators roam and the law of the jungle operates. This today, as in the past, before and after the industrial revolution, is the real home of capitalism."[8] There, in that jungle of primitive accumulation in the Americas, cats roamed, too.

Along the eastern coastal and woodland areas of North America dwelled the two largest groupings of First Nations, the Algonquin and the Haudenosaunee. Many Algonquin nations, including the Ojibwe, believed in the power of the Mishipeshu, a mythical underwater panther whose disposition ranged from protective to warlike and whose name translates as Great Lynx. Another mythical cat of these nations was the Gichi-anami'e-bizhiw, "which translates as 'the fabulous night panther' ... and is also referred to as the 'great underground wildcat' or 'great under-water wildcat.'"[9] However these feline names are transliterated, it was a powerful cat whose lexical root may be seen today in a variety of indigenous languages.

The Haudenosaunee attributed the creation of the earth to yet another cat.[10] The Haudenosaunee story of creation "traces this nation's descent from the Sky People through Sky Woman and her daughter, the Lynx. The Lynx, also known as Jigon-saseh, begins back in the mists of creation, with First Woman, She Who Fell from the Sky, and her beloved daughter, most usually called the Fat-Faced Lynx, the Panther, the Wild Cat."[11] In this tale of beginning, Sky Woman's daughter, Lynx, is seduced by North Wind, and she ultimately dies while giving birth to four children: North, South, East and West.

As the epic develops, Sky Woman grieves Lynx's death until, "at last, she buried her beautiful Lynx, watering the grave with tears." As historian Barbara Mann relates, "The Earth embraced The Lynx, winding its beautiful elements about her, nourishing her so that she could shoot up all the crops of Earth. The Three Sisters sprouted from her fingers, and potatoes—that special creation of The Lynx—from her toes. Eventually, The Lynx sank down, down into the Earth. The first burial, she changed the ground from ordinary dirt into the remains of our ancestors. The Lynx lives now as Our Mother, the Earth."[12]

The Haudenosaunee confederation was of special interest to Marx, who believed its confederated models of governance not based on property ownership offered a potential path around the tragedies of capitalist development. Marx referred to the confederation as "a masterpiece of Indian wisdom." According to one historian, "it doubtless fascinated [Marx] to learn that, as far in advance of the revolution as 1755, the Iroquois had recommended to the 'forefathers [of the] Americans, *a union of the colonies similar to their own*.'" It was not simply the model of confederation that offered what Marx perceived as Indian wisdom; it was also the matter of their material relations. Marxist historian Franklin Rosemont details Marx's sense that "primitive communities had *incomparably greater vitality* than the Semitic, Greek, Roman and *a fortiori* the modern capitalist societies."[13] He argues that Marx had come to realize that when measured according to the "wealth of subjective human sensuality ... Iroquois society stood *much higher* than any of the societies 'poisoned by the pestilential breath of civilization.'"[14]

Marx had learned of various First Nations primarily through the work of the nineteenth-century American ethnologist Henry Louis Morgan and his book, *Ancient Society*. His was a work scattered with references to something that Morgan called the "Cat-nation."[15] Morgan was the best authority Marx could hope for on the matter. Yet Morgan was also someone from whom elements of Haudenosaunee society and culture, including certain feline aspects, remained hidden. As Mann relates, the "main goal of the missionaries from the moment European 'explorers' first set foot in Iroquoia was to disempower Haudenosaunee women, whose socioeconomic and political clout had outraged 'Old World' male authority."[16] To this end, "the important two-thirds of Sky that belonged to women and the stories of Sky Woman and her beloved daughter, The Lynx, were drastically rearranged and/or suppressed outright." Nonetheless references to tigers and "Wild- Cats" appear in Marx's ethnological notebooks, as does the fact that Haudenosaunee offered greater political equality between the sexes than did Euro-American society.[17]

The English colonists sometimes sought to placate indigenous nations, aware as they were of their dependence on them. But more often they sought to expropriate indigenous knowledge and garner indigenous communities' support for their own wars and skirmishes with the French, Spanish, Dutch, and so on. First Nations held the land; poor whites and black slaves held the labor. As the white colonial elite began to consolidate into an emerging class, they became rightly wary of managing these coalitions across race and bondage. Elite whites could offer poor whites land to prevent them from joining with blacks and revolting. But they were offering First Nations land. Colonial animals played a role here, as cattle became "creatures of empire."[18] As indigenous people turned to actual and figurative lynxes and panthers for sustenance and protection, white settlers used livestock as land colonizers. Cows and pigs, animals unknown to indigenous nations, grazed on their lands, forever altering the landscape. Fences were placed to, in the words of one Massachusetts municipality, "keep cows in and Indians out."[19]

The white colonial elite got a preview of what might await them if they failed in this balancing act during Bacon's Rebellion of 1676, in which black and white servants, slaves, and freed mulattos united to fight against their common overlords and exploiters, burning down the Virginia state capitol of Jamestown. This rebellion was against the British colonial government, but it was also a demand for access to more First Nations land. In other words, a slowly consolidating proletariat — those without land — united not only against a bourgeoisie that controlled land but also against the indigenous nations on whose land the British colonists lived. After that uprising colonial elites began to craft a properly stratified society in which race, class, and bondage merged. Their efforts included "a 1676 act that declared captured Indians to be enslaved for life as property of their captor; a 1682 act that eliminated status distinctions among non-Christian servants brought into the colony, reducing them to the common condition of slavery; a 1691 act on miscegenation whose most detailed proscriptions concerned white women bearing mulatto offspring." Together these laws began "to curtail the rights of Blacks, Mulattos, and Indians, free and enslaved, to self-protection, property, and suffrage as it began to recognize the claims of poor white Virginians to these same liberties."[20]

Yet even as the nascent American colonial elite became a landowning, land controlling bourgeoisie and began to break slowly away from its English roots, certain feline elements of the Old World remained. Cats still functioned as witches' familiars, and witch trials spread throughout the Massachusetts Bay colony. In one scene from 1688, "four exemplary Boston children, the sons and daughters of a devout Boston stone-layer named John Goodwin," suffered from a baffling disorder. "'They would bark at one another like dogs, and again purr like so many cats,' noted minister Cotton Mather, who observed Goodwin's family and wrote of their afflictions in *Memorable Providences, Relating to Witchcraft and Possessions* the following year."[21] When not diagnosing and exorcising the possessed, Mather turned his attention to a shortage of circulating money in the colonies and, in his 1691 treatise, *Some Considerations of the Bills of Credit Now Passing in New-England*, began to agitate for paper currency. Mather's concerns with witchcraft and paper money represent problems from the old and new worlds, respectively, and he will not be the only settler colonist in the Americas to dwell between cats and currency. Indeed, we will see in chapter 5 a connection emerge between the two.

In Stamford, Connecticut, the problem of feline demonic possession took hold in 1692. A servant named Katherine Branch "began relaying stories about a cat that spoke to her, offering to take her to a place where she could have fine things and meet fine people." As in medieval Europe, cats here marked class position. This servant used the cat to imagine access to a kind of life denied to her but that could prosper only because of workers like her. "Sometimes, Kate declared, the cats turned into women and then back again," a report noted.[22] "In April of 1692, Branch fell to the ground, her body contorting strangely. The local midwife, Sarah Bates, examined Branch, concluding her illness could be due to natural causes. But after an unsuccessful bleeding—a common medical practice for ailments in those days—Bates concluded that Branch was bewitched."[23]

A bourgeois revolution, however, is about getting rid of such superstitions, and these were some of capitalist prehistory's last witch trials. Marx writes of the coming of capitalism that "all fixed, fast-frozen relations, with their train of ancient and venerable prejudices and opinions, are swept away."[24] There is a reason that when Marx writes of capitalist value, he often jokes about witches and sorcery. The bourgeoisie are rational—they even produced an "era of reason," the so-called Enlightenment. The bourgeoisie do not believe in witches; they believe in private property. And as the eighteenth century began, the bourgeoisie had more and more property to their name. Of course, too strong a belief in property produces its own forms of sorcery, as we will see.

Marx and Engels saw in America a context "rich, vast, expanding, with purely bourgeois institutions, unleavened by feudal remnants or monarchical traditions and without a permanent or hereditary proletariat." As a result, Engels observed, "everyone could become, if not a capitalist, at all events an independent man, producing and trading with his own means, for his own account."[25] That understanding is incomplete—the land abounded with slaves, formerly indentured whites, and disinherited indigenous people. Engels's claim is true for certain white men, and for far more of them than could be found in Europe. But Marx understood quite well the role of slavery in producing the wealth of the American state and its European partners. And when Marx and Marxists say there was no feudalism in colonial America, they should add it wasn't for lack of trying.

Marxist historian Neil Davidson asks, How revolutionary were the bourgeois revolutions? in his book of the same name; and he answers: Not very. In the American case, he notes, "There were three genuine attempts to install or revive systematic feudalism in the new colonial context . . . [including] a constitution involving hereditary serfdom."[26] He continues, "Feudal projects collapsed not because America was too progressive to endure them, but because it was too primitive to sustain them."[27] When New World feudalism didn't pan out, elite colonists began to imagine a different kind of state. They desired a state to protect them and their belongings as one once protected those of their feudal lords. Thus, they needed a new kind of state, one that could guarantee not the interpenetration of crown, religion, and accumulation—as feudal fiefdoms had done—but land claims and labor contracts. More specifically they envisioned a state that protected land and labor for them against the claims of others, including nobles back in England and the poor rabble of the New World.

Davidson is only one of many Marxists to note the constrained revolutionary spirit—"reluctant revolutionaries," as popular histories sometimes call the actors—of the American case. We now consider it, too, but we will approach its conservatism somewhat differently: we will trace the founding fathers' use of felines, from lions to lynxes to domestic cats. In doing so we will be able to confirm Marx's fundamental critique of the bourgeois order: that it combines the revolutionary and the reactionary in a historically novel manner. Such bourgeois novelty applies to cats as well.

THE LION-CAT REDUX OF
THE AMERICAN REVOLUTION

By the late eighteenth century one out of every four English people lived in the thirteen British colonies. These colonies were Britain's wealthiest possession, and that wealth was beginning to produce a new social world whose problems had a distinctly American flair. For the emergent American bourgeoisie to develop into a class strong enough to break the bonds of absolutism they needed land and labor. They got both, but neither was rightly theirs. The labor came from a steady stream of slave importation and from the work of poor whites, who were themselves an emergent class of proletarians. The emergent proletarians needed land—that's what it meant to be a proletarian during American capitalist development before wage labor. It was the land that served, in Marx's words, as colonists' means of production, or what enables an individual, community, or society to satisfy its subsistence needs, produce wealth, and maybe even grow and flourish from one day to the next. What was unique about colonial America was that colonial elites could offer their underlings other people's land. It is this very kind of purloining that Marx says constitutes "the secret of primitive accumulation"—or the beginning of capitalism.[28] For Marx, this secret reveals the great hidden truth of capitalism: if someone possesses something today, it's most likely because someone else took it by force yesterday.

In the American case, however, the "secret of primitive accumulation" was no metaphor. Here is founding father, lion admirer, and genocidaire George Washington describing one of his own transactions in stolen Indian land to a prospective partner: "All of this [transaction] can be carried on by silent management and can be carried out by you under the guise of hunting game, which you may, I presume, effectually do, at the same time you are in pursuit of land. When this is fully discovered advise me of it, and if there appears a possibility of succeeding, I will have the land surveyed to keep others off and leave the rest to time and my own assiduity. . . . Keep the whole matter a secret."[29] In their land dealings one notices a difference between the bourgeoisie and feudal kings and lords of yore, the latter of whom would simply conquer and take land as their own. Washington, in contrast, knew it is sometimes better to tread quietly. Once they had seized indigenous land they could offer it to white settlers. It was hardly a case of bourgeois altruism, even though the bourgeoisie does love altruism. The American bourgeoisie realized the way to avoid another Bacon's Rebellion was, as founding father James Madison said, to "extend the sphere"—to continue to take land away from indigenous nations and offer it to poor white settlers, whom one British governor described as "the overflowing Scum of the Empire" and another as "the Scum of the Gaols."[30]

The translation of the classic Marxist story in which the two great classes of history, bourgeoisie and proletariat, face each other requires that certain amendments be made in the American context of settler colonialism. There was ample land to give and the secret of primitive accumulation was real. There was also a class of enslaved people who couldn't be placated with land or exterminated because the economy required their ongoing enslavement. As their profits from slavery and empire continued to grow, the nascent American bourgeoisie began to wonder: Why send part of these profits back to the Crown, when we could keep them for ourselves? Why have a government that supports a whole noble class of king and lords in England when we could develop our own middle management here? Marx tells us that "each step in the development of the bourgeoisie was accompanied by a corresponding political advance of that class" and "at a certain stage of development, the material productive forces of society come into conflict with the existing relations of production.... Then begins an era of social revolution."[31] It was about to begin in colonial America as elites tired of paying duties to England and grew frustrated with limits on seizing indigenous land. As they begin to agitate for a radical break with King George III of England, even a break with the idea of kings themselves, we can now properly be introduced to the bourgeoisie.

The bourgeoisie is a revolutionary class. In an age of revolutions, Marx believes "the bourgeoisie has played the most revolutionary role."[32] In the colonies, in Europe, everywhere, the bourgeoisie is a global class with global designs. But the bourgeoisie is a derivative class, too. Marx writes, "On the level plain, simple mounds look like hills; and the imbecile flatness of the present bourgeoisie is to be measured by the altitude of its great intellects."[33] In the American case those mounds were even smaller. This was not the *haute bourgeoisie* of Europe, to use that class's own language. Rather, this is what the German sociologist Max Weber called the "backwoods small bourgeois circumstances" of eighteenth-century colonial America.[34] There was no Scottish enlightenment to offer up a skeptical thinker like David Hume or a truly great capitalist philosopher like Adam Smith. There was no French Enlightenment to produce a Jean-Jacques Rousseau (admittedly Swiss-born) to proclaim the need for a social contract or a Voltaire to offer the class a reflection of itself through satire. Instead, the American bourgeois awakening ponied up to posterity a few slaveowners who read French. George Washington didn't even do that. Backwoods small bourgeois, indeed.

Marx insists it doesn't matter. It is their skill for combining revolution and recalcitrance that distinguishes the bourgeoisie and that, in the American case, set the thirteen colonies on a road to independence and enabled world history to leap into a new epoch. While revolting against those of higher social status, they would have to ensure they were not revolted against by the proletarians, those of lower social status. That is the real trick of any bourgeois revolution: to be freed from one's rulers but not from those whom one rules.

The bourgeoisie, those great shoplifters of history, began to borrow from cats as well. They had appropriated from First Nations the land and many of the skills to live in the New World. They also borrowed the lynx, which, during colonization, entered American English vocabulary as an animal known to possess an uncommon keenness, with penetrating sight both real and metaphorical. For the Haudenosaunee the lynx was a god; for the British and now Americans, God was like a lynx. Thomas Carlyle noted in *Criticism and Miscellaneous Essays* that God with "His lynx-eye discerns the true relations of the world and human life."[35] John Sylvester claimed God "sees all secrets and his Lynx-like eye doth every thought describe."[36] In their negotiation of the lynx we note an important bourgeois habit: they begin to desacralize nature, to render it a less spiritual place; but they do so slowly: the lynx begins as God, then becomes godlike, then a secular cat.

From the English, colonial American elites lifted a leonine element. It seems that everywhere we look among the founding fathers we find not only slavery and genocide but lions. We begin with George Washington, under whose military guidance the thirteen American colonies became an independent nation through bourgeois revolution. General of the Revolutionary army, torturer of humans and animals, and first president of the United States, Washington, along with his wife, Martha, kept a plantation of hundreds of slaves in Virginia. Among his slaveholding confederates Washington was distinguished by his cruelty. One historian reports, "It was the sense of all his neighbors that he treated [his slaves] with more severity than any other man."[37] Not content to abuse only his slaves, Washington orchestrated a mass hanging of his slaves' dogs, which he felt were encroaching on his sheep. As another historian laconically put it, "The barbarous, insidious nature of American chattel slavery really did infect everything in Colonial life, even dog ownership."[38]

A statesman and military tactician, Washington is often depicted with his sword. Yet since the inventions of muskets, long rifles, and bayonets, swords had ceased to be used in warfare and certainly their employment was minimal during the American Revolutionary War. For Washington, then, the sword was a symbol of martial art and masculine comportment. It was an accessory whose function was its appearance. The sword appeared as a lion.

A cuttoe whose handle was cow bone but aspired to ivory, Washington's lion sword was a replica in more ways than one. As he styled himself as a new kind of ruler, an American imbued with a spirit of sacrifice and freedom, he turned to the past

FIGURE 3.4. For the first American president, a leonine relic of the past: Washington's silver lion-headed sword.

to craft his new style and represent himself as a revolutionary. While Marx had little to say about Washington, he had plenty to say about this kind of bourgeois revolutionary. "Just as [the bourgeoisie] seem to be occupied with revolutionizing themselves and things, creating something that did not exist before, precisely in such epochs of revolutionary crisis they anxiously conjure up the spirits of the past to their service, borrowing from them names, battle slogans, and costumes in order to present this new scene in world history in time-honored disguise and borrowed language."[39] Washington adopted the feudal lion, that sign of mastery, bravery, and dominance. This sort of guise did not fool Marx, however. "But unheroic though bourgeois society is," he wrote, "it nevertheless needed heroism, sacrifice, terror, civil war, and national wars to bring it into being."[40] The bourgeoisie makes amendments and turns history into theater.

In his quest for democratic independence and human freedom, Washington was joined by man of science and fellow slaveholder Thomas Jefferson, to whom the task fell to articulate the revolutionary discourse some months into the colonists' military rebellion against the English king. In his class's formal *Declaration of Independence*, Jefferson began by stating the new bourgeois rules of government: "When in the course of human events," this enslaver of his own children wrote, "it becomes necessary for one people to dissolve the political bands which have connected them with another ... a decent respect to the opinions of mankind requires that they should declare the causes which impel them to the separation."[41] He went on to reject the idea of the divine right of kings to rule. People get their rulers from their own consent, just as they consent to contracts. When they no longer consent, they are entitled to radical change.

And then came one of most famous bourgeois statements, ventriloquized through Jefferson: "We hold these truths to be self-evident, that all men are created equal, that they are endowed by their Creator with certain unalienable rights, that

FIGURE 3.5. Lion at Jefferson's slave plantation, Monticello, in Charlottesville, Virginia. Source: Rufus W. Holsinger, Monticello Exterior, Holsinger Studio Collection, Special Collections, University of Virginia Library.

among these are life, liberty and the pursuit of happiness."[42] As lofty prose, Jefferson's words are hard to match. Yet it is the material conditions from which such rhetoric springs that form Marx's estimation of them. Jefferson wrote these words while overseeing a plantation of slaves and directing a genocide. Thus Marx claims, "The democratic petty bourgeois, far from wanting to transform the whole society . . . only aspire to make the existing society as tolerable for themselves as possible."[43] Jefferson was aware of what universal freedom would mean for his bottom line. To describe the paradox of slavery Jefferson turned to the natural world. Using a language of animality, he imagined black slaves as dangerous, unpredictable beings. "We have the wolf by the ear," he wrote of the slave, "and we can neither hold him, nor safely let him go. Justice is in one scale, and self-preservation in the other."[44]

Washington copied old European swords and symbols. Jefferson copied newer European philosophy, up to and including an emergent kind of natural history that had replaced the animal knowledge once found in bestiaries. Jefferson styled himself as a renaissance man, a humanist equally at home in science as in government and arts. His scientific pursuits led him to believe he had identified lion skeletons in Virginia. In 1796 a certain Colonel John Stuart sent Jefferson several fossilized bones: a femur fragment, an ulna, a radius, and foot bones, including three large claws. Jefferson soon after presented a paper on "Certain Bones" to the American Philosophical Society in Philadelphia on March 10, 1797.[45] In the paper he theorized that the bones represented the remains of a lion, which he named *Megalonyx*, or "giant claw." Jefferson asked Meriwether Lewis and William Clark, as they planned their famous expropriation of Western indigenous lands from 1804 to 1806, to keep an eye out for living specimens of his *Megalonyx*. They found none. Jefferson had misidentified his fossils and located a lion where, in reality, there was a sloth. Nonetheless, lions were placed at his plantation, Monticello, in Virginia, likely after his death, and from there they arrived on the Jefferson two-dollar bill.

The actual appellation of *lion* fell to the man who devised the financial infrastructure of the early United States. Alexander Hamilton was a member of the revolutionary gang of founding fathers who advocated for continued monarchy. Appropriately he was called the "Little Lion" by his colleagues, a particularly important fact considering his role in developing the first American national banking system. If Washington and Jefferson made the United States modern through war and declarations of independence, Alexander Hamilton did so through monetary and fiscal policy. As secretary of the

Treasury, Hamilton sought to use Revolutionary War debt to create a financial system that would promote American economic growth. In his *Report on Public Credit* he urged Congress to consolidate state and national debts into a single debt that would be funded by the federal government. Congress approved these measures in July 1790. Marx's words on public debt were as true for the early United States as they had been for the sixteenth-century Republic of Venice: "As with the stroke of an enchanter's wand, it endows barren money with the power of breeding and thus turns it into capital."[46] Furthermore, once established, the public debt takes on a life and history of its own. "The modern fiscal system contains within it the germ of progress," Marx continues. A new American history begins here, and it was Hamilton, the "Little Lion" and slaveholder, who laid out a truly capitalist path for the novel country. George Washington grew so fond of Hamilton that he and Martha named one of their two domestic cats Alexander Hamilton.[47]

Then there was John Adams, the second American president, who recalled a solemn day on a transatlantic voyage in his journals. In reading his entry today we see the historical ambivalence of the bourgeoisie as a class. He begins by noting, rightly, his fundamental mediocrity. "By my Physical Constitution, I am but an ordinary Man." This would never have been written by a king, who in no sense understands himself as ordinary. Adams continues, "The Times alone have destined me to Fame—and even these have not been able to give me, much." In Adams's writing we get a sense of the bourgeois mind, both self-conscious and made unique by world historical events in which it participated. Adams elaborates, "Yet some great Events, some cutting Expressions, some mean Hypocrisies, have at Times, thrown this Assemblage of Sloth, Sleep, and littleness into Rage a little like a Lion. Yet it is not like the Lion—there is Extravagance and Distraction in it, that still betrays the same Weakness."[48] Adams realizes that the lion is a fantasy, and such awareness enables him to be both drawn to it and skeptical of it. Adams and his colleagues were more clear about what kind of government they needed. They designed a state insulated from democratic impetuousness. They limited voting. They protected slavery. And they made sure Americans could not directly elect a president. Thus Marx says of the new capitalist democracies, "The executive of the modern state is but a committee for managing the common affairs of the whole bourgeoisie."[49] It was the bourgeoisie for whom the liberty bell rang, even if the actual bell cracked and was rendered mute. Banished was the king of England, George III. Consigned to history were the inherited titles and the House of Lords. But there is more to this story, and now, in due course, enter the lion dissenters and the domestic cat lovers as our reenactment of feudal glory and terror continues.

In New England a little-known anti-lion rebellion in Boston, Massachusetts, took place at the height of American revolutionary activity. On July 18, 1776, the Declaration of Independence was first proclaimed from the statehouse balcony to citizens of Boston. In response a group of revelers removed the statehouse's rooftop statues of a lion and unicorn, along with other symbols of royal authority, and consigned them to a bonfire.[50] In a different kind of rebellious act, the commonwealth of Massachusetts put the lion back up. Today it still stands, sheathed in gold leaf and wearing a crown laden with crosses.

There were other moments of leonine criticism during the American Revolution and after, and in those moments we find domestic cats and kittens. We now introduce founding father Thomas Paine, a political pamphleteer, poet, and, yes, a lover of cats—too much of one, according to some of his more scornful critics. But we start with not his affection for cats but his displeasure at lions.

FIGURE 3.6. Royal relics still in residence today at the Massachusetts State House, Boston.

In his 1776 call for revolution, *Common Sense*, Paine returns to the dark scene that began feudal English history, William the Conqueror's invasion. We know, as did Paine, that William was a lion who brought with him generations of Lyons. Paine rebukes his readers, "If there are any so weak as to believe [in] hereditary right, let them worship the ass and the lion."[51] So as royals understood their genealogy as one of lions, Paine uses a language of animality to describe how they understand their subjects. Royals, he wrote, "inherit the People, as if they were flocks and herds."[52] Unlike kings, and perhaps many of his band of founding fathers, Paine understood well that aristocratic leonine appearance was a mark of longing, not of fact. He insisted that most of the king's subjects "jeered [at the royals] as an ass rather than dreaded [it] as a lion."[53]

Paine's view of royalty did not necessarily distinguish him from most of the founding fathers, but he did suspect a few of royal longings. Of John Adams he said, "His head was as full of kings, queens, and knaves, as a pack of cards." Adams returned the compliment with his own bestial vocabulary and described Paine as "a mongrel between pig and puppy, begotten by a wild boar or a bitch wolf, never before in any age of the world was suffered by the poltroonery of mankind, to run through such a career of mischief."[54]

What did distinguish Paine from his revolutionary colleagues was his appreciation of animals, cats in particular. In his pamphlet in support of the French Revolution, *The Age of Reason,* he argues that "the moral duty of man consists in 'imitating the moral goodness and beneficence of God, manifested in the creation toward all His creatures ... everything of persecution and revenge between man and man, and everything of cruelty to animals, is a violation of moral duty.'"[55] His opposition to animal suffering is also evident in his poetry, as the cat-centric "Cruelty to Animals Exposed" demonstrates.[56]

> Occasioned by a real circumstance
> A Pale and wrinkled wretch I saw one day,
> Whom pale disease had wither'd half away,
> And yet the sad remaining half seem'd curst
> With all the mis'ries that befell the first;
> While death, impatient to unite the two
> Pursu'd him hard, and kept him in his view.
> This half-dead wretch with pain and palsy shook,
> Beneath his arm a captived kitten took,
> Close to his savage side she fondly clung,

And unsuspicious, kindly purr'd and sung;
While he with smiles conceal'd his black intent,
And gentle strok'd her all the way he went.

In an act of trans-species solidarity the kitten offers love and
respect to the poor wretch, who, as the title of the poem indicates, ultimately betrays the kitten. In Revolutionary America, a genuine land of plenty for white elites, Paine argued
that "a great portion of mankind . . . are in a state of poverty
and wretchedness . . . far below" that of preindustrial societies.
"The present state of civilization is as odious as it is unjust,"
Paine argued. "It is absolutely the opposite of what it should
be, and it is necessary that a revolution should be made in
it."[57] Yet the revolution that was made took a quite different
form: slavery was enshrined, voting was restricted, and nothing like Paine's proposed scheme of a basic income for all was
included.[58]

Paine's colleagues had many reasons to hate him—his political radicality, his desire for an economic democracy, his
debts, his charge that George Washington was a corrupt em-
bezzler. One of his detractors, however, chose an anachronistic
charge to level at him: cat sodomy.

Paine's enemies, like his revolutionary spirit and publications, existed on both sides of the Atlantic. In England "a counterfeit letter supposedly from Paine's mother was circulated,
complaining of his debts, his terrible treatment of his wife, and
his 'undutiful behavior to the tenderest of parents.'" Its author,
Charles Harrington Elliot, went on to charge that Paine was
known to "engage in carnal relations with his 'maiden wife,'
and a cat."[59] As the colonies became the United States and developed into a slaveholding plutocracy, Paine's vision of economic democracy became ever more distant from historical
reality. He died in debt with rumors of cat sodomy swirling
about him, but his words—and his corpse—continued to cir-

FIGURE 3.7. Thomas Spence's cat coin for a utopian economy, 1796. The text on the coin reads: "I among slaves enjoy my freedom."

culate in both the United States and England. We'll meet his remains again in chapter 5. When revolutionary sentiment began to appear in France, Paine traveled there to join the efforts but was almost killed as a reactionary; indeed, he was almost killed by a tiger.

While Marx didn't engage directly with Paine's work, "the American revolutionary's followers on both sides of the Atlantic played an enormous role in forging the nineteenth century's workers movement that supplied Marx with the empirical politics that he provided . . . philosophical understanding of."[60] Some of the first known American worker radicals were indeed called "Painites." The fact that his feline defamation originated overseas alerts us to his popularity there; Paine was born in England. But it also alerts us to the fact that the American Revolution is not simply the story of one country but of two: the United States and England. And in England we meet additional radical cat lovers and Paine contemporaries who looked to the revolutions in the United States and France and agitated to replicate them at home.

Englishman Thomas Spence, for example, both followed and critiqued Paine. Spence's writings call for the end of "landlordism," or rent; freedom for children; universal political representation; and a jubilee from debt. And, like Paine, he turned away from the lion and toward other felines. Spence imprinted a series of coins for his imagined utopian economy, many of which depicted animals (see figure 3.7). It fell to the domestic cat to celebrate freedom.[61] Like Paine as well, Spence's social criticism extended to his poetry, where the lion is removed from his royal position and other animals and children emerge to take that beast's place. As he imagined a postrevolutionary society of equals, Spence predicted that

> The Golden Age, so fam'd by men of yore, Shall now be counted fabulous no more.
> The tyrant lion like an ox shall feed, And lisping Infants shall tam'd tygers lead:
> With deadly asps shall sportive sucklings play, Nor ought obnoxious blight the blithesome day.
> Yes, all that prophets e'er of bliss foretold, And all that poets ever feign'd of old,
> As yielding joy to man, shall now be seen, And ever flourish like an evergreen.

> Then, Mortals, join to hail great Nature's plan, That
> fully gives to Babes those Rights it gives to Man.[62]

For his political writings and speeches Spence was convicted
of sedition and hauled off to Newgate Gaol, that infamous
prison from whose door, we remember, prisoners could once
see a statue of Dick Whittington's cat. While incarcerated
Spence continued with his compositions, producing poetry
that rued the day that the lion William the Conqueror arrived
in England. He tarried with leading conservatives of his time,
especially on the question of revolution in France, and in doing so bolstered the position of animals as agents of change.
When reactionary Irish philosopher Edmund Burke claimed
the French Revolution was porcine and christened its revolutionaries a "swinish multitude," Spence started a periodical
called *Pig's Meat; or, Lessons for the Swinish Multitude*, which
advocated the nationalization of land.

Spence was not a fallen founding father like Paine, whom
he ultimately criticized for maintaining a notion of private
property and for not supporting the 1780 prison uprising at
Newgate. Unlike Paine, Spence had no elite associations from
which to be exiled. Marx considered Spence a practical utopian and noted that "only a German could be so insular not
to have heard of Thomas More, the Levellers, Robert Owen,
John Minter Morgan or Thomas Spence."[63] But few Marxists
today, save Peter Linebaugh, know the historical import of this
cat lover.[64] Like Paine, Spence moved through a world of 1790s
radical printers that included William Blake, whose poem *The
Tyger* remains one of the most revolutionary cat incantations
ever published. It is the tiger that will guide us through revolutionary France, Haiti, and the larger Atlantic world in our
next chapter, and it is the tiger that introduces our next dialectic as well.

INTERMEZZO 2

———————

THE TIGER-TYGER DIALECTIC

Through the lives and work of Tom Paine, Thomas Spence, and now William Blake, and their cats, we encounter the outlines of a history that existed but went partly unfulfilled. In an age of empire and revolution, these cat admirers offered visions of a liberatory future for women, the enslaved, the indebted, children, animals, and colonized peoples. Theirs was a future that might have been, and indeed still might be, and it is this distance between what happened and what might have happened that guides any historical study. Marxism in particular has long asked, How can history be written otherwise to present new possibilities? *Marx for Cats* narrows the question and renders it a feline inquiry: How can cats, both great and small, lead us to a radical history anew?

There's no better guide to this question than twentieth-century Marxist philosopher Walter Benjamin, both because he asserted that "to articulate the past historically does not mean to recognize it 'the way it really was'" and because he suggested that the animal we should follow to discover that long gone newness is a feline. Benjamin advises locating the past we seek by "seiz[ing] hold of a memory as it flashes up at a moment of danger."[1] Benjamin wrote those words during his own dangerous moment, the coming of Nazi fascism to Germany, an event that would end his life. Ours is a dangerous moment as well. As I write, the world is in the grip of a global pandemic whose origin lies in the brutality of capitalist animal agriculture. Paine, Spence, and Blake lived in their own dangerous moments of revolution and empire. For Benjamin, a precarious present may guide the historian to an emancipatory past whose identification might transform the future. As Benjamin emphasizes, "Only that historian will have the gift of fanning the spark of hope in the past who is firmly convinced that *even the dead* will not be safe from the enemy if he wins."[2]

His vision of history requires a powerful and idiosyncratic guide. For this journey, Benjamin selects a cat. He writes:

> History is the object of a construction whose place is formed not in homogenous and empty time, but in the fulfilled here-and-now.... It is the tiger's leap into that which has gone before. Only it takes place in an arena in which the ruling classes are in control. The same leap in the open sky of history is the dialectical one, as Marx conceptualized the revolution.[3]

The text from which these lines are taken, *Theses on the Philosophy of History*, has generated multiple speculative stories and histories, and Marxists have long been captivated by the text's despairing figure of "the angel of history" to the neglect of the text's tiger and its leap. This neglect has occluded not only Marxism's feline archive but one of its crucial figures of social transformation, namely the leap. Why has the tiger's leap into history been forsaken by Marxists in favor of a doomed angel? Why has the tiger been an outcast in the menagerie of

FIGURE 12.1. N-gram: Tiger overlaid with tyger. Source: Author created.

the historian's conceptual tools as she seeks to spring free of the past? The immediate answer is one of identification: in an age of bourgeois revolution, the tiger we seek is in fact a tyger.

As they refer to the striped feline, the terms *tyger* and *tiger* are one and the same. They differ only in their orthography, or a language's writing system. In eighteenth-century English, then as now a developing hybrid of a language, *y* was used as often as *i* for a simple economic reason: it was cheaper to print and easier to read. As printing technology became more standard and efficient, English witnessed a gradual replacement of *y* with *i*. The *y* endured in certain word groups, for example those of Greek origin such as *etymology*, as well as in in certain feline names, such as *lynx*, but in others, like *tyger*, it was slowly abandoned.[4] In the period of revolutionary activity under discussion here, from the 1770s through roughly 1805, *tyger* and *tiger* overlap, with *tyger* overtaking *tiger* perhaps only momentarily in the mid- to late eighteenth century. By the 1850s, *tyger* had essentially become a relic.

Blake and Spence were printers who were driven to the margins of society by their political views. The *y* they printed was cheaper, but it was also more revolutionary. Indeed, Spence was so devoted to transforming the English language as a political project that he developed his own phonetic and orthographic systems that he believed would enable the poor to learn more easily to read and write. Benjamin likewise was a philosophical outcast from the German academy, for the creativity of his thought, and from Germany as it became a Nazi state, as a Jew. Each of these thinkers recognized the tiger as a potential partner. But much of that potential has been buried under the y. Our task in chapter 4 is to undertake our own *Tigersprung* and leap back into the past as the tyger both becomes and resists the tiger in France, Haiti, and the English language. Once we locate the work that the tiger does for revolutionary transformation we will be in a better position to recognize that feline's crucial addition to our archive, its leap. What was lost with the tyger was a world of feline possibility and, just as importantly, a critique of an impossibility, too.

4

Revolutionary Tigers

"The tiger is, perhaps, the only animal whose spirit cannot be subdued."

— GEORGES-LOUIS LECLERC, COMTE DE BUFFON,
NATURAL HISTORY

 t the height of French revolutionary activity in 1793, Jean-Paul Marat, radical journalist and physician, leading supporter of the Jacobin leftist political group, defender of the poor and enslaved, lay soaking in his Paris tub. He suffered from an unknown skin ailment and took medicinal waters for treatment. During his bath his wife granted a certain Charlotte Corday entrance to their home. Corday explained that she brought news of his political opponents. She was escorted to meet a still-bathing Marat, whom she then stabbed and killed. The assassination of Marat soon took on symbolic importance in the work of painter Jacques-Louis David, whose

haunting image of the aquatic death scene has become synonymous with the French Revolution itself and who, in the words of one Marxist art historian, ushered in the first truly modern painting with his depiction of Marat.[1]

The first announcements of Marat's death, however, came not via painting but the speedier medium of print. Throughout eighteenth-century France and England, an increasing number of newspapers transmitted events to a similarly increasing readership. In life, Marat had circulated in the same revolutionary print culture as had Thomas Spence. Indeed, he had launched his publication, *The Chains of Slavery*, in Newcastle, Spence's hometown, and visited its Philosophical Society, which Spence helped to found and at which Spence spoke, perhaps to Marat.[2] Witnessing growing revolutionary turmoil in France, Marat returned home to join the struggle with violent verve. In death, however, Marat was transformed. He became a tiger. On July 13, 1793, the London *Times* published a searing memorial of him as "a fine portrait of [a] chief murderer with eyes of a tyger cat and . . . looks that corresponded to that animal."[3] Two weeks later the *Courier de Londres* provided its own feline assessment of Marat: "Ses yeux étaient d'un verd pale, semblable à ceux d'un chat tigre, même férocité dans le regard" (His eyes were a pale green, resembling those of a cat tiger, [with] the same ferocity in this regard).[4] Jean-Paul Marat was not the only one of many revolutionaries of the francophone world, in France and its rebellious colony Saint-Domingue, who would earn the epithet *tiger*. He was only the first to die.

In this chapter we leave the backwoods bourgeois world of the English colonies and arrive in the native land of the bourgeoisie, France. The French Revolution, a bête noir of conservatives in its own day and still in ours, was, according to Marx, "the most colossal revolution that history has ever known."[5] At the height of their historical radicalism, French revolutionaries abolished slavery, denuded France of the influence of the Cath-

FIGURE 4.1. Buffon Georges-Louis Leclerc, *Der Tiger*, from the German edition of *Natural History*, 1750–72.

olic church, executed their king and queen, and liberated their big cats from the royal menagerie. But that height was short-lived, and no sooner did the regal blood dry on the guillotine than the executioners became the executed, slavery was re-established, and a new emperor, the cat hating, lion loving Napoleon Bonaparte, emerged from the revolutionary detritus.

If the American founding fathers were a pride of lions, the French revolutionaries were an ambush of tigers. The American colonists had written a letter to their king explaining the reasons for their political separation. The French revoked their king's title and staged his public decapitation. Unlike lions, tigers are solitary creatures and form groups, called ambushes, only while in captivity. Perhaps the radicals of the French Revolution were in a kind of captivity as they attempted to break the bonds of the French monarchy and to initiate what Marx claims was nothing less than the "victory of a new social order."[6]

Part of the new social order of which Marx speaks was the dawning of a secular philosophy and literature, of transformed humanistic ideas of citizenship and friendship, and a novel kind of science called natural history. In each of these emergent knowledges we find a series of reinvented cats. In the natural histories of the animal world, for example, most religious references were jettisoned, but the cataloguing of multiple felines remained. In this period's philosophy, freedom became assumed as both a condition for and an end of human flourishing. Cats offered the template. Jean-Jacques Rousseau thought of loving cats as a kind of litmus test for humans' abilities to resist tyranny and nurture social and political equality. In literature and art cats began their entry indoors, where they appeared sitting on tables and surreptitiously visiting banquets, all the while continuing their contribution to a new totality, something now called "society," namely, their mousing and ratting work.

Like the American Revolution and its felines, the French Revolution and its felines resonated abroad, perhaps even more so. The British monarchical state and much of its press looked on, horrified, from across the English Channel as turmoil erupted in France and went on to transform the European continent. Some of the American founding fathers paternalistically weighed in as well; Thomas Paine traveled to France to join the Revolution and was almost guillotined himself. Most importantly, Saint-Domingue, the Caribbean colony that generated huge wealth for France, declared its freedom and launched its own revolution in which cats played an important role.

So we traverse the Atlantic again to arrive in Saint-Domingue, present-day Haiti, where perhaps the most revolutionary of revolutions occurred as a French colony of slaves rose up and became the first black republic in the world. Its execution of a slave revolt is without parallel in modern history. Haiti, too, is a unique and enduring case. If the French Revolution is traditionally hated, the Haitian Revolution has been traditionally ignored, including by many Marxists. Through these francophone revolutions we will be introduced to a new species of feline, the tiger (or tyger), a beast who haunts the French Revolution and guides the Haitian Revolution. The tiger does not replace the lion—no animal, feline or otherwise, could—but offers instead an addition to our bestiary. And we will contend with numerous *chats domestiques*, felines who undergo their own French revolution as they are welcomed into philosophy, painting, poetry, and class struggle. Each of these felines—lion, tiger, tyger, lynx, domestic cat—is present for the world-transforming class struggle that produced the French Revolution and all that that event has come to represent.

Domestic felines were despised by certain vocal elements of the aristocracy, but certainly not by all; anyway, the whole point of the French Revolution was to do away with the aristocracy. The same domestic cats were mostly embraced by the emergent bourgeoisie, who launched an assault on the political power of rent-seeking nobles, whom Marx refers to as a "parasitical excrescence." Where were the proletarians in this struggle? It is the prospect of their freedom that animates Marx's and Marxist critique. The proletarians had their own class resentments against domestic cats, who in many cases received better treatment from the bourgeoisie than they did. Yet they also advocated for forms of animal freedom distinct from the emerging bourgeois concern with "animal welfare." This age truly is one of conflicting alliances, and historical contradiction applies no less to cats than to other subjects of history.

CAT ALLIANCES, CLASS ALLIANCES

As France began developing into an absolutist state governed by a monarch with broad administrative reach, cats began to shed their devilish connotations. In 1484 Pope Innocent VIII had declared the cat a favorite animal of witches. Some hun-

FIGURE 4.2. Charles Édouard Delort, *La distraction de Richelieu* (*The Cardinal's Leisure*), before 1885. Collection of Detroit Institute of Arts.

dred years later, French essayist Michel de Montaigne delighted in the mutuality of cats' playfulness and wondered why humans insist on our moral superiority over them and indeed all animals. Of their communication, Montaigne noted, humans assume it is animals with whom they cannot speak rather than realizing that communication is a menagerie of styles and possibilities.[7] This kind of feline horizontality came from a man whose family had been able to purchase its own noble position, which he inherited.

There is some historiographical debate about whether the absolutist state that opens our chapter constituted the same kind of domination by a class of landowners that ushered us through feudalism or whether it represented a sort of negotiated settlement between an expiring nobility and an emergent bourgeoisie. French aristocrats certainly felt some jealous concern as an emergent capitalist class began to reap profits in industry, banking, and trading, all of which offered new paths to enrichment outside of noble control of land ownership. At the same time nobles' own power through their governing position in the Estates General remained unfettered, at least until the Revolution. In fact, we may address this question of precisely what kind of class composition the absolutist state engendered through a consideration of domestic cats, where we will find a similar negotiation between old and new orders as well as an auspicious set of class contradictions.

Consider the role of chief architect of that state form, Cardinal Armand Jean du Plessis, Duke of Richelieu. Effectively the ruler of France in the mid-seventeenth century, Cardinal Richelieu installed a cattery at the seat of government, the Palais Royal, to house his fourteen Persian and Angora felines. One of his amendments to the French state was to begin the process of clearing out the deadweight nobility from government by selling off governmental posts. As Marxist historian Perry Anderson explains in his classic work, *Lineages of the Ab-*

Quand les francois prendront
ARRAS les Souris mengerons
les Chats, les francois on pris ARRAS
et si les Souris non poinct mange
les Chats

ARRAS Pris Par Les Francois Le 10 Aoust
1640.

Chaque chose a son tour Matou tu le Verras   Vn prouerbe fatal, ta fait prise des Rats
En vain si grauement tu gagne la campagne   car puis que les francois ont enfin prins Arras
Ton corps sera mange deuant qu estre en Espagne.   J - laOnd ex

FIGURE 4.3. Anonymous artist, *Le chat du siège d'Arras*, 1640. The
work depicts the French capture of Arras from Spain during the
Thirty Years' War.

solutist State, "by making the acquisition of bureaucratic position a market transaction, and vesting ownership of it with
rights of inheritance, [the] sale of offices blocked the formation of grandee clientage systems within the State."[8] Anderson notes that Richelieu stressed the "critical 'sterilizing' role of
[selling positions] in putting the whole administrative system
beyond the reach of tentacular aristocratic lineages."[9]

Even more interesting for our purposes is the fact that
Richelieu included provisions for his cats in his will, although
they were offered only monetary allotments and not positions
in government. One of the architects of the French absolutist
state whose destruction was the goal of the French Revolution,
Richelieu's feline appreciation demonstrates a real historical
distance from the feudal order. As a passing swipe at that me-

dieval heritage, he seems to have jokingly named one of his cats Lucifer.[10] The Spanish had their own feline joke with Richelieu; during the Thirty Years' War, a cartoon circulated in the contested city of Arras with the caption "Quand les Français prendront Arras, les souris mangeront les chats" (When the French take Arras, mice will eat cats).

Unlike in the work and lives of Montaigne and Richelieu, in the natural history and physiognomy of the late seventeenth and eighteenth centuries, domestic cats and some of their wild brethren remained suspect. Court painter and founder of the Académie royale de peinture et de sculpture, Charles Le Brun, produced a remarkable series of human-animal hybrid studies in which multiple species of felines as well as boars, camels, and donkeys made appearances. "Of course, there were 'noble' characteristics to be found in the lion," writes historian Peter Sahlins of that big cat's requisite inclusion.[11] In the lion we see the lineages of the absolutist state as it was still connected to a feudal history and expressed through an appreciation of the regality. In men who possessed leonine features, the lines of classical Greco-Roman busts predominate in facial features and in form.

But not so the for the domestic cat. Around his sketches of the animal's head Le Brun jotted disparaging adjectives such as "obstinate and fearful" (*opiniâtre et méfiant*) and "obstinate, wild" (*au piniarete* [sic] *farouche*).[12] Such concerns also applied to the lynx, whom he described as "timid, obstinate" (*timide, opiniâtre*). In Le Brun's cat-man hybrid study, the rounded, perfectly proportioned face of the lion-man gave way to sharp angles and errant whiskers. In Le Brun's work we see that cats continued to index social disorder, but no longer through the language of heresy. Instead they began to "represent subjects of the lower social orders, peasants or artisans, those social groups most likely to exhibit the bestial behavior that was the opposite of [the kind of] *civilité* and civilization" that was emerging in a certain slice of France. Representations of them suggested "the

FIGURE 4.4. Charles Le Brun, lithograph, lion-man study from notebook "The relation between the human physiognomy and that of the brute creation," 1671.

bestiality of men from the lower classes, those who were not part of the civilizing process at the court of Louis XIV and in the Parisian salons."[13]

In the more robust and influential developing science of natural history, the cat likewise could not fully shed its aura

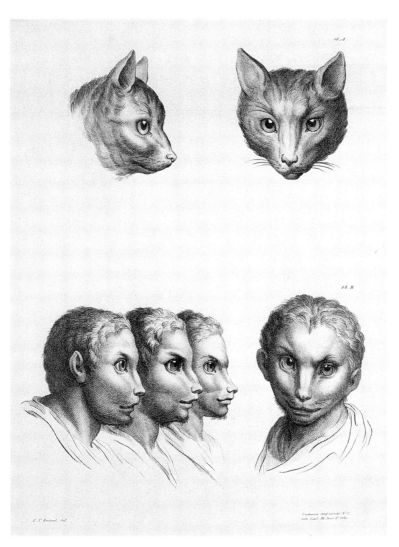

FIGURE 4.5. Charles Le Brun, lithograph, cat-man study from notebook "The relation between the human physiognomy and that of the brute creation," 1671.

of suspicion. Natural historian Georges-Louis Leclerc, Comte de Buffon, whose multivolume work *Natural History, General and Particular with a Description of the King's Cabinet* was published between 1749 and 1789 and was one of the most widely read books in the eighteenth century, took some exception to the domestic feline. Buffon explains of the beast:

> The cat is a faithless domestic, and only kept through necessity to oppose to another domestic which incommodes us still more, and which we cannot drive away; for we pay no respect to those who, being fond of all beasts, keep cats for amusement. Though these animals are gentle and frolicksome when young, yet they even then possess an innate cunning, and perverse disposition, which age increases, and which education only serves to conceal. They are naturally inclined to theft, and the best education only converts them into servile and flattering robbers; for they have the same address, subtlety and inclination for mischief or rapine. Like all knaves they know how to conceal their intentions, to watch, wait, and choose opportunities for seizing their prey; to fly from punishment, and to remain away until the danger is over and they can return with safety.[14]

His description showcases an obvious dislike, but it also evidences a kind of prose that is at some historical remove from the bestiaries and papal bulls we saw in chapter 2. Buffon's cat is not a satanic companion but a petty thief. The bestiary had become the natural history, still a mix of images and descriptions but now without an omnipresent Christ to guide the symbolism. The writing does not possess the same dispassionate scientific tone we are familiar with today, nor does it possess the divine reach of animal compilations under feudalism. But Buffon was not unreasonable, and despite his clear misgivings about the domestic cat, he offered some context for its failings. He noted that the cat was in a compromised position

FIGURE 4.6. Buffon Georges-Louis Leclerc, *Le chat domestique*. From Buffon's *Natural History*.

because of its domestication, namely, that it had been "reduced to slavery."[15]

Nonetheless, Buffon's tussles with domestic cats are revealing, and as Engels says, "historical struggles, whether they proceed in the political, religious, philosophical or some other ideological domain, are in fact only the more or less clear expression of struggles of social classes."[16] Indeed, in Buffon's writing about cats we sense his lack of comfort with those of lower status, those who might work for him, those who might live with him. Likewise, one can glimpse the self-persecutory feelings of the French nobles and aristocracy as they increasingly found themselves in competition with an emergent bourgeoisie who, more and more, embraced the domestic cat.

By the first half of the eighteenth century we encounter what cat-focused historians Amy Freund and Michael Yonan call "a key moment in feline history."[17] It was then, they note, that "cats first entered elite social circles as beloved companions . . . when Enlightenment ideas of human selfhood and society were spreading across the French cultural scene."[18] Cats did not enter elite social circles as a multitude, of course; they made their way in furtively, sneaking through the back door of history. Once they arrived their reception by no means was consistently warm, nor was it consistent with the class positions of those who received them.

The emergent bourgeoisie had its own class-oriented feline struggles to contend with. The French Revolution is well-known for its public trials and executions, but the first jurisprudence of death we encounter in this chapter attends not to humans but to cats. This history comes from Robert Darnton's book, *The Great Cat Massacre*, whose cover shows a mischievous calico peering over the corpse of a chicken.[19] Yet it is not cats' well-known proclivity for killing birds to which the massacre in the title refers; the historical episode that concerns us involved a public slaughter of cats themselves.

The culling took place in the Latin Quarter of Paris in the late 1730s. Several apprentices in a small printing shop were upset that the bourgeois shop owner (bourgeois because he owned such a business) was treating his and his wife's domestic cats better than his employees, who were without businesses of their own, who had to work for wages, and whom Marx calls proletarians. During mealtimes at the shop the workers were offered food that had been rejected by the cook as not suitable for the madame's cats. Worse, the proletarians were exhausted. They reported their sleep was frequently interrupted by howling alley cats. The contours of their working days and nights were recounted by apprentice Nicolas Contat in his chronicle of quotidian life, *Typographic Anecdotes Where We See the Description of the Customs, Mores and Singular Uses of the Fellow Printers.*[20]

Contat reveals how these proletarian apprentices finally sought their revenge. They began a ritual of sneaking up on the roof by their shop owner's bedroom window and howling like crazed cats night after night. Their nightly caterwauls worked, and they convinced their shop owner's wife that certain local cats had been demonically possessed. Then, as a "favor" to their bourgeois bosses, the proletarians offered to round up and execute the possessed cats; they were given instructions not to include the madame's pets in their massacre. For Buffon the cat was an untrusty domestic worker, but for these workers the cat was an untrusty boss. For Marx this is the period in which we first see "two great classes directly facing each other—Bourgeoisie and Proletariat." They faced cats with a similar oppositional stance.

According to Darnton the proletarian apprentices "dumped sack-loads of half-dead cats in the courtyard [and then] gathered around and staged a mock trial, complete with guards, a confessor, and a public executioner. After pronouncing the animals guilty [of satanic tendencies] and administering last rites, they strung them up on improvised gallows."[21] Included in their massacre was the madame's favorite cat, La Grise, who was left dangling on a noose. This bloody act of workers' rebellion points both backward and forward in time. It points backward in that throughout the late Middle Ages, especially in France, animals had been put on trial. In figure 4.7, for example, a French pig stands trial for infanticide in 1494.

In those closing scenes of feudalism, if an animal ate a farmer's crop, he could stand trial for robbery. If an animal killed her young she could stand trial for infanticide.[22] Cats, it seems, were never given the benefit of trial, although one does make an appearance on the docket. There is a record of a rat's trial for grain theft in which the lawyer—seventeenth-century Swiss attorney Bartholomew Chassenee—was able excuse the rat from a court appearance after arguing that the rat would have had to endure the presence of cats, not in the court but on the way to it.[23] Now, in a new age of capitalism and bourgeois ascendency,

FIGURE 4.7. *Trial of a Sow and Pigs at Lavegny*, from Chambers, *The Book of Days*, 1869.

FIGURE 4.8. Profile of "Black Cat the First, born in 1725," used to mock the French nobility. Charles Nicolas Cochin, Comte de Caylus, 1727.

the Great Cat Massacre included a mock trial. The animals were already guilty because they belonged to the bourgeoisie. The massacre points forward in time as well: soon France would be engulfed in the public trials and executions of many more beings.

While workers attacked the cats of the bourgeoisie, the bourgeoisie used their cats to mock the nobles along with aristocratic portraits, titles, and other artifacts of privilege. The frontispiece of a folio boasts "a black cat's head, shown in antiquising profile in the manner of a Great Man" and is labeled "Black Cat the First, born in 1725"(see figure 4.8).[24] The motto reads, "Knowing whom I please, know what I am worth." Royals and aristocrats had continued to style themselves with and as lions, and now the bourgeoisie mocked them for it, as if to say, You thought you were a lion but in fact you're a domestic cat. The bourgeois cat knows its value, its worth—and, like the bourgeoisie, the bourgeois cat puts a price on everything, including itself.

Proletarian against bourgeoisie, bourgeoisie against aristocracy; by the mid-1750s French society was being pulled in more directions than one. Amid the kind of increasing class conflict that the Great Cat Massacre exemplified, philosopher Jean-Jacques Rousseau began to consider how a society so divided by class, governed by a monarch who sold shares in his government, should organize itself. What, Rousseau wondered, do people of such different stations owe to each other in life? Why? How could an economically unequal society develop a kind of political equality? How could humans overcome their own *amour propre*, or self-love, which led them to desire riches, fame, and power, and which ultimately, Rousseau believed, led some of them to tyranny?

"Man is born free, and everywhere he is in chains," the famous first sentence of Rousseau's *The Social Contract* declares.[25] And yet on the book's cover is not a man but a woman and a cat. The feline is hardly incidental. For Rousseau, a per-

FIGURE 4.9. Detail of the frontispiece to Jean-Jacques Rousseau's *The Social Contract*, 1762, one of two originals; both had cats on their covers.

son's relations with cats were a kind of index for their sensibility toward freedom and tyranny. The Scottish philosopher and biographer James Boswell recalls being asked by Rousseau whether he was fond of cats, to which he replied that he was not. Rousseau then returned that the question was "my test of character" and explained that those who don't enjoy cats "have the despotic instinct of men." Rousseau continued, "They do not like cats because the cat is free and will never consent to be a slave. He will do nothing to your order, as the other animals do." Boswell then offered the objection that a hen also did not follow human orders. Rousseau replied, "A hen would obey your orders if you could make her understand them. But a cat will understand you perfectly and still not obey them."[26]

Rousseau presents an interesting case for Marxists. He clearly found economic inequality problematic but had little to offer in the way of overcoming it or analyzing it in anything but a descriptive register. In lieu of the kind of class-based analysis of human inequality that Marx would offer some hundred years later, Rousseau offered a moral one. And yet that morality included cats, and indeed all animals, to whom Rousseau believed some sort of social contract applied. Rousseau, an abstainer from flesh and animal advocate, observed a growing French empire whose profits resulted from tyranny and slavery and asserted, "It is certain that great eaters of flesh are, in general, more cruel and ferocious than other men." As he concerned himself with the civic cultivation of children, who might be raised to be kinder and therefore freer than his own generation, he noted, "It is of the last importance . . . not to render them carnivorous, if not for health reasons, at least for the sake of their character."[27] We have now met the vegetarian and cat enthusiast philosopher of the French Revolution. Rousseau's concerns articulated and supplemented a growing revolutionary ferment that, according to Marx, would soon transform Europe and make it modern by substituting an "owner's mastery of the land over the land's mastery of its owner," introducing "enlightenment over superstition," and placing "civil law over privileges of medieval origin."[28]

A REVOLUTION OF TYGERS

"Like the fall of Rome or the rise of capitalism, the origins of the French revolution have been debated again and again," writes Marxist historian George Lefebvre in his famous study *The Coming of the French Revolution*.[29] It was he who coined the phrase that inspired generations of Marxist social historians, "history from below." To write a history of a society one must look to its lowliest members. Lefebvre looked to French peasants; we look to French cats, who, as we've seen, were sometimes held in higher esteem than peasants and proletarians, but who will nonetheless be our entry point into this subterranean history.

What kind of change precipitated the French Revolution, or what kind of change augurs any revolution? There are multiple levels on which such a question may be explored, to say nothing of answered. A sudden and unexpected event could be the source, such as a poor harvest. That concrete local level applies here, as France suffered a series of bad growing seasons and was beset by the so-called Flour Wars in 1775. Peasants demanded a reduction in the price of flour, the basis of their diet, which consumed, on average, 50 percent of their meager wages.

We also must consider a festering sense of class resentment of both the proletarians toward the bourgeoisie and of the bourgeoisie toward the nobles and royals. That's another level on which to organize an analysis, a class-based one in which effects germinate rather than erupt. Sure enough, the coming of capitalism had the effect of introducing into history the bourgeoisie and the proletariat, both of whom rightly viewed the royals and nobles as holding monopolies over land, church, and state, taxing everyone and taking a cut of everything. It was members of the more radical left wing of the French bourgeoisie who, looking at social strictures both past and present, introduced in this period the word and concept that guided our first two chapters, feudalism, or *féodalité*. They declared they would be bound by it no longer.[30]

Finally, there is another level, the path of world history itself as it unfolds in a direction of greater self-consciousness, according to a contemporaneous onlooker in France, G. W. F Hegel. Marx would both adopt and amend this understanding of historical time some years later. Human history becomes not more self-conscious but more free, Marx insisted. That wasn't their only difference; both saw the French Revolution as necessary and emancipatory, but Marx admired its bourgeois beginning and Hegel appreciated its Napoleonic end.

There is a case to be made for each of these levels of interpretation and for including all of them in our analysis. But there is also occasion to add another level, a feline one. Among the most important actors in France's revolutionary transformation both at home and abroad was the tiger. Meanwhile, lions remained on the historical scene as creatures of noble accoutrement and as increasingly popular sites of spectacle when they showed up at parade grounds around prerevolutionary Paris. Perhaps there was no more famous a celebrity animal in eighteenth-century Paris than Woira, a Senegalese lion. Natural scientists such as Buffon sought to compare and distinguish lion and tiger, a project that had the effect of maintaining the dignity of the former and diminishing that of the latter as well as of offering a feline vocabulary in which to understand revolutionary conflict. "In the class of carnivorous animals, the lion stands foremost, and he is immediately followed by the tiger, who, possessing all the bad qualities of the former, is a stranger to his good ones," Buffon wrote in what can almost be read as a prediction.[31] He and other onlookers had the opportunity to observe these beasts at Versailles, the royal palace, whose menagerie paralleled both the ascent and decline of the Bourbon monarchy in which the long line of kings Louis—the XIV, XV, and XVI—ruled.

Louis XIV had installed the collection of exotic animals and enjoyed a long and prosperous reign as France warred with its European rivals and established an empire. He not only imported animals from around the world; he exported France to the world. Under his reign the sun came to revolve around France, as colonies were established in India, North America, the Caribbean, and Africa. The menagerie continued to develop under the reign of Louis XV, as did France's colonialism and capitalism. Cats great and small now roamed the grounds at Versailles. The beasts delighted the imaginations of painters such as Le Brun, sculptors, and all manner of royal onlookers. It was then that Woira arrived from Senegal with a dog in tow. Their friendship captivated the French elite.[32] Handlers who had ventured to Paris from Senegal with Woira testified to his character and his love for his canine ward.

Court painter Nicolas Maréchal represented Woira both alone and with *son chien*. The relationship between the two animals served as an example of the kind of fraternity and respect that different social orders might have for each other. "Never have I seen such generosity in a lion and such amiability in a dog," Bernardin de Saint-Pierre noted at the time.[33] But the stability between classes for which this interspecies friendship was made to stand in did not endure. And it was a foreboding sign that Woira swiftly devoured the next dog given to him after his

FIGURE 4.10. The interspecies friendship that captivated Paris: Nicolas Maréchal, *Le lion avec son chien* (The lion and his dog), ca. 1794–95.

LE LION *du Muséum d'Histoire Naturelle avec* Son Chien. *Dessiné d'après nature*.

first canine friend passed. Finally, under Louis XVI, sometimes called Louis the Last, the menagerie, and the royal palace and court that supported it, came to a revolutionary halt.

When the French elite were not contenting themselves with their exotic beasts, they took note of the changes that were sweeping the world. They, too, became involved in the American Revolution, supporting the American colonists against the British in order to weaken their old imperial rival. They offered the Americans money and aid, which soon played its own role in bankrupting the French state and with it the Bourbon monarchy. By the late 1780s, time was running out for the ancien régime, that old order of church and crown that ruled France.

On the cusp of revolution in France the old order could no longer be maintained, yet it was unclear in what form a new order would emerge. Shifting coalitions between multiple classes struggled to solidify and grasp political power within France and sought either to avoid or to intensify war abroad. It was from this scene of conflict and transformation, Marx noted, that the class that would assume the ultimate mantle of history, the proletariat, begins to come into being. He wrote, "The struggle of the proletariat assumes clearer outlines . . . they have only to take note of what is happening before their eyes and to become its mouthpiece . . . so long as they are at the beginning of the struggle, they see in poverty nothing but poverty . . . [but soon they see] in it the revolutionary, subversive side, which will overthrow the old society."[34] The process is a long one, and for Marx it began then.

French workers stormed an armory, the Bastille, and collected gunpowder. Poor women began marching and making their own demands. Among the most crucial mobilizing moments in the revolution was in October 1789, when thousands of women in Paris marched in the pouring rain to Versailles to demand bread and force the king to leave his palace. In crisis, the king summoned the Estates General, an advisory meeting of all representatives of France. It had the following composition: the first estate, the clergy, who owned about 10 percent of French land and collected taxes from the peasants; the second estate, the nobility, who owned about 25 percent of French land and also collected taxes on peasants; and the third estate, the petty bourgeoisie, who owned the remaining land and collected rent from the peasants. What's the common theme here? No wonder this was the moment revolutionaries declared they were done with that sclerotic order they now called feudalism.

When the Estates failed to unite in support of the monarch, it was dissolved, and the crisis of the French absolutist state edged closer, thus opening a real path for the bourgeoisie to take the reigns of history. It was a moment that also produced a wonderful series of animal cartoons, including one in which the regal lion is tamed by the music of a revolutionary.[35]

We can follow the revolutionary course of action through a series of vignettes. The famous but apocryphal line "let them eat cake," uttered by a soon to be decapitated Queen Marie Antoinette, was in response to the peasants' ongoing demands for flour. In fact, she said, "Let them eat brioche," which was more expensive than bread. She was given a nickname that marks an important historical point: Madame Déficit. She was known for her exorbitant royal spending, and her sobriquet alerts us to an important transformation. As Engels says, "The economic facts, which have so far played no role or only a contemptible one in the writing of history, are, at least in the modern world, a decisive historical force."[36] To follow history requires following the money, but also following the cats.

The French Constitution of 1791, which created the National Assembly in the wake of the collapse of the ancien ré-

ADIEU BASTILLE

FIGURE 4.11. Anonymous artist, *Adieu Bastille*, 1789.
Source: Library of Congress Prints and Photographs Division,
Washington, D.C.

gime, was memorialized with both a lion and a domestic feline
in the work of engraver Jacques-Louis Copia, who followed
Pierre-Paul Prud'hon's drawing, *The French Constitution*.

Prud'hon's original drawing contained in its legend a description of the scene: "Un Chat, emblème de l'indépendance
est assis aux pieds de la Liberté" (A cat, symbol of independence, sits at the feet of Liberty).[37]

The insurrection of August 10, 1792, when armed revolutionaries in Paris stormed the Tuileries Palace, was another key
event of the French Revolution. By this point revolutionaries
wanted more than bread. They demanded an end to church
taxation, an end to seigneurial privilege, and an end to the
Bourbon monarchy; they sought the broad dechristianization
of society and a republic to replace the monarchy; and they

launched a new history represented by a new calendar. Gone were the twelve months of the Gregorian scheme and the old days of the year, each of which had been named for a particular saint of the Catholic church. Now each day in the year was dedicated to a plant, animal, or earthly element. In the new French Republican calendar, 25 Nivôse (our January 14) became the day of the cat.

As in the American Revolution there were multiple factions, some more bourgeois, some more proletarian. The two most radical of the French revolutionary groups were the Jacobins and their even more radical offshoot, the sansculottes, a name whose translation, "without pants," suggests a certain philosophical disposition. Jean-Paul Marat, for example, pre-

FIGURE 4.12. *Constitution Française*: A feline constitution. Engraving by Jacques-Louis Copia, after the painting by Pierre-Paul Prud'hon, 1796.

sented himself in a "disheveled and unbathed appearance" and explained that he did so in order "to live simply and according to the precepts of Rousseau."[38] From their ranks emerged a new group of revolutionary leaders, many of whom were philosophically loyal to cat lover Jean-Jacques Rousseau, some of whom were executed, and most of whom were decried as tigers.

Maximilien Robespierre remains the most notorious of the bunch. Described by Marx as the "real representative of revolutionary power, i.e., the class alone which was truly revolutionary, the innumerable mass," it was he who established a secular religion glorifying Rousseau, he who lead the French revolutionary government under the auspices of the Committee on Public Safety, and he who initiated what is now known as the

FIGURE 4.13. Michel Hennin, *Greuelscenen der Jacobiner*, 1794 or 1795. The work depicts Robespierre (*left*) next to a tiger. Source: Bibliotheque nationale de France.

Terror.[39] Marxist historian Eric Hobsbawm presents him in a more laconic fashion as a "dandyish, thin-blooded, fanatical lawyer with [a] somewhat excessive sense of private monopoly in virtue."[40] Either way, Robespierre embodied the most revolutionary qualities of the moment, and he dared others to do likewise. "Citizens," he asked, "do you want a revolution without a revolution?"[41] For him it was a rhetorical question. According to Marx, he sought to exterminate a "swarm of state vermin" and remove the "enormous governmental parasite" that was the French state. And according to Marx, such actions were imperative. "This revolution is necessary, therefore, not only because the ruling class cannot be overthrown in any other way, but also because the class overthrowing it can only in a revolution succeed in ridding itself of all the muck of ages and become fitted to found society anew."[42]

Robespierre campaigned for universal suffrage and the abolition of slavery. He supported the Women's March on Versailles. Robespierre, the radical, unlike his American counterparts (one of whom, Paine, was jailed by him), argued for expanding rights for women and the poor and for an end to France's imperial wars. He likewise advocated for various excluded classes and groups, including Protestants, Jews, blacks, and servants. Under his leadership the National Convention indeed abolished slavery in all French colonies, including Haiti, and made all inhabitants of the colonies French citizens.

If Robespierre is routinely cited as the most radical of the revolutionaries, he is also cited as the most feline. These feline-tinted denouncements came from onlookers in France as well as in two countries famous for never having had proper bourgeois revolutions—Germany and England—as their elite inhabitants began to worry that their own countries might be next. One German publication produced an image of the Jacobin leader adorned with gnarling tigers. A few weeks after Robespierre's execution during the Thermidorian Reaction,

Portrait of Robespierre was published by Antoine Merlin de Thionville, a deputy who had sat alongside him in the National Convention. Following a physiognomic logic similar to that of court painter Le Brun, Thionville explained:

> People who like to find relationships between faces and moral qualities, between human faces and those of animals, have noted that . . . Robespierre had the face of a cat. But the face altered its physiognomy; at first [Robespierre's] was the anxious but fairly soft look of a domestic cat; then the wild look of a feral cat; and then the ferocious look of a tiger.[43]

In calling Robespierre a tiger, critics might have been influenced by Buffon's description of the moral failings of the tiger, particularly in comparison with the lion: "To pride, bravery and strength, the lion conjoins nobility, clemency and magnanimity; while the tiger is low and ferocious, and cruel without justice, that is to say, without need." Seemingly for the sake of it, the tiger "desolates the country he inhabits, . . . he kills and devastates herds of domestic animals and he slaughters all wild beasts [he encounters]."[44] From across the English Channel, British chronicler John Adolphus noted in 1799 "that the ferocity of Robespierre's gaze led an accurate observer to compare his general aspect to that of the cat-tyger." Other revolutionary witnesses claimed that "'the tiger Robespierre' had presided over a revolutionary politics that was in essence . . . a 'cadavero-faminocratic government' and a 'tigrocracy.'"[45]

Before his execution Robespierre had defended the animal. When critics charged him with disobeying the will of God for attempting to secularize society, he returned, "How edifying is the piety of tyrants! . . . Who is the God they are talking of? They call themselves images of God, perhaps, in order to cause all the world to desert his altars. They assert that their authority is his work. No! God has created tigers, and kings are the master-pieces of human corruption."[46]

Indeed, it was in a discussion of Robespierre that Walter Benjamin introduced his conception of the *Tigersprung*. In his consideration of how revolutionary activity collapses past and present in order to transform present and future, Benjamin noted that

> for Robespierre, Roman antiquity was a past charged with the here-and-now, which he exploded out of the continuum of history. The French Revolution thought of itself as a latter-day Rome. It cited ancient Rome exactly the way fashion cites a past costume. Fashion has an eye for what is up-to-date, wherever it moves in the jungle of the past. It is the tiger's leap into that which has gone before. Only it takes place in an arena in which the ruling classes are in control. The same leap in the open sky of history is the dialectical one, as Marx conceptualized the revolution.[47]

It is the strength of the tiger's leap—up to fifteen feet from a standing position—that may break through the ruling class's imaginative and material infrastructure. Unlike a tiger, however, the historian who seeks a revolutionary past to guide her to an emancipatory future cannot simply leap forward; rather, she leaps backward to retrieve a new history. Once she has secured it she begins to reorder the world. Such was the *Tigersprung* of Robespierre, who Benjamin seems not to have known was repeatedly called a tiger. According to one scholar, Benjamin, a fan of bicycle races, was referring to the moment of final acceleration toward the finish line, called *Tigersprung* in German in the 1930s and still used today as historical reference.[48] Another Benjamin scholar understands the term differently: "I think [Benjamin] means (people commonly in the 1930s mean) real cats—circus tigers who leap through hoops, and from stool to stool."[49] The *Tigersprung* both is and represents the Benjaminian historical conjecture: multiple threads of cats, all coming alive at similar moments in history, with no clear causal connections between them. This will not be our last consideration of this beast's leap.

Through revolutionary violence and imagination, this oddly counterintuitive group of French vegetarians and tigers began to craft a new society from the ruins of the old one. They acted in accordance with one of Marx's laws of history: "History is the judge—its executioner, the proletarian."[50] It was they who stripped King Louis XVI of his royal title. Calling him Citizen Louis Capet—they had to dig through a thousand years of medieval history to find a last name—they guillotined him and Madame Déficit at the Place de la Révolution, formerly called Place Louis XV. They renamed that, too. And they declared what propertied American, English, and German onlookers so feared: their revolution would spread. Jacobin leader Antoine Saint-Just predicted, "Soon the enlightened nations will be put on trial [by] those who have hitherto ruled over them. The kings shall flee into the deserts, into the company of the wild beasts whom they resemble."[51]

Above and beyond any individual revolutionaries such as Marat or Robespierre, the whole event of the French Revolution was condemned as a tigerish affair. On January 7, 1792, the London *Times* declared that the French had become set "loose from all restraints, and, in many instances, more ferocious than wolves and tigers." Sir Samuel Romilly reflected on the new French republic and noted that "one might as well as think of establishing a republic of tigers in some forest of Africa."[52]

At the height of 1793, that revolutionary year, the *True Briton* published a poem by pseudonymous author, "Tacitus," that both prefaced Benjamin and exhorted his fellow Britons to avoid the example of the French and their animalistic revolution:

FIGURE 4.14. George Stubbs, sketch of a tiger in human posture, ca. 1795–1806.

O Britons! To YOURSELVES be true! Despise the vile
   and lep'rous Crew,
From Apes and Tygers sprung,
A Monkey Race, ferocious bred,
That snap the hand by which they're fed,
Their deeds till now unsung.[53]

Sometime between 1795 and 1806, English painter George
Stubbs produced an uncanny human-tiger sketch that might
be said to rival the hybrids of Le Brun (figure 4.14).

Even the American founding fathers weighed in. En-
sconced in the safety of their slaveholding republic, they, too,
noted animal features abroad. According to Hannah Arendt,
who despised the French Revolution on thinly philosophical
grounds, John Adams "was convinced that a free republican
government [in France] 'was as unnatural, irrational, and im-
practicable as it would be over elephants, lions, tigers, panthers,
wolves, and bears, in the royal menagerie at Versailles.'"[54]

Tell that to the Jacobins who liberated the menagerie of
Louis VXI and invited its animals into their struggle. On
August 11, 1792, a group of Jacobins marched to Versailles and
declared to the menagerie's director that they had come "in the
name of the people and in the name of nature in order to liberate the beings that had emerged free from the hands of the Creator and had been unduly detained by the pomp and arrogance
of tyrants."[55] The lions, tigers, and elephants thus liberated,
they marched with the beasts back into Paris and stationed
them at Jardin des Plantes, which later became that perversion
of revolution known as a zoo. Some historians claim that this
tale of animal solidarity is apocryphal, yet it is hardly the only
such animal act the revolutionaries undertook.

With the outbreak of the French Revolution the Scotsman
John Oswald traveled to Paris and joined the Jacobins. He, too,
considered animals part of the oppressed classes. Influenced

FIGURE 4.15. George Cruikshank, *The Radical's Arms*, 1819. Print with tiger on a guillotine blade.

by Rousseau, Oswald argued in his 1791 text, *The Cry of Nature; or, an Appeal to Mercy and Justice, on Behalf of the Persecuted Animals*, for vegetarianism and political solidarity with all animals. The time had come, he said, "to protect the mute creation from those injuries which the powerful are but too prone to inflict upon the weak."[56] Oswald called for the universal arming of the masses to fight oppression; he died in the battle of Ponts-de-Cee in September 1793.

But tell it to the Marxists, too, including Hobsbawm, whose 1962 work *The Age of Revolution,* one of the foremost Marxist studies of the period, neglects the feline features of the French Revolution entirely. Hobsbawm and his study are well-known for a different omission: that of Haiti and its world-turning revolution. What we are now in a position to realize is that attending to the former would have helped him attend to the latter. For by the time the tyger Robespierre had ended slavery in all of France's colonies and the "blood-thirsty tiger" Gracchus Babeuf, whom many cite as history's first communist revolutionary, had voiced his support for "our brothers the blacks," the revolution in France's colony Saint-Domingue was well underway.[57] There, too, the tiger predominates—but in Haiti it does so in multiplicity. In Haiti a true *Tigersprung* emerges.

If capitalism's conservative bourgeois and aristocratic sympathizers were appalled at the French Revolution, the Haitian Revolution was so grave as to be never mentioned in polite company. In France's wealthiest colony, whose slave-produced sugar had transformed European palates, a group of formerly enslaved black revolutionaries began to raze plantation after plantation, town after town, until they had killed many and driven most of the French colonists away. The beginning of their revolt was accompanied by the usual chorus of anti-French, anti-black, anti-animal reactions from British onlookers, one of whom composed this poem:

FIGURE 4.16. Marxist historian Eric Hobsbawm and Tricia. Source: *The Guardian*, February 10, 2019.

> St. Domingo's bloody journal
> Tells of those who would be free,
> Points to slaughter heaps diurnal,
> That is French fraternity.
> What has France for Europe, done, sir,
> Set a savage tyger free,
> Armed the father 'gainst the son, sir,
> That is—French equality.[58]

But the empire's denunciation soon gave way to a discursive refusal. By the time the free government of Haiti wrote to the United States to establish diplomatic relations in the 1820s, John Quincy Adams's response was indicative of all of history: "not to be answered."[59]

It was Trinidadian Marxist C. L. R. James who, bearing his own feline name—the *L* stands for Lionel—was first able to represent this radical feline history. And everywhere James saw the tiger. Indeed, the *Tigersrpung* with which Benjamin referred to Robespierre in 1940 had already been revealed as a practice for writing and conceptualizing history in James's 1938 study of the Haitian Revolution, *The Black Jacobins*.

No Marxist had analyzed this, the most radical event in an age of revolution, and James had to contend with the newness of an archive as well as of an approach. Revolution is always a collective eruption, and even as James singles out former slave and revolutionary general Touissant Louverture, he also asserts that leaders matter little to Marxist method: "Toussaint did not make the revolution. It was the revolution that made Toussaint. And even that is not the whole truth."[60] There are fewer leaders in Marxist method than there are those through whom we may see with a bit more detail how history unfolds. Indeed, it's almost better for our telling that historical cats don't have names (royal ones excepted); they lead us anonymously through history.

When the revolution on the island reached its pinnacle and victory was imminent, Louverture declared to his forces, "This is no longer a war. It is a fight of tigers. It is no longer bravery I want from you. It is rage." He got it. Thousands of mixed-race mulattos, some free and others enslaved, joined the revolution against the French colonists. James tells us they "fought like tigers." When Louverture died in French captivity, Haitian revolutionary Jean-Jacques Dessalines succeeded him and declared a free Haitian republic to the world. But while Louverture was alive, he was so feared and admired that James reports "even Dessalines, the Tiger, was afraid of him." Dessalines, a tiger, was afraid of Louverture, who moved like a tiger. In James's study, however, we notice a certain feline divergence. He uses the language of the tiger in appreciation of revolutionary fortitude. Yet the received antisocial association of the tiger is likewise present in his archive. For example, when James describes the moment in which Louverture heard of Napoleon's order to reverse emancipation and restore slavery to Haiti, he reports that Louverture "could not believe that the French ruling class would be so depraved . . . he could not admit to himself and to his people that it was easier to find decency, gratitude, justice, and humanity in a cage of starving tigers than in the councils of [French] imperialism."[61] He thus incorporates a certain antitiger perspective. The Haitian revolutionaries did so as well.

When Jean-Jacques Dessalines proclaimed Haiti a free republic in his "I Have Avenged America" speech of late April 1804, he justified violence against colonizers as a reaction similar to that needed to defend against a tiger. Dessalines asked of his country's populace, "Who is that Haitian so vile, so unworthy of his regeneration that he does not believe that he has fulfilled eternal [laws] by exterminating these bloodthirsty tigers?" He went on, "What do I say, look for your children, your suckling babies? What has become of them . . . I shudder to say it . . . the prey of these vultures . . . these tigers still covered with their blood."[62] Throughout these years of rebellion there was a contest between black revolutionaries and French colonists over who was most deserving of the epithet *tiger*.

One French chronicler, Laure Junot d'Abrantès, noted of Dessalines in her *Mémoires* that "[he is a] bloodthirsty tiger, and one can say that without any metaphor."[63] Her point is somewhat baffling—Dessalines was clearly a human—but it does show the limits of metaphor as a figure of speech. D'Abrantès desired to banish Dessalines beyond the world of humanity. A metaphorical operation, however, requires that separation be maintained between the objects of comparison: "when this person runs, she is a cheetah," for example, necessitates a distinction between human and feline so that the latter's speed can be transposed onto the former—she runs quickly (like a cheetah).

But d'Abrantès refuses to maintain the separation. She provides a metaphor, "he is a tiger," and then negates it: "my claim is not metaphorical." In fact, d'Abrantès offers in reactionary form a lesson that James hints at in *The Black Jacobins* but would not fully articulate until ten years later in *Notes on Dialectics*: to revolt one must become a tiger because one must leap.

What James, what Benjamin, what our archive here instructs us is that the tiger is not a metaphor but a dialectic, and dialectics are a different creature; they do not separate; rather, they unite in contradiction, and in doing so they make sense where none before was to be found. To move from one object to another, from one state of being to another, from one kind of historical moment to another, requires a leap. James recounts how Louverture moved by "tigerish leaps" as he commanded a rebel army to dispatch the French colonial powers. For James there is no more dialectic a term than *leap*, which, fittingly, takes both noun and verb forms and which appeared to him in his analysis of Haiti through the language of thetiger.

As James's own Marxism developed in the 1940s he moved away from the tiger and trained his focus on that beast's signature move, the leap. In narrative language unusual for a theoretician, James explains how he came to this figure. He recalls reading cat-loving Russian revolutionary Vladimir Lenin's exposition of Hegel, who (we recall from our lion-cat dialectic) isolated the leap as a figure of both categorical and historical transition. Lenin, too, noted that passage, and on reading it, James recounts, "I was particularly struck by this in Lenin. Hegel is very irritating. He sticks to method. He does not shout. But every single one of his transitions involves a *leap*." James emphasizes that Lenin's notebook devoted to *The Science of Logic* contained in its margins a repetition of this word:

In reading [the section] on Quality in the Doctrine of Being, Lenin writes in very large writing:

LEAP

LEAP

LEAP

LEAP

This obviously hit him hard.[64]

Lenin highlighted the term in his marginalia, and for James the materiality of the spacing, capitalization, and repetition all accentuate how crucial the leap was for understanding dialectics and ultimately for understanding radical social change. James continues, "This is a passage of great importance and Lenin has summarized it perfectly with his LEAP LEAP LEAP LEAP. The new thing LEAPS out.... [Lenin] didn't have to wait to see anything. That was there. It would LEAP up."[65]

James already knew this and, for him, reading Lenin was an affirmation of truth, not a discovery of it. In Haiti the revolution was there; it leapt up through the collective consciousness of a group of radical tigers. And yet, that leap, so dramatic, so unable to be thought, would not be assimilated into the imperial archives of France, the United States, England—"not to be answered" represents not a negation but a refusal of recognition.

Haiti's is a history that has been silenced, overlooked, and destroyed by capitalist imperialism and racism. James was able to reconstruct it through the archive of the tiger. Benjamin, two years later but seemingly independently, suggested a historical methodology for retrieving this kind of history by mimicking the actions of the tiger. But it was radical printer and poet William Blake, for whom animals were always a muse, whose writing unites the tyger and the tiger and who presents Haiti like few others, for he saw the brilliance of its eruption before the moment had materialized. His 1794 poem *The Tyger* opens with an urgent invocation:

FIGURE 4.17. William Blake, "The Tyger," 1825. Plate from *Songs of Innocence and of Experience*. Source: The Metropolitan Museum of Art, New York.

Tyger! Tyger! burning bright
In the forests of the night,
What immortal hand or eye
Could frame thy fearful symmetry?
In what distant deeps or skies
Burnt the fire of thine eyes?
On what wings dare he aspire?
What the hand, dare seize the fire?

Blake's tyger was a powerful animal, but in the poem fear of the feline gives way to respect for it. This poetic tyger reveals futures and possibilities rather than forecloses them. One literary critic argues that "the poem expresses the leap of thought which ... provocatively cast the unthinkable quality of the Haitian Revolution."[66] Other scholars have read the poem as an homage to New World slave rebellions more generally.[67] Either way, Blake's tyger was an animal of historical revelation. Blake himself had said "the history of all times and places is nothing else but improbabilities and impossibilities."[68] For Haiti that impossibility is framed by the tyger, and once we realize that it is so, a feline Marxist history becomes a little less impossible. Blake was not alone in his appreciation for the revolutionary possibilities of the tyger. Thomas Spence, too, had presented the power of the tyger in the form of a real-world utopia. Representing an as yet unrealized moment of freedom, that cat lover had imagined that "lisping Infants shall tam'd tygers lead."[69]

CONCLUSION: NAPOLEON

Where do we find ourselves at the end of this revolutionary tigrocracy? The French royals? Executed. The French radicals? Executed. The bourgeoisie, both liberal and conservative, confused and embittered. Haiti, independent but impoverished

FIGURE 4.18. Nineteenth-century engraving of Napoleon Bonaparte with lion.

and silenced (still.) And who finally emerges from the French Revolution's decade of guillotining and warring both external (with other states and colonies) and internal (as economic classes battled each other)? None other than Napoleon Bonaparte, a lion lover and domestic cat hater. He was antiroyalist and suspicious of religion, like the radical revolutionaries. And he was a modern state builder of infrastructure, education, and public health in the best bourgeois tradition. But he was also an imperialist and warmonger. As a general and ultimately self-declared emperor he assembled a French empire that rivaled Charlemagne's. In crafting that empire he reversed some of the most liberatory decrees of the French Revolution; he hollowed out suffrage and restored slavery in France's colonies. He attempted but failed to recapture Haiti. Marx said that he substituted permanent war for permanent revolution.

In his own words, but with obvious reference to Machiavelli, Napoleon explained how he governed: "I am sometimes a fox and sometimes a lion. The whole secret of government lies in knowing when to be the one or the other." Thus the figure 4.18 engraving seems the correct image to conclude this ghastly chapter in French national history. He is still hailed today as a brilliant military strategist, and Napoleon's understanding of military leadership was in part feline. "If you build an army of 100 lions and their leader is a dog," he wrote, "in any fight, the lions will die like a dog. But if you build an army of 100 dogs and their leader is a lion, all dogs will fight like a lion." Perhaps the most important animal assessment of Napoleon came from none other than Hegel himself, who witnessed Napoleon when he entered Hegel's home city of Jena. Hegel said that he had seen "world history on horseback."

Our Dumb Beasts

———

THE RISE OF THE BOURGEOISIE
AND ITS APPROPRIATION OF CATS,
1800–1900

PART III

5

Wildcats

"A stout farmer might hope to 'whip' a wild cat or two; but once in the grasp of a 'wild cat bank,' his struggles were unavailing."

—CAROLINE MATILDA KIRKLAND,
A NEW HOME — WHO'LL FOLLOW?

n 1845, the escaped slave turned abolitionist Frederick Douglass published *Narrative of the Life Frederick Douglass, An American Slave*, a trenchant account of the racist terrors of nineteenth-century capitalism. Feline incidents and references dot Douglass's book. In one scene he rides on a schooner called *The Wildcat*. In another recollection, certainly one of the most famous passages in nineteenth-century American literature, Douglass resists a brutal assault from his master's overseer, Mr. Covey, and thus begins his path to liberation. He reports that Covey "rushed at me with the fierceness of a tiger."[1] As was customary at the time, the text of Douglass's autobiography was preceded by introductions from noted interlocutors, including

one from abolitionist Wendell Phillips, whose words to Douglass begin with the salutation "My Dear Friend." Phillips then recounts an aphorism: "You remember the old fable of 'The Man and the Lion,' where the lion complained that he should not be so represented when 'the lions wrote history.' I am glad the time has come when 'the lions write history.'"[2] Phillips's point was twofold. First, as the West African version of the story insists, the history of the hunt glorifies the hunter and will do so until lions become their own historians. The second meaning was more direct: Frederick Douglass was a lion. Indeed, this letter marks the beginning of a long feline association for Douglass, who was sometimes described as "leonine in appearance" but was also referred to as "The Lion of Anacostia" for the neighborhood in Washington, DC, where he ultimately settled as a freeman. The lion had become a force of liberation.

In England, too, by the mid-nineteenth century, the lion would become a critical animal, one used to dissent from that country's own political repression. That the lion was transformed from a creature of oppression into one of freedom was only one of the many convulsions of a bourgeois age in which premodern values were radically reevaluated. Marx captured this quality perhaps better than any other critic with his claim that as capitalism takes hold, customs and beliefs are overturned to the effect that "all that is holy is profaned" and "all that is solid melts into air."[3] Indeed, the fate of the lion represents many of the social upheavals occurring as the age of bourgeois revolution continues into the nineteenth century and gives way to its own series of counterrevolutions and reverberations. In the United States slavery and empire expand, but fierce opposition to these orders takes root as well. In England riots and political uprisings ensue. In those moments the slave turns on the master, the freedom fighter confronts the state, and the lion leaves the companionship of the king to join his rebellious subjects. These events, too, are part of the coming of capitalism, and Marx explains that as capitalism develops, humans are "at last compelled to face with sober senses" their "real conditions of life" and their real "relations with [their] kind."[4] Those moments of "at last" are many, it turns out, and still ongoing. They transpire throughout the nineteenth century as the bourgeoisie solidifies its historical domination and relies on a new revolution, that of industry, to support itself. Yet the same industrial revolution also empowers proletarians in their efforts to overcome the bourgeoisie.

In this chapter we track how these contradictions of capitalism after the bourgeois revolutions of the eighteenth century take material form in money, technology, control of land,

FIGURE 5.1. John James Audubon, *Common American Wildcat Male*, 1842.

forms of culture, and, yes, in cats. We will trace how cats were instrumental in realizing, stabilizing, and critiquing many of these contradictions. Wildcats now enter our bestiary as creatures of accumulation in the ever-expanding United States.

American and indigenous wildcats both enabled and resisted the spread of the American empire. As that empire expanded, wildcats appeared in multiple roles: as animals to be eliminated, as people who resisted American incursion, and as a new type of banking known simply as "wildcatting." All the while, lions and domestic cats continued their own historical transformations, and with them circulated a new set of conflicting meanings. Now the domestic cat appears as a muse and philosopher, hardly the rebellious animal Thomas Spence had imprinted on coin; the lion becomes an ally in political freedom for African Americans, workers, and political dissidents as well as a leader in technological innovation.

As nineteenth-century felines develop contradictory meanings and associations, so do key concepts of capitalist modernity. Take freedom, for example. It refers to free trade, which is needed if capitalism is to flourish, as well as to political freedom, which arrives with the great bourgeois revolutions. But trade is rarely free—people and countries are forced into it by the spread of capitalist competition. And most people do not have political freedom; this is an age of slavery, after all. Rather, many unfree people developed a new idea of freedom, and from Marx's vantage point, that's something. Or consider the wondrous new technologies of the Industrial Revolution: factories so powerful and able to produce goods so quickly and at such a scale that it would have been possible to free many people from the toil and misery of work. In practice, however, more people were forced to work more hours in worse conditions. Yet another contradiction emerges in the political disposition of the bourgeoisie: this class, which both organizes and benefits from this state of affairs, now joins the chorus denouncing it. The bourgeoisie emerges as a class of concerned citizens worried about the welfare of others: children, factory workers, slaves, and animals.

No less shaped by the contradictions of capitalism than any other human or feline, Karl Marx arrives in the present but in retrospect. Marx, like the continuing revolutions of and against the bourgeoisie, will be with us for the next two chapters. As his own political and critical sensibilities developed, he became persona non grata in his Prussian homeland. In 1843 he applied for a permit to immigrate to Texas but instead left for France and took over the editorship of a newspaper. There he also began a lifelong collaboration with the son of a factory owner, Friedrich Engels. Their work together resulted in their being asked to leave France. They headed for newly independent Belgium. In Brussels they wrote the *Communist Manifesto*, in which they responded to the revolutions sweeping Europe and predicted not only more to come but the arrival of a genuinely democratic postcapitalist society. When they were subsequently instructed to leave Belgium, they headed for London, the capital of capital and the economic seat of Great Britain, where a new science of inquiry was being developed: political economy, or the study of national wealth. As Marx slowly and studiously developed what we know today as Marxism, he became first a political economist and then a critic of that field. And as he made his way through the various texts of German philosophers including Hegel, of the utopian socialists like Spence, and of the various British political economists whom we will soon encounter, Marx wondered, What separates human animals from other animals, and how does this separation allow humans to organize themselves economically? The answer involves cats.

We remember that when Marx examined the United States he saw a growing country of "rich vast expanding [territory] with purely bourgeois institutions, unleavened by feudal remains or monarchical traditions."[5] More land meant different things to different people, however. For white southern elites, more land meant more slavery and therefore more wealth. For white northern elites, more land meant less class conflict as poor whites could be nudged west. For white militias and their associated adventurers, more land meant the possibility of property and prosperity. For white settler colonists, the plan for possession was twofold. It required indigenous removal and the expansion of white supremacy. There was some genuine contest over how newly colonized land should be incorporated into the United States, as either slave territory or free territory. Some whites believed slavery drove down white wages and thus contributed to the exploitation of all workers; others were appreciative of an invitation to join a racial and economic elite. There was no disagreement, however, about the necessity of indigenous removal as white settler colonists spread across the continent.

We can trace their path west, a crucial journey for the emergence of American capitalism, by following the trails of the wildcat. Missouri is well-known for its role in the famous 1820 Missouri Compromise over slavery, but our focus on that territory will be more feline. In 1816 the governor of the Missouri Territory approved an act "to encourage the killing of wolves, panthers, and wildcats." The Territory of Missouri set specific values for wildcat corpses. "Panthers which shall exceed the age of six months [are] two dollars, if under that age the sum of one dollar and in the case of wildcats the sum of fifty cents each, regardless of age." To claim the money white settlers killing either "panther, or wildcat as aforesaid, shall exhibit the

FIGURE 5.2. A satirical wildcat bank note, the "Cleveland," ca. 1892.

scalp with both ears . . . to some justice of the peace within said county." A wildcat killer received a certificate from a local justice of the peace that was deemed "legal tender for any county taxes levied within said county."[6] Wildcat certificates began to circulate as paper money in the Missouri Territory as well as in other territories not yet admitted into the union, such as Michigan, Kansas, and Nebraska.

The systematic killing of these cats became a crucial site of capital accumulation as the United States expanded. What at first seemed like an impediment—a land filled with predatory cats—became an opportunity as the state began to transform cats into currency. Wildcat death certificates became an important form of money in these years of specie, or gold, being in short supply, particularly on the frontier. Wildcat destruction became culturally significant as well. Famed imperialist frontiersman Davy Crockett is well-known for his "coonskin cap," but he, too, paid homage to wildcat killing: in fact he wore a wildcat on his head.

For Crockett, a dead wildcat possessed what Marx called a use value. Crockett killed the wildcat for his own purpose: to wear it. For the settler capitalists who killed wildcats in order to receive wildcat bank notes, the dead cats possessed what

FIGURE 5.3. The cover of *Davy Crockett's Almanack*, 1837, with wildcat hat.

Marx labeled an exchange value. They killed wildcats to obtain something other than wildcat corpses; they desired the certificates that they would use as money. These two aspects of value come to structure capitalist society, and as the system of capitalism continues its development, exchange value comes to displace use value.

Marx offers a helpful equation to understand this transposition. In the early years of capitalist development there was not a true sense of monetary accumulation. Members of society needed commodities such as food, clothes, and shelter in order to survive, and they sought to exchange their commodities for money for the purpose of acquiring other commodities. Marx schematizes this stage of development as: C-M-C, or commodities-money-commodities. At a certain point, however, monetary accumulation began: people had money and with it they bought commodities in hopes of exchanging those commodities for even more money, which Marx expresses as M-C-M', money-commodity-money prime. Unlike commodities, money does not expire or become obsolete; one can seemingly accumulate it forever, as indicated by the prime symbol. Thus Marx jokes that in a capitalist society M-C-M', becomes a kind of religion. "Accumulate, accumulate! That is Moses and the prophets!" he says in describing how a capitalist understands heaven and earth.[7]

In the American case, Marx's formula neatly tracked the arc of the wildcat; we could just as easily discuss how cat-money-cat became money-cat-money'. Indeed, the language of wildcats on the genocidal frontier became the language of money, and soon enough a new kind of capitalist enterprise began to dot the southern midwest plains and northern midwest woods: the wildcat bank. Made possible by a mix of white frontier vigilantes, the US military, and lands emptied of felines, wildcat banks became part of the formula for expanding the United States. Wildcat banks helped to destroy indigenous nations, dispossess them of their land, and integrate such land into the circuits of capital emanating from East Coast cities.

So began the era of "free banking" in the early to mid-nineteenth-century United States in which anyone could start a bank as long as the money the bank issued was redeemable for gold. Of course, to redeem that money for gold, you had to be able to find the bank.[8] And this was the crucial invention of wildcat banks: they could be located to accept deposits but not to redeem them. It was open season not only for killing wild-cats but for starting wildcat banks. Soon wildcat banks run by "wildcatters" spread across the country.

One 1830s account of this banking, as it took root in Mich-igan, notes that

> some thirty banks or more were the fungous growth of the new political hot-bed; [they were located in] some part of the deep woods, where the wild cat had hitherto been the most formidable foe to the unwary and defenceless. Hence the celebrated term 'Wild Cat,' justified fully by the course of these cunning and stealthy blood-suckers; more fatal in their treacherous spring than ever was their forest proto-type. A stout farmer might hope to 'whip' a wild cat or two; but once in the grasp of a 'wild cat bank,' his struggles were unavailing. Hopeless ruin has been the consequence.[9]

"What is robbing a bank compared to founding a bank?" the great Marxist playwright Bertolt Brecht once asked.[10] It's a pithy question but he misses the mark: bank foundings of-ten *are* bank robberies. Indeed, what better way to rob a bank than to found your own? The swift fleecing of United States government bank insurance that savings and loan bank op-erators undertook in the 1980s had been engineered in na-scent form a century and a half earlier by wildcatters. With their uncertain comings and goings, wildcatting introduced the same kind of boom-bust experience that we find in the Roaring Twenties, the dot-com era, the 2007–2008 mortgage crisis, and so on. Marx could already perceive how such cycles worked: "everyone knows that some time or other the crash must come, but everyone hopes that it may fall on the head of his neighbour, after he himself has caught the shower of gold and placed it in safety."[11]

Still, for a boom and bust cycle to run its course, to say nothing of other economic activity, someone needs to protect the most basic lubricant of a capitalist economy, the money system. The whole thing can't be a swindle, only select parts of it. In the midst of the wildcatting, the US federal government began issuing a weekly *Specie Circular* to provide guidance on which banks were trustworthy and which were pure wildcats. The language of animality saturated the wildcat and larger free banking movement as it would also come to structure a financial vocabulary from brands to stocks to Celtic and Asian tigers. Certain banks, selected to receive state support, were called "pet banks," while other banks simply disappeared like a black cat into a dark night. United States president and genocidaire Andrew Jackson was a backer of free banking and thus of wildcat banking, a fact to which numerous cartoons of the era attest; and he participated in the so-called Bank Wars, in which he supported free banking against federally controlled banking. Cats played their own part in Jackson's struggle, as in figure 5.4, in which Jackson (Old Hickory) faces off against the United States bank president Nicholas Biddle (Bully Nick).

The cartoon is catalogued in the Library of Congress, and its participants and their symbolic import are described therein. The cartoon is introduced as a "satire on the public conflict between Andrew Jackson and Nicholas Biddle over

FIGURE 5.4. Note the spectator's wildcat hat in Anthony Imbert's 1834 *Set To between Old Hickory and Bully Nick*, satirizing the Bank Wars. Source: Library of Congress Prints and Photographs Division, Washington, DC.

the future of the Bank of the United States, and the former's campaign to destroy it. The print is sympathetic to Jackson, portraying him as the champion of the common man against the moneyed interests of the Bank." As the description continues, however, we note an odd feline discrepancy. "On the right are Jackson's supporters: Martin Van Buren, Major Jack Downing and 'Joe Tammany,' [and] a frontiersman in buckskins and raccoon cap."[12] Reader, in what world is that a raccoon? As with Crockett, the supposed coonskin cap described in the cartoon's exposition is in fact a wildcat cap; here it appears to be simply a cat. This repeated mistaking of cat for raccoon, which is twentieth-century in origin, raises its own questions. The archival substitution of raccoon for cat evidences a retrospective effort to sanitize nineteenth-century American capitalism, to render it a little less appalling. In the nineteenth century itself, as our archive attests, no such substitution was necessary, and cats were only one more of the many victims of empire.

In white supremacist frontier society in the West the wildcat was an object of speculation and accumulation. In Florida territory, a Seminole leader named Wildcat fought against the invading United States Army. The United States had acquired Florida from Spain and used this acquisition to continue its genocide of First Nations during a series of wars against the Seminole in the mid-nineteenth century. Over the course of several years Wildcat led the resistance against the growing American empire. He was sometimes joined by a black Seminole named John Horse, one of many mestizos in Florida, a land of First Nations, escaped slaves, free blacks, and Spanish colonizers. But Wildcat's resistance could endure only so long, and soon he and his comrades followed the path of another Seminole leader, Tiger Tail, who had been offered and had taken passage to Louisiana. But whereas Tiger Tail's displacement had ended with his suicide, Wildcat ultimately made his way to Mexico, where he helped to establish a community of escaped slaves, free blacks, and members of First Nations.[13] His death in 1857 attracted notice throughout the Midwest.

As wildcats of all sorts coursed through various American frontiers, their lowly cousin, the domestic cat, was a rarity, but one whose mousing and ratting work was continually sought. Settler colonist Laura Ingalls Wilder of *Little House on the Prairie* fame reports her Pa having to buy a kitten too young to be separated from its mother for fear that there would be no more domestic cats available on the Great Plains.[14] During the San Francisco gold rush of 1849, cats were imported from Mexico (which the US Army was occupying) to help stamp out rodents.[15]

FIGURE 5.5. *Cat Drinking from a Bowl*, perhaps the world's first cat photo, an undated daguerreotype by an unknown photographer. Source: Houghton Library, Harvard University.

Meanwhile, in the industrializing Northeast, the reverse feline situation prevailed. Wildcats had begun to vanish and domestic cats to appear in everything from philosophical speculations to gothic horror stories to the results of a new invention, photography, with the world's first cat photo likely taken in the mid-1840s.

In 1843, cat lover Edgar Allan Poe published his short story "The Black Cat" in *The Saturday Evening Post*. Poe, whose misattributed if not apocryphal quotations include "I wish I could write as mysterious as a cat," was a new kind of writer.[16] He was waged and middle class, and he wrote a new kind of prose, the mystery or detective story, which would soon become a favorite of Marxist literary critics. Marxists like Benjamin and his contemporary Siegfried Kracauer saw in the detective story the very play of capital. As exchange value becomes dominant, so-

FIGURE 5.6. Charles Mills Sheldon, *Edgar Allan Poe with Catterina*, 1910.

cial relations become obscured. We remember that Marx says in feudalism such relations can be seen and grasped, while in capitalism they are often obscured. The detective story dramatizes a loss of knowledge as its protagonists seek to find the truth of a great mystery. In Poe's work it falls to the black cat to organize that search. The black cat, who led medieval inquisitors on the search for the devil, now leads nineteenth-century middle-class readers on a fantastic search for the guilty parties of the various crimes of capitalism.

In New England, Transcendentalist philosopher Henry David Thoreau both mourned the loss of wildcats and celebrated the flourishing of domestic ones. "When I consider that the nobler animals have been exterminated here—the cougar, the panther, lynx, wolverine, wolf...—I cannot but feel as if I lived in a tame and as it were emasculated country," he wrote.[17] As he bemoaned the loss of big cats he took pleasure in the company of smaller ones. "What sort of philosophers are we, who know absolutely nothing of the origin and destiny of cats?" he inquired. His was a question that one could still ask of so much American philosophy, particularly in comparison to its French counterpart. Enjoying his self-imposed solitude at Walden Pond in Massachusetts, Thoreau offered that "it often happens that a man is more humanely related to a cat or dog than to any human being."[18]

Walden Pond was owned by another transcendentalist philosopher, Ralph Waldo Emerson, who likewise positioned a domestic cat as his interlocutor. "Do you see that kitten chasing so prettily her own tail?" he inquired. "If you could look with her eyes, you might see her surrounded with hundreds of figures performing complex dramas, with tragic and comic issues, long conversations, many characters, many ups and downs of fate."[19] Delighted by these animals and the company they provided, Thoreau and Emerson were also vegetarians. "The carcasses of some poor squirrels," Thoreau memorialized, "the same that frisked so merrily in the morning, which we had skinned and embowelled for our dinner, we abandoned in disgust, with tardy humanity, as too wretched a resource for any but starving men."[20]

Theirs was the kind of empathy that would drive Karl Marx and subsequent generations of Marxists mad. Thoreau and Emerson were opposed to all the right things: slavery, imperial aggression in Mexico, and animal cruelty, including the slaughter and eating of animals. But their Transcendentalist vegetarianism was not like that of John Oswald, who took up arms with the Jacobins of the French Revolution and fought for a cause that included freedom for animals. Thoreau, in particular, was more interested in withdrawing from the old capitalist society than in creating a new communist one—he lived, according one literary scholar, in a "utopia of one."[21]

As a critic, Marx was beginning to realize that "a part of the bourgeoisie is desirous of redressing social grievances in order to secure the continued existence of bourgeois society." He and Engels then specified, "To this section belong economists, philanthropists, humanitarians, improvers of the condition of the working class, organisers of charity, members of societies for the prevention of cruelty to animals, temperance fanatics, hole-and-corner reformers of every imaginable kind."[22] They did not include vegetarians here, but Engels would make a similar remark about them elsewhere, and subsequent Marxists would return to this point: bourgeois sympathy is not enough. Indeed, one of the chief freedoms that capitalism provides the bourgeoisie is the freedom to criticize the unfreedoms of capitalism. Could Thoreau and Emerson have done better? Perhaps. By the early 1850s a wave of socialists and communists—one might even say Marxists—had begun to immigrate to the United States as a result of the fallout of a series of failed revolutions in Europe. Once stateside, they founded socialist organizations and newspapers and began to offer critiques of the existing system of imperial, slave-based capitalism. This history we will rejoin in the next chapter, but for now we stay with the bourgeoisie as they begin to put cats to work.

FELINE FORCES OF PRODUCTION
AND THEIR ANTAGONISTS

The concerns of vegetarian Transcendentalists in the United States were a response to more than the loss of the lynx and the wildcat or the violent adventures of the ever-expanding empire. They were a response to the most important of capitalist revolutions, the Industrial Revolution. This revolution began in England with the transformation of water into steam, fossils into fuel, workers into a working class. From each of these sources of energy the capacity of humans to erect a new infrastructural world whereby each generation could dwarf the productive power of the previous one took hold. Factories could transform raw materials, steam could power trains and ships faster and for greater distances, and humans could organize into exponentially more powerful groupings than any other social form of history as a result of what Marx calls their labor power, a quality that takes its most magnificent form in large-scale industry. Marx notes again and again that the ability to labor is unique to humans. He writes, "We are not now dealing with those primitive instinctive forms of labour that remind us of the mere animal. . . . We pre-suppose labour in a form that stamps it as exclusively human." For Marx, only humans could produce industry, even though "a spider conducts operations that resemble those of a weaver, and a bee puts to shame many an architect in the construction of her cells," because only humans think before they act.[23] Yet Marx did note how the reorganization of human labor during capitalist industrialization had begun to affect animals. "Disgusting!" Marx exclaimed of new industrial farming methods. "Animals are born [in pens] and remain there until they are killed off. The question is whether or not this system connected to the breeding system that grows animals in an abnormal way by aborting bones in order to transform them to mere meat and a bulk of fat—whereas earlier animals remained active by staying under free air as much as possible—will ultimately result in serious deterioration of life force."[24]

Marx extols human labor and rejects the ability of animals to contribute to the erecting of a new industrial world. Yet the names chosen for the leading technological innovations of early industry hew to a certain feline theme of lions. In the United States the first steam-powered railroad engine bore the name Lion of Stourbridge. The train powered through Pennsylvania with the front grille of its engine emblazoned with a gold lion. But it was in England where the real industrialization—and reaction against it—took hold, and there, too, a lion was the star. The first truly powerful English waterwheel was named the Lion of Catrine. Marx gives the totality of these new technological powers a simple name: the forces of production. It was these industrial forces of production, more than any political revolution, that transformed nineteenth-century lives, both human and animal.

Animals never left their pens and workers rarely left the factories. They began to work longer days. They relocated to be closer to the factories that began to spring up around the English countryside. The English government made laws against working-class "blacking," or hunting, one form of proletarian self-sufficiency. The government persecuted various petty crimes of survival—starving children stealing bread or eggs, for example. Localities forbade barter in order to ensure that a money economy, and thus a capitalist economy, would flourish. The state established workhouses—so orphans could support themselves through factory work—and debt prisons for adults who couldn't work enough. Yet even in such trying and constricted circumstances workers developed knowledges, routines and relationships with each other, which Marx calls the relationships of production. From this dichotomy a new contradiction emerges: the forces of production come into conflict with the relations of production, and in England foremost, social conflicts emerged over how to inhabit this new industrial world.

English workers and radicals witnessed the French Revolution and began to form Jacobin clubs in England, until such clubs were banned. They read the works of cat lovers Thomas Paine and Thomas Spence, until those texts were banned. Emboldened, they began to agitate for political representation so that they might have a say in the organization of their lives. While mass gatherings were rare—they, too, were banned—one took place in 1819. It became a massacre, one of England's most infamous, the so-called Peterloo Massacre. It transpired near Manchester, which was both symbol and center of the country's capitalist industry and thus its immiseration. The United States had the animal-loving Transcendentalists to record its political concerns about industrialization in artful language. The United Kingdom had the animal-loving Romantics, whose sentiments were similar but whose writerly sensibilities were considerably better. Workers' political agitation and Romantic lyricism would unite after the Peterloo Massacre in the work of poet and abstainer from animal products Percy Bysshe Shelley.

Shelley turned to felines to memorialize the slaughter of political agitators by producing one of the greatest political poems ever penned, "The Masque of Anarchy." The poem did not appear in print until 1832, ten years after Shelley's death. Shelley had sent the manuscript off to newspapers in 1819, immediately following the massacre, but no press would run it, fearful as they were of the censorious state. In this land of empire, royalty, heraldry, and now public slaughter, Shelley turned his poetic language to those unrepresented in history:

> Men of England, heirs of Glory,
> Heroes of unwritten story,
> Nurslings of one mighty Mother,
> Hopes of her, and one another;

Shelley calls out to those whose lives and doings remain invisible. Their unwritten story possesses a history, but one so far not told. How do they become visible? Through becoming aware of their power, through collective action, through uprising, and lastly, through a big cat. Now the poem's most heralded stanza, in which the unseen rise up and collectively become undefeatable:

> Rise like Lions after slumber
> In unvanquishable number,
> Shake your chains to earth like dew
> Which in sleep had fallen on you—
> Ye are many—they are few.

Before the 99 percent and the 1 percent electrified our contemporary political discourse, there were Shelley's lionlike many and unlionlike few. Shelley not only memorialized those many; he sought to liberate the lion from the clutches of that most oppressive entity, the British monarchy. Shelley himself was hardly proletarian, but his sympathies lay with that class. He wrote poems condemning Napoleon, he celebrated the French Revolution, and he saw England as a country governed by "tyrants." Why should the many not shape their own political worlds? Why should they not have access to the force and beauty of the lion, even if only symbolically? In his poem Shelley predicted that not only would the power of proletarian mobilization expand, but his verses on lions and their potential force would resonate and become "Eloquent, oracular; / A volcano heard afar." The poem would resound through space and time:

> And these words shall then become
> Like Oppression's thundered doom
> Ringing through each heart and brain,
> Heard again—again—again—

At its close, the poem repeats its mesmerizing incantation:

FIGURE 5.7. Roger Peet, *Shake Your Chains*, 2019. Image courtesy of the artist.

Shelley was correct. His poetic lions laid the ground for a different kind of feline, whom we will meet in chapter 7: the worker's black cat, an animal of twentieth-century political-economic critique.

Meanwhile, back in the nineteenth century, Marx, ever a literary critic, weighed in on Romantic poets including Shelley and Lord Byron. Marx *always* weighed in. "The real difference between Byron and Shelley," he wrote of England's two most famous lyricists, "is this: those who understand them and love them rejoice that Byron died at thirty-six, because if he had lived he would have become a reactionary *bourgeois*; they grieve that Shelley died at twenty-nine, because he was essentially a revolutionist, and he would always have been one of the advanced guard of Socialism."[25] But Marx also made another point: "Social revolutions . . . cannot take their poetry from the past, but only from the future."[26]

Romantic English printer William Cobbett's response to the Peterloo Massacre was located squarely in the past, however. Cobbett had distinguished himself as his own kind of printer, a populist but not a Spence-like radical. Still, his works had been banned and he had been imprisoned, and thus he had immigrated to the United States. He was a proponent of the theory that large wildcats roamed England, a question still unsettled to this day.[27] Cobbett had another, more pressing feline association, however. In 1798 he had published the pamphlet *French Arrogance; or, "The Cat Let Out of the Bag;" A Poetical Dialogue between the Envoys of America, and X.Y.Z. and the Lady,"* in which he staged a dramatic rhyming exchange between vaunted American revolutionaries and arrogant French ones. The Americans exclaim:

> Cat's paws nor tools we'll never be
> But are determin'd to be free

As the title suggests, the French are not accorded similar respect. But while Cobbett participated in anti-French feline rhetoric, he also grew concerned about what one scholar calls a "linguistic animalisation of the working class" of the sort in which Edmund Burke had engaged by declaring French revolutionaries a "swinish multitude."[28] Cobbett now wondered whether events like Peterloo meant such animalization had accelerated from description into the kind of "institutionally sanctioned violence" regularly committed against animals.[29]

Cobbett's own political antagonists had long referred to him as the Hampshire Hog. Now, when Cobbett heard the news of the Peterloo Massacre, his thoughts turned to animal lover and accused cat sodomite, Thomas Paine.

Still in the United States when the massacre transpired, Cobbett engaged in his own revolutionary *Tigersprung*: he leaped back into history, ventured to Paine's grave site in New Rochelle, New York, and exhumed him. We remember that Benjamin explained the *Tigersprung* with the claim that "only that historian will have the gift of fanning the spark of hope in the past who is firmly convinced that *even the dead* will not be safe from the enemy if he wins."[30] Cobbett decided that, in the wake of the slaughter at Peterloo, Paine was not safe from the ravages of history and that he must be re-remembered. The man had died in debt and alone, an unfitting end for a defender of humanity and animals, Cobbett surmised. He reported in a letter, "I have done myself the honour to disinter [Paine's] bones ... they are now on their way to England. When I myself return, I shall cause them to speak the common sense of the great man."[31]

Thomas Paine then crossed the Atlantic again, this time in skeletal form. The journey of Paine's bones did not proceed as smoothly as Cobbett had anticipated. He was barred from bringing Paine's remains into Manchester by customs officials. Cobbett seems to have secreted them in regardless, but he was forced to forgo a public reburial or other commemoration of Paine. Lord Byron, who Marx thought would turn into a reactionary, commented on the affair and demonstrated the tendencies that alerted Marx to his political disposition:

> In digging up your bones, Tom Paine,
> Will Cobbett has done well;
> You visit him on earth again;
> He'll visit you in hell

Who's ultimately to say who ended up in hell? Byron died young of a disease contracted while fighting for Greek independence. When Cobbett died his oldest son took to selling his estate but was legally unable to include Paine's remains as part thereof. One historian reports that the "bones then were passed to a day laborer, then Cobbett's secretary, then a furniture dealer, then oblivion. Over the years, several people have claimed to be in possession of parts of the bones—a rib in France, a jawbone in England, a skull in Australia."[32]

While still alive, however, Cobbett participated in the production of emergent knowledge of political economy. He had published the pamphlet *Paper against Gold and Glory against Prosperity*, in which he argued against the gold standard so as to support greater economic well-being for more of England's populace. He had advocated against the Poor Laws, England's attempt to attend to the poverty and misery that industrial capitalism had produced by setting up workhouses for orphans and the impoverished. Publications like Cobbett's and other efforts were part of the relations of production, too. This knowledge represented a new method of inquiry that could explain how a nation's wealth was produced and how the value therein should be distributed. "As a writer he has not been surpassed," Marx noted of Cobbett's popular style. Regarding his substance, however, Marx had concerns. "His intellect rarely broke through the boundaries of middle-class reform." That was because Cobbett "did not see the modern *bourgeoisie* ... he saw the machine, but not the hidden motive power."[33] A clearer, more condensed critique of the problem with bourgeois morality and criticism has seldom been put to page. Marx published these words in the *New York Tribune,* where he worked as a journalist and wrote European dispatches for years.

Engels, too, had worked as a journalist. Son of an industrial magnate, he had ample opportunity to visit English factories and inspect how their laborers lived and work. He collected these writings into *The Condition of the Working Class in England,* a book beginning with the claim "The condition of the working class is the real basis and point of departure of all social movements of the present because it is the highest and most unconcealed pinnacle of the social misery existing in our day."[34] It's not only that the industrial forces of production are in conflict with the social relations of production, but that capitalism's misery germinates another possible future. Thus, dialectically, the very conditions required for industrial capitalism to emerge also form the conditions for resistance to it. In the twentieth century English historian E. P. Thompson would modify Engels's title to render it more active in his field-defining book, *The Making of the English Working Class,* in which he anglicized the method of historical inquiry we first witnessed in Georges Lefebvre's work on the French Revolution, a history written "from below." Shelley had proposed something similar in his poetic attempt to capture the "heroes of unwritten story." But whereas Shelley had included animals in his project, Thompson neglected them, even though, as with Hobsbawm, a cat assisted his writerly efforts.

England has long been of importance to Marxists, as it was to Marx. Just as his ancestor Meir Ben Isaac Katzenellenbogen had fled northern Europe for Venice, in the early sixteenth century the most capitalized and most cosmopolitan city of Europe, Marx fled the continent for London, the most capitalized and thus most cosmopolitan city of the nineteenth century. England's liberal immigration laws attracted a mass of fleeing revolutionaries from the continent who did not make their way to the United States. Venice was distinguished by its lions and so was England. Radical exiles and immigrants flocked to one of many leonine pubs where, one historian reports, "for the roughly 1,000 German refugees in London in the early 1850s, a key social and political centre was the Red Lion at 20 Great

FIGURE 5.8. E. P. Thompson and his cat, writing *The Making of the English Working Class* (1968).

Windmill Street. [It] housed the Communist League, a small but international organisation for which Marx and Engels had written *The Communist Manifesto*."[35]

England was likewise important because the country was the cradle and crucible of industrial capitalism, and that was the real object of Marx's critique. Finally, England was central to early Marxist critique because no one likes to document their deeds and misdeeds like the English bourgeoisie. Even without Engels's familial access to the terrors of textile factories, the Factory Act of 1833 required that inspectors visit fac-

FIGURE 5.9. The Red Lion pub, Soho, London. Source: Flickr, undated.

tories and produce reports detailing the conditions they found. These reports demonstrated that children worked all hours into the night, that whole families trudged off to the mills, and that they left the factories with barely enough time or calories to get back again for another working day.

It was this kind of living and working that generated the demand for a ten-hour workday, among other working-class hopes like free schooling and political representation. Of course, the bourgeoisie opposed working-class aspirations, to say nothing of the English aristocrats' opinions. Marx took note of who formed a coalition that was determined to keep workers working for as much of the day and night as possible: "all fractions of the ruling classes, landlords and capitalists, stock-exchange wolves and shop-keepers, Protectionists and Freetraders, government and opposition, priests and freethinkers, young whores and old nuns, under the common cry for the salvation of Property, Religion, the Family and Society."[36] But opposing the working day through political coalition was not enough. The bourgeoisie wanted to explain reasonably and scientifically the problem with shortening the working day.

Enter political economist Nassau Senior and his famous "last hour." Factories can't give up the eleventh hour and go down to ten, he explained, because the eleventh hour is when profit is made. According to Senior, profit slowly accumulates throughout the day but is not claimed until that crucial last hour. This economic law posed obvious trouble for the working class since whichever "last hour" workers sought to reclaim would be the hour in which profit was made. Then there was Say's Law, claiming that every purchase is also a sale and every sale is likewise a purchase. Thus supply and demand form equilibrium conditions, and from there a general social equilibrium takes root. Senior and Say were representatives of the same tradition as Cobbett, political economy, or the study of national wealth. Political economists began to produce theories to rationalize a bourgeois world as quickly as English textile factories processed slave-produced cotton. This is the intellectual world in which Marx found his métier. He would critique political economy. But there was so much of it.

Exasperated by having to reject every lunacy that bourgeois economics put forward, Marx specified that he would narrow his focus to genuine political economists like Adam

Smith and David Ricardo. He would exclude those like Nassau Senior and others whom he labeled "vulgar economists" and whom he said did not investigate "the real forces of production" but "only flounder[ed] around within the apparent framework of those relations . . . for the domestic purposes of the bourgeoisie."[37]

For Marx it was not only the case that the vulgar economists provide the wrong answer, for example:

QUESTION: During which hour is profit made?
ANSWER: In the last hour.

Of course, the answer *is* wrong. But, and here is Marx's point, so is the question. How, then, can one ask the appropriate questions, questions that investigate rather than reflect the existing conditions of the world? Such an interrogation brings us to the telltale heart of *Marx for Cats* because it evokes the question, How did Marxism become the mode of philosophical investigation that we know it as today and what, precisely, do cats have to do with it?

INTERMEZZO 3

———

THE CAT-MOUSE
DIALECTIC

Marx became Marx through the study and combination of English political economy, French utopianism, and German philosophy. Each of these fields had its own consideration of animals, and as Marx sought to distinguish himself from his pack of contemporaries, he also turned to beasts as he began to elaborate an idea of "species being." Humans, he proposed, are distinct from other animals in that they create a world with "life activity itself an object of will and consciousness."[1] Animals make the world their own, too, Marx understood, but he qualified that they do not think about the construction before they do it, nor do they consider their activities retrospectively; other species, Marx said, do not develop a concept of history.

Yet humans, including Marxists, use animals to develop both the fact and the narration of human history. For example, in *Dialectics of Nature,* Engels found recourse in cats to consider the relationship between diet and evolution. "Just as becoming accustomed to a plant diet side by side with meat

FIGURE 13.1. Banksy dialectics. Image courtesy of Alamy.

has converted wild cats and dogs into the servants of man, so also adaptation to a flesh diet, side by side with a vegetable diet, has considerably contributed to giving bodily strength and independence to man in the making."[2] For Engels, human omnivorousness frees humanity and sets it on a path toward historical development; feline and canine omnivorousness, however, condemns those species to servitude. Engels continues with a gratuitous barb about human herbivores the kind of which has continued to appear in Marxist writing and no doubt has had the effect of denigrating vegetarianism as a Marxist practice. "With all respect to the vegetarians," Engels notes, "it has to be recognised that man did not come into existence without a flesh diet [and that vegetarianism] has led to cannibalism at some time or another."[3]

But even as Marxists like Engels distinguished humans from cats, the same felines were called on by Marx and Engels for the development of one of their most important philosophical contributions: their reconstitution of the problem of abstraction through their critique of its presence in the work of extant German philosophy. To critique capitalism, Marx insisted, one must contend with its abstract character. One cannot ask the right questions of capitalism until one has the correct categories, and one cannot have the correct categories until one's own theory of abstraction is pitched at the appropriate level. To locate that level Marx and Engels introduced cats into their work. We turn to their critique of philosophical idealism in *The German Ideology*. They begin by criticizing Ludwig Feuerbach's method, which they describe as a process in which, "first of all, an abstraction is made from a fact; then it is declared that the fact is based upon the abstraction. A very cheap method to produce the semblance of being profound and speculative in the German manner."[4]

Marx and Engels here argue that an investigation cannot begin with a fact. Facts are only possible because of preexisting abstract categories. One must be able to identify the relevant category. Yet too often thinkers, both then and now, presume a fact can win an argument or form the basis of an assertation without realizing the web of abstraction in which any given fact is already imbricated. Indeed, "facts" are themselves a product of capitalism, coming into being around the mid-1700s and deriving from early Scottish political economy.[5]

Now, Marx and Engels proceed down a feline path of exemplarity:

> For example:
> *Fact:* The cat eats the mouse.
> *Reflection:* Cat—nature, mouse—nature, consumption of mouse by cat = consumption of nature by nature = self-consumption of nature.

Philosophic presentation of the fact: Devouring of the mouse by the cat is based upon the self-consumption of nature.[6]

No, no, no! We can almost hear them insisting. It is our conception of nature that leads us to see in the cat's activities certain truths and not the reverse. Agreed-on facts only become possible in "the midst of general abstractions," just as ideas are a result of material conditions and not an exception from them. There is a cat. It eats a mouse. Such empiricism will get us nowhere. Hegel critiqued this style of philosophy as being the equivalent of seeing "a dark night in which all cows are black."[7] Now Marx and Engels continued his work; Marx said of Hegel that his philosophy was "standing on its head. It must be turned right side up again."[8] In addition to inverting Hegel's work, Marx and Engels added a cat to the menagerie of animals to be wielded against other philosophers, but they did so on the condition that such animals be rendered dialectically as both abstract and concrete.

For now, however, we note that it was a cow to whom Marx turned to distinguish his thought from that of the Scottish progenitor of political economy, Adam Smith, and to elaborate the relationship between abstraction and labor, both of which, Marx argues, are uniquely human habits. "We are not now dealing with those primitive instinctive forms of labour that remind us of the mere animal," Marx explains. Rather, "we pre-suppose labour in a form that stamps it as exclusively human."[9] Marx specifies a kind of "human labor in the abstract." He then cites Smith, for whom "no equal capital puts into motion a greater quantity of productive labour than that of the farmer. Not only his labouring servants, but his labouring cattle are productive labourers." Marx issues one of his famous retorts to Smith in *Capital, Vol. 2*: "How much Adam Smith barred his own way to an understanding of the role of labour-power in the valorization process is shown by [that] sentence, which puts the labour of the worker on the same level as that of draught cattle." And what "a charming compliment" Smith bestows on workers, Marx concludes, not bothering to note the long etymological entwining of cattle and capital in Latin, Old English, and Old French.[10]

Human "species-being" is defined by the fact not only that humans have history but that it is abstract human labor that produces that history. As humans labor to reproduce themselves and their societies, they necessarily become historical beings. Engels made reference to this co-constitution in his unfinished *Outline of The General Plan*, which included a section titled, "The Part Played by Labour in the Transition from Ape to Man."[11] But as the development of Marx's thought continued throughout the nineteenth century, he moved away from species-being and shifted his investigation from humans as a distinct animal to capitalism as a distinctly abstract economic system whose value is generated by human labor power. That shift has had the effect of obscuring the work of all animals—cats in particular—in the archives of Marxism. The cat-mouse dialectic enables us to begin the long process of recovering some of these animal participants and allows us to answer Donna Haraway's lingering question: "Where is our zoological Marx when we need him?"[12] Reader, he is right here!

6

Domestic Cats, Communal and Servile

"The horse and the cow, the wild rabbit and the cat, the deer and the hare—these are more valuable to us as friends than as meat."

—ÉLISÉE RECLUS, *ANARCHY, GEOGRAPHY, MODERNITY*

n 1867, after the conclusion of the American Civil War, animal welfare supporter and author Harriet Beecher Stowe relocated from New England to Jacksonville, Florida. Famous for her antislavery novel, *Uncle Tom's Cabin*— Abraham Lincoln had joked to her that the novel had caused the war—Stowe also published the article "Rights of Dumb Animals," in which she encouraged greater care of both working and domestic beasts and which spurred a nascent animal rights movement in the United States. Per-

haps out of deference to cats' well-known dislike of travel, on her move Stowe left her cat, Calvin, in Connecticut with essayist, man of letters, and editor of the *Hartford Courant* Charles Dudley Warner. He soon turned his pen toward his adoptee and in 1870 published *"My Summer in a Garden" and Calvin: A Study of Character."* The book contained a lengthy examination not of a species of cat, as so many natural histories did, but of a single feline: Calvin.

"His individuality always made itself felt," Warner wrote. Calvin, he explained, was belletristic; he knew of *Uncle Tom's Cabin*; he always received a mention in epistles sent to the Warner house; seeing himself as distinguished, he disliked other cats. In so describing Calvin, Dudley was drawing attention not only to his essay's approach—his is perhaps one of the first nonfiction studies of a specific feline—but also to that of his class—the nineteenth-century bourgeoisie. There is no truer a bourgeois form than the individual: solitary, unique, in possession of a worthy past and an unknown future, and endlessly describable. Calvin possessed yet another bourgeois trait; he had a secret noble lineage. "He was of royal mould and had an air of high breeding," Warner wrote. "He was large but had nothing of the fat grossness of the celebrated Angora," he continued. "In his finely formed head, you saw something of his aristocratic character." Calvin was a gentleman as well. "I think he was fond of birds . . . but he never killed, like sportsmen do, for the sake of killing, but only as civilized people do, from necessity."[1]

In Warner's study of Calvin we meet a new, liberated, if ultimately doomed, bourgeoisie. We saw in the previous chapters how members of the bourgeoisie broke free from their aristocratic overlords. They never did emancipate themselves from the desire to be like them, however. Cats continued to be the muses of poets and storytellers; social reformers began to worry about their safety; and, finally, as must be included in any consideration of the bourgeoisie, those in business learned a lesson still with us today: cats sell. There is nothing more important to the bourgeoise than to transact; labor, land, stocks, trinkets, people, animals, everything everywhere must go to market. The lion, that noble beast, becomes one of their calling cards as the bourgeoisie can't help but cheapen everything they touch. "Sweeter than honey and stronger than a lion," they biblically declared of their slave-produced commodity, sugar. Marx says of this class, "It has resolved personal worth into exchange value."[2] Looking out on a world becoming increasingly connected by the bourgeois inventions of steam power, railroad, and telegraph, the bourgeoisie declares that everything has a price. This class, Marx explains, "compels all nations, on pain of extinction, to adopt the bourgeois mode of production; it compels them to introduce what it calls civilisation into their midst, i.e., to become bourgeois themselves. In one word, it creates a world after its own image."[3]

While the bourgeoisie styles and reinvents itself in its novels, portraits, salons, and businesses, the proletarians go to work (for the bourgeoisie). As Marx describes these two classes meeting each other, he resorts to the terms of an animal skin: of the bourgeoisie he writes that they comport themselves with "an air of importance, smirking, intent on business"; of "the other," the proletarians, he writes that they seem "timid and holding back, like one who is bringing his own hide to market and has nothing to expect but a hiding."[4] But the bourgeoisie is no less riven by contradiction now than it was when we made its acquaintance in previous chapters. Its members knew full well that the revolutions of France, the United States, and Haiti had settled little; that revolutions would continue; that slavery in its then-current form could not endure; that not every petty bread or egg thief in England could be sent off to Australia or strung up on the gallows; that European empires could not expand forever. But, as Marx intimates, they know this and persevere nonetheless.

FIGURE 6.1. The 1800s was a century of bourgeois cats. Frederick Dielman, *Uncle Toby and the Widow*, 1878.

Facing near-certain revolutions against itself, the bourgeoisie follows long-dead King Louis XV and declares — in language just as suited to our own era of climate change as to the 1860s — "après moi, le déluge."⁵ After me, the flood. A class that is individualist and stubborn, Marx insists that this is the bourgeois mantra. The bourgeoisie, he predicts, will only learn the lessons of their own history "as a man learns the law of gravity when his roof collapses on him."⁶ Simmering tensions between class factions intensify in the second half of the nineteenth century. We will witness civil war erupt in both France and the United States and address the pressing questions of whether republic or empire, democracy or slave-state, would endure. Marx weighed in on both events; he corresponded with Abraham Lincoln. In those harrowing years of imperialism and war emerged moments of political radicalism that remain celebrated to this day: a great labor stoppage in the southern United States and the emergence of an internationalist commune in Paris led, in part, by a great cat lover.

In London Marx continued his life's work: his critique of political economy. He watched as Britain became the world's first global capitalist empire whose leonine symbol endures to this day. After years of study in the British Museum's reading rooms, in 1867 Marx published his masterwork, *Capital*, which he claimed would "deal a theoretical blow to the bourgeoisie from which they will never recover."[7] He was right about that. Our present-day bourgeoisie still cannot explain economic inequality, which they see as a nagging glitch to be corrected through reform and legislation. For Marx, however, inequality is not a by-product of capitalism but rather both the condition for and the chief result of any capitalist economy. But as correct as he was about the laws of capitalism, he was wrong about other things—the role of animals in the revolution, for example.

Marx debated everything with everyone. Philosopher, revolutionary, and commentator, he left a prolific journal of the nineteenth century, to which he was both witness and interlocutor. During Marx's time in London the city emerged as place of cats; the world's first recorded cat show was staged there in 1871. Cat fancier associations began forming, and cat-themed books and hymns tumbled out of commercial printing presses. In an era of the *haute bourgeoisie* the lives and roles of animals were changing as antivivisection societies formed along with organizations for the prevention of cruelty to animals; vegetarian societies emerged in London and Manchester. How should humans relate to nonhuman animals, from cats to cattle? critics wondered. As friends? Housemates? Fellow workers? Property? In these debates Marx did not engage, and as his critique of capital developed, he seemed to leave animals behind. Some of his comrades followed his lead; others developed their own thought to be more inclusive of animals. Cats allow us to trace the paths of both and to wonder what might have been.

THE RADICAL AND PRIVATE LIVES OF
FRENCH CATS AND CAT LOVERS

Bourgeois is, of course, a French word. A *bourg* is a space inside the city wall, and those within are urbane, cultured, and (their word) civilized. They are of the bourg rather than of the country, with its farms, beasts, and peasants. Marx argued that the bourgeoisie uses "the price of their cheap commodities" to "batter down Chinese walls" and other barriers the world over.[8] But, alas, as it batters down others' walls, the bourgeoisie retains its own. Its members lead private lives. Their interiors become antithetical to their spaces of work; their homes become refuges for their families and their new site of emotional cathexis, their pets.

On the weekends—their own invention, which they would deny the proletarians who worked for them—they enjoy leisure and hobbies. They read novels; they discuss newspapers; they wander through urban space, taking in the new sensorium of capitalist commodities found in arcades, department stores, parks, and parades. They stroll on the grand Parisian boulevards, newly created by architect Georges-Eugène Haussmann after civil strife and designed to make Paris wholly visible, organized, and modern, and to evoke, in Haussmann's own words, the power and beauty of a straight line.[9] Members of the Parisian bourgeoisie might enroll in a painting class at the Jardin des Plantes, which hosted a public zoo whose first animals had been repurposed from Louis XVI's menagerie decades earlier during the height of the French Revolution. Representing fearsome cats with their own hand is the perfect bourgeois exercise: as they stare at these cats in cages they paint them in the wild; in others' captivity they experience their own freedom.

FIGURE 6.2. Bourgeois cats and commodities. Advertisement for Bourgeois Frères absinthe, 1902.

FIGURE 6.3. The bourgeoisie painting large cats at the Jardin des Plantes. Artist unknown, 1902.

It was this sense of bourgeois contradiction that motivated French caricaturist J. J. Grandville in his illustrations for P. J. Stahl's *Scènes de la vie privée et publique des animaux*. Stahl's book opens with a scene of an international congress of animals. Their assembly is led by a lion; a domestic cat and "parroquet" borrow a quill from an attending goose and use it to record the proceedings. "Shaking the dewdrops from his mane," the lion ascends the podium. "He denounces in a voice of thunder the tyranny of mankind." Then the lion speaks to this palaver of beasts and invites them to imagine a different world, free of humans.

> There is but one way of escape open for all! Fly with me to Africa, to the sweet solitudes of boundless deserts and primeval forests, where we can hold our own against the inroads of degenerate humanity. Far from sheltering walls, man is powerless against the noble animals I see around

me. Cities are men's refuge and there are few lion-hearted among them, if I may use the expression (ironical cheers from the Tiger).[10]

Producing a recursive narrative structure that could rival any postmodern novelist, at the conclusion of their congress the animals vote that the Ape, Parroquet, and Village Cock will become editors of a book called *The Public and Private Life of Animals*. A series of tales and accompanying drawings begins, including "Love Adventures of a French Cat" and "Journey of an African Lion to Paris"—perhaps a nod to Woira.

Marx lived in Paris from 1843 to 1845, until he was forced into exile, again. Like Grandville, he worked in that city's burgeoning print culture as the coeditor of a radical newspaper, *Deutsch-Französische Jahrbücher*. Marx may well have glanced

FIGURE 6.4. J. J. Grandville, *Congress of Animals*, 1842. Lion presiding; cat as scribe. Source: Stahl, *Public and Private Life of Animals*, 1977.

through Grandville's popular caricatures. But it was tiger enthusiast and Marxist Walter Benjamin who became captivated by Grandville and who noted that, under Grandville, "nature is transformed into specialties."[11] We see his point in Grandville's animal congress, in which each animal is given a role, so much like the division of labor that began to characterize French capitalist society. Benjamin correctly identified the split between "the utopian and cynical elements [in Grandville's] work": utopian because animals are free to run their own lives and everything can be transformed; cynical because animals can be imagined only as mirror images of the bourgeoisie.[12]

Grandville participated in a broader reimagining of society contemporaneous with French utopianism, a tradition that included the likes of Henri de Saint-Simon as well as Charles Fourier, socialist and subject of Marx's criticism. Some utopians likewise recruited animals to depict social transformation as they conceived of a different, more equal world. Yet they did so without understanding the need to confront class antagonisms, which, once overcome, could bring such a world into being. Fourier suggested that lions could be put to work and would participate in the development of more perfect societies. He believed lions and sharks would soon die out and be replaced by "anti-sharks" and "anti-lions."[13] Fourier's anti-lions "would transport travelers from one end of France to the other in barely three hours and assist in the delivery of mail. And, most famously of all, he claimed a shift in cosmic conditions would change the chemical makeup of the earth's oceans, so that they would taste like lemonade."[14] Marx's collaborator, Friedrich Engels, translated Fourier into German and editorialized that "French nonsense is at least cheerful, whereas German nonsense is gloomy and profound."[15]

While in Paris and after his banishment therefrom, Marx was captivated by the doings and undoings of French political and economic life. The country's first revolution had ended in Napoleonic imperialism. In 1848, amid high food prices, imperial adventurism, and lack of political representation (or even the right to demonstrate for it) for many, another revolution seized France and toppled another monarch. This was the so-called February Revolution, which, through both electoral and popular (including peasant) support, installed Napoleon's nephew, Louis Bonaparte, as president of what was declared the Second Republic of France.

Like his imperious uncle, this Bonaparte enacted a series of progressive and state-building infrastructural projects and reforms. Slavery was abolished, again. Universal male suffrage was enacted, again. Women did not have the right to vote, yet a proliferation of political clubs emerged, including women's organizations. Relief for the unemployed was achieved through the creation of the National Workshops, which guaranteed French citizens a "right to work," always a mixed blessing. The right to work meant the right to wages, but it also meant the right to be frustrated, exhausted, or, in Marx's own phrasing, alienated.

The culture of enfranchised alienation that emerged during the Second Republic has been well captured by twentieth-century Marxist philosopher Jacques Rancière in his book *Proletarian Nights*. His investigation will likely remind readers of the world of printing apprentice Nicolas Contat and his great cat massacre of the 1730s; the days of toil, misery, and overwork are the same. It is their nights that differ. In the eighteenth century Contat produced cat dramas after sunset. Looking from the twentieth back into the nineteenth century, Rancière finds workers who are likewise determined to seize the night through their own poetry, prose, and narrative. He resurrects the words of joiner Louis Gabriel Gauny, who both longs for the breezy cheapness of bourgeois culture and identifies with the animals such culture degrades. He imagines an address to Dante Alighieri, that composer of beautiful poetry of the damned: "You did not know the sorrow of sorrows, the vulgar sorrow of a lion caught in a trap," Gauny accuses his interlocutor. He then explains in his own words the pain of a proletarian working day, "the commoner subjected to horrible sessions in the workshop. . . . Ah Dante, you old devil, you never travelled to the real hell, the hell without poetry! Adieu!"[16]

After a few years of governing France as a republic, Louis Bonaparte launched a coup—against himself. He took the name Napoleon III and declared himself ruler for life. France became an empire for the second time. These events allowed Marx to witness, from his perch in London, a revolution transformed, not from his historical studies but in real time. After the revolutionary intensity of 1848 he and Engels had declared in *The Communist Manifesto* that "a spectre [was] haunting Europe, the spectre of communism." Three years later, continental revolutions had seemingly collapsed, and France was now ruled by Napoleon lite, a man famous for his mistresses and his fear of cats. Gone was expanded male suffrage and returned was the influence of the Catholic church, on education, for example. The upper crusts of the bourgeoisie again enjoyed state support for their various monopolies and rackets. Opponents of Napoleon III ridiculed him in animal language, one comparing him to "a turkey who believes he's an eagle."[17]

How could such a radical French revolution become a revanchist counterrevolution not once but twice? Under what conditions would the bourgeoisie give up their own political rights to secure their property? Was the bourgeoisie still playing the role of a progressive historical force?

Marx considered these questions in *The Eighteenth Brumaire of Louis Bonaparte,* which, it must be said, constitutes the most comedic of Marx's writing. This is also the work of Marx in which cats take the most central role; indeed, we can hardly imagine *The Eighteenth Brumaire* without them. The text opens with Marx's famous evocation of his old antagonist, G. W. F. Hegel: "Hegel remarks somewhere that all great

Chez ROSSIGNOL II Rue Taitbout • DÉPOSÉ ___ Tous droits réservés

LA CHATTE (Souplesse-Rouerie)

FIGURE 6.5. Paul Hadol, *Marguerite Bélenger La Chatte* (*Souplesse-Rouerie*), ca. 1870–71, depicts the mistress of Napoleon III. Victoria and Albert Museum Department of Prints and Drawings and Department of Paintings, London.

world-historic facts and personages appear, so to speak, twice. He forgot to add: the first time as tragedy, the second time as farce."[18] Napoleon was the first world-historical tragedy of French democracy; Napoleon III represents the return of that tragedy, now in farcical form.

It's fitting that Marx opens this text with different literary genres. The whole of *The Eighteenth Brumaire* is saturated with references to comedy, theater, and performance. Many scholars have noted how such idioms structure it. What few have noted, however, is that such language is repeatedly feline in nature. Who precisely was Louis Bonaparte? In explaining one man's hollow historical repetition of another's statecraft, Marx takes recourse to the lion and offers, "Bonaparte answered the party of Order as Agesilaus did King Agis:—I seem to thee an ant, but one day I shall be a lion."[19] Sometimes given over to repetition himself, Marx offers the analogy twice. He returns to the noblest of big cats: "For [Bonaparte's] irruption into Boulogne he puts some London lackeys into French uniforms. They represent the army. In his Society of December 10, he assembles ten thousand rascals who are to play the part of the people as Nick Bottom that of the lion."[20] Louis Bonaparte, now Napoleon III, thinks of himself as a lion, but in fact he is only a satire, a pale imitation, of both a lion and Napoleon. He is the lion of Shakespeare's comedy *A Midsummer Night's Dream*, in which the character playing a lion during the play within a play worries he won't remember his lines. But he has only to roar.

The most important feline distinction in *The Eighteenth Brumaire*, however, is located in Marx's analysis of different types of revolution. Marx writes, "Bourgeois revolutions, like those of the eighteenth century, storm more swiftly from success to success, their dramatic effects outdo each other, men and things seem set in sparkling diamonds, ecstasy is the order of the day."[21] Think back to our own discussions of bourgeois revolutions in the previous chapters: "all men are created equal," "liberty, equality, fraternity," and so forth. But what kind of equality is established? Soon enough it's back to the capitalist grind of slavery and factory, of lords of lash and lords of loom.

Marx turns to the cat to explain why. "Bourgeois revolutions," he explains, "are short-lived, soon they have reached their zenith, and a long *Katzenjammer* takes hold of society before it learns to assimilate the results of its storm-and-stress period soberly." I've left the crucial German term *Katzenjammer* untranslated for dramatic effect. It means, literally, "cat's wail." More colloquially it translates as a hangover after a night of drunkenness. While members of the bourgeoisie fall under the spell of a cat's piercing howl in their revolutions, proletarian revolutions are different. Marx says that they "constantly criticize themselves, constantly interrupt themselves in their own course, return to the apparently accomplished, in order to begin anew."[22] In their newness and radicality, proletarian revolutions avoid the dreaded *Katzenjammer* of history.

As astute and feline as Marx's political retrospective of France was, *The Eighteenth Brumaire* has, as its concluding words, a call that twenty years later became a reality and thus can be read as a prognostication. Referring to Paris's Vendôme Column, a phallic monument erected to commemorate Napoleon Bonaparte's victory at the Battle of Austerlitz, Marx declares, "When the imperial mantle finally falls on the shoulders of Louis Bonaparte, the bronze statue of Napoleon will come crashing down from the top of the Vendôme Column."[23] Marx now saw history not through the lens of "species-being" but through that of class struggle. The rule of Napoleon III and France's second empire would not endure. Perhaps Marx saw the French future as Walter Benjamin imagined the French past some seventy years later in his essay "Paris, Capital of the Nineteenth Century": "With the destabilizing of the market economy, we begin to recognize the monuments of the bourgeoisie as ruins even before they have crumbled."[24]

Written in German, *The Eighteenth Brumaire of Louis Bonaparte* was first published in New York City by Marx's colleague and comrade Joseph Weydemeyer. As a result of failed socialist and democratic revolutions, radicals like Weydemeyer had begun to flee Europe for the United States, where they established socialist clubs, workers' organizations, and socialist presses. It is here that we can begin to speak of Marx's followers as perhaps the first generation of Marxists. Weydemeyer had launched an American Labor Federation in 1853 and declared its ranks open to all "regardless of occupation, language, color, or sex."[25] Such claims became central to the politics of Marx's followers in America.

AMERICAN REVOLUTION REDUX

While civil strife gripped France as revolutions emerged and departed, the United States was moving toward civil war. To secure his own meager wages, Marx worked as a newspaper correspondent, transmitting his analysis of the United States to Europe and of Europe to the United States. He maintained an active correspondence with Weydemeyer and followed the development of an American labor movement keenly during the country's prelude to war. Marx clearly realized there could be no powerful labor movements in the United States while slavery was still operative. "In the United States of North America, every independent movement of the workers was paralysed so long as slavery disfigured a part of the Republic. Labour cannot emancipate itself in the white skin where in the black it is branded," he commented.[26]

In his writings on the productive and social relationships in the American South, Marx did not employ felines, but he could have. Cats were put to work torturing slaves. Plantation

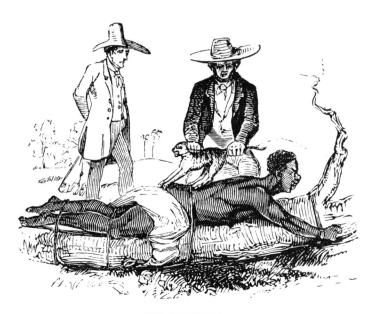

CAT HAWLING.

FIGURE 6.6. Illustration from the pamphlet "The Horrors of Negro Slavery," 1843, printed by the Quaker abolitionist Samuel Wood in New York.

overseers' whips were called cat-o'-nine-tails; in the 1700s these instruments had been used to torture those who had been impressed into the British navy. Now they were used in the labor-management relationships of slavery.

But cat-based torture went beyond metaphor in southern life. One southern visitor reported, "When other modes of punishment will not subdue [slaves, the owners] cat-haul them; that is, take a cat by the nape of the neck and tail, or by its hind legs, and drag the claws across the back until satisfied; this kind of punishment, as I have understood, poisons the flesh much worse than the whip, and is more dreaded by the slave."[27]

Southern plantation elites, for their part, resorted to big game to degrade people of African descent and to justify slavery. Frederick Douglass, in his 1845 autobiography, had claimed that both his overseer and his owner exhibited tiger-like qualities. In 1860 a group of slavery proponents explained in *Cotton Is King and Pro-Slavery Arguments* that "Nigritians" were not "tiger" enough:

> The innate love to act as body servant or lacquey is too strongly developed in the negro race to be concealed. . . . If Nature had intended the prognathous race for barbarism as the end and object of their creation, they would have been like lions and tigers, fierce and untamable. So far from being like ferocious beasts, they are endowed with a will so weak, passions so easily subdued, and dispositions so gentle and affectionate, as readily to fall under subjection to the wild Arab, or any other race of men.[28]

In their more private musings, however, slaveholders recorded a certain nervousness in the language of yet another feline. One wrote, "If they [slaves] want to kill us, they can do it when they please . . . they are noiseless as panthers. . . . We ought to be grateful that anyone of us is alive, but nobody is afraid of their own Negroes."[29] In their images and fantasies they presented a southern gentility, but at night they worried the stealthiest of cats might come for them: the black panther, a cat we will meet again in chapter 8.

As the United States began to face its revolution's second act, the Civil War, Marx analyzed the situation. "In my view, the most momentous thing happening in the world today is the slave movement," he wrote.[30] Despite an ostensibly free North, Marx noted that the United States as a whole was run for the propagation of slavery. "In the foreign as in the domestic policy of the United States, the interest of the slave-holders served as the guiding star," he wrote.[31] Slavery, like all aspects of capitalism, was riven with contradiction. Marx realized that "without slavery, north America, the most progressive country, would be transformed into a patriarchal land."[32] He meant by this that slavery was an economically progressive force, able to generate enough wealth to fundamentally transform society. But that was far from an endorsement—Marx understood that economic "progress" is often deeply reactionary and requires bloodshed, torture, and colonialism to "advance."

It wasn't just that American president Abraham Lincoln "let the cat out of the bag" as the cartoon in figure 6.7 claims, or that Lincoln had a cat named Dixie whom he declared smarter than most of his cabinet; rather, it was that the contradictions of capitalism, which make that system productive and possible, also make it doomed and impossible. New World slavery generated enough wealth to transform the world, but some of its transformations included the undoing of New World slavery. The revolutions, inventions, and social transformations that brought the bourgeoisie to power would keep developing, and Marx suggested they would ultimately develop beyond the bourgeoisie itself.

That is the case because the bourgeoisie, Marx explains, "cannot exist without constantly revolutionising the instruments of production, and thereby the relations of production, and with them the whole relations of society."[33] As capitalism brought this kind of systematic slavery into being, a new class of workers would, like they had done in Haiti, fight to the death to end it. In *Harper's Magazine* (figure 6.8) this civil war was staged as a battle of cats with the Confederate States of America facing off against the United States of America while Union general Ulysses S. Grant looked on. Like proverbial Kilkenny cats, only the tail would be left at the fight's conclusion.

Marxists have tarried over how to characterize American slavery. Marx and Engels wrote about it a great deal and their writings have recently been collated and published anew.[34] But

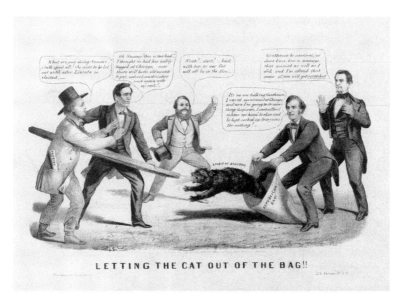

FIGURE 6.7. Lincoln confronts slavery in Louis Maurer's *Letting the Cat Out of the Bag!!*, 1860. Library of Congress, Prints and Photographs Division.

for years some Marxists suggested that slavery was not a capitalist institution because it was not based on wage labor; it was more akin to feudal bondage, they argued. We will follow the lead of sometime Marxist W. E. B. Du Bois, who claimed the Civil War was brought on not solely by structural contradiction but by slave revolt. In the years prior to the war Du Bois argued a great labor action had been systematically taking place throughout the South, where the three million slaves who toiled under torture had undertaken a general strike. Du Bois, who correctly noted in the 1920s that Marxism had a "negro problem," also used Marxist methodology to reveal that before the Civil War slaves were slowly but surely sabotaging the plantation economy. And Du Bois correctly realized that, given the chance, slaves would "turn like uncaged tigers on the rebel hordes."[35]

They did.

Marxists like Weydemeyer fought for the North and were in regular correspondence with Marx himself. Marx weighed in on the vicissitudes of civil war in a series of letters to his uncle, Lion Phillips, a Dutch tobacconist and sometime patron of Marx and his family. In one such letter Marx accurately predicted the course of the war's denouement: "The south will score early victories," due to its "property-less white adventurers [who form] an inexhaustible martial militia." But, he continued, "in the long run the north will win for in case of necessity it can play its last card, that of a slave revolution."[36]

FIGURE 6.8. This 1864 cartoon from *Harper's Weekly* depicts a Civil War catfight: the United States of America versus the Confederate States of America as General Ulysses Grant looks on.

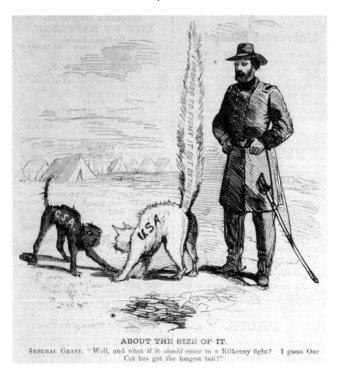

ABOUT THE SIZE OF IT.

GENERAL GRANT. "Well, and what if it *should* come to a Kilkenny fight? I guess Our Cat has got the longest tail!"

It was also in a letter to his uncle Lion that Marx noted one of the effects unique to capitalism: a seeming speedup of historical time. Revolutions throughout the world had erupted, and revolutions upon revolutions continued; never had history changed so quickly and radically as it had after the generalization of the capitalist mode of production. "When you think, dear Uncle, that three and a half years ago, at the time of Lincoln's election, the problem was making no further concessions to the slaveholders, while now the abolition of slavery is the avowed . . . aim, you must admit that never has such a gigantic upheaval taken place so rapidly. It will have a beneficent effect on the whole world."[37] Indeed, Marx noted in *Capital* that "a new life, immediately arose from the death of slavery. The first fruit of the American Civil War was the eight hours' agitation, which ran from the Atlantic to the Pacific, from New England to California, with the seven-league boots of the locomotive."[38]

Slavery was abolished. Railroads were constructed. Financial scandals proliferated. Worker actions took hold. Moments of genuine emancipatory potential for labor against capital seemed possible, briefly, after the Civil War. Former slaves were enfranchised and offered some form of equality, even more briefly. Of the United States in the 1870s there is so much to say, and we will say more in the next chapter on the rise of the labor movement and its turn toward cats. But, for now, we will leave it at this: Marx's uncle was named Lion.

FELINE FRIENDS AND COMRADES

By the end of the reign of Napoleon III in 1870, France too was gripped by war. Its sparring partner this time was Prussia under the rule of Chancellor Otto von Bismarck. While military historians still debate who enticed whom into war and under what conditions, Marxists insist that such wars are all but a foregone conclusion as competing empires chase new spoils. Regardless, the result of this conflagration was the capture of Napoleon III and the collapse of France's second empire. The grand bourgeois city of Paris was under military siege for months; buildings were destroyed, much of its population starved, and zoo animals (save the large cats) were eaten. The desperate French government relocated its headquarters from Paris to the southwest city of Tours.

Then in 1871, amid (quite literally) the ruins of the bourgeoisie, certain members of the Parisian National Guard refused to accept the terms of surrender to Prussia. They shot and killed two French generals, a discrete action whose outsized outcome revealed deeper revolutionary forces at work. And again a revolution began as certain workers of Paris turned against France. Paris, home of hundreds of thousands of radical laborers and artisans, declared a new political community, a universal republic of working people they called the Commune. The city's Federation of Artists' manifesto explained their new political project: "We will work cooperatively toward our regeneration, the birth of communal luxury, future splendors and the Universal Republic," a place in which wages, nationalism, imperialist war, and bourgeois trinkets would cease their domination of everyday life.[39] Again we are faced with the historical question of how such an event could occur and what kind of historical conditions might manifest such a break. Historian Stewart Edwards offered this conclusion on the occasion of the Commune's centennial in 1971: "The Commune as a revolution was not just one stage in a gradual social progress, but a 'tiger-leap,' one of those moments that cancel historical time. . . . In this the Commune was a revolution of more than just its own time."[40]

Celebrated by cat lover Vladimir Lenin as a "festival of the oppressed" and by Marx as a true "dictatorship of the proletariat," the Paris Commune has been justifiably extolled for its radical break with history in the midst of the most dreadful capitalist horrors. Looking on from London, Marx realized a new Paris was forming before his eyes. He wrote, "No longer was Paris the rendezvous of British Landlords, Irish absentees, American ex-slaveholders and Russian ex-serfowners"; rather, it was a people's republic open to all who arrived. And just as white workers could not be free amid black slavery, the Communards of the Paris Commune understood that one nation's workers cannot be free in an international order of capitalism. Thus all people were welcomed into the Commune, were they willing to work toward collective social betterment and the elimination of capitalist imperialism, were they prepared to be free as equals. Bourgeois Paris was expropriated and replaced by a scheme of "from each according to [their] abilities, to each according to [their] needs."[41] Education was reimagined, the Catholic church was again exiled, and, as Marx had predicted, the imperialist column at the Place Vendôme was toppled by the Communards and its location renamed the Place International.

Marx approved. The French bourgeoisie, however, felt the same horror the English had summoned toward the French Revolution some eighty years earlier. Marx was as right about this in his day as he still is in our own: given the choice between genuine democracy and capitalist imperialism, the bourgeoisie will choose the latter every time—even if they are on the receiving end of it! The French bourgeoisie certainly would not stand for a workers' democracy in Paris. Its war against Prussia lost, the French state now turned its guns and cannons on the Paris Commune and the tens of thousands of Communards who organized it. Over the course of a bloody week in May 1871 the French Army entered Paris and slaughtered up to 25,000 workers.

Generations of Marxists and radical historians have celebrated the beauty and possibility of the Paris Commune coming into being as they have mourned the mass murder by the

French state that ended the Commune's material existence. What is less known about the Paris Commune is that it was organized in part by a cat lover and produced a generation of radical vegetarians. Indeed, its members' vision of radical equality under the direst of circumstances included interspecies communism and political vegetarianism as forms of social practice. Even Marx missed this angle in his writings on the Commune, collected in *The Civil War in France*.[42]

One of largest and most effective organizations of the Commune was the Women's Union for the Defense of Paris and Aid to the Wounded. This union was in part organized by writer, soldier, teacher, and cat lover Louise Michel. Reflecting on her time defending the Commune on the barricades, Michel recollected, "I was accused of allowing my concern for animals to outweigh the problems of humans at the Perronet barricade at Neuilly during the Commune, when I ran to help a cat in peril. The unfortunate beast was crouched in a corner that was being scoured by shells, and it was crying out." Assisting a cat during shelling by the French military? For Michel the link was obvious. "The more ferocious a man is toward animals," she wrote, "the more that man cringes before the people who dominate him." Michel went on to credit her opposition to the death penalty to witnessing the slaughter of an animal as a child. "As far back as I can remember, the origin of my revolt against the powerful was my horror at the tortures inflicted on animals," she said. "I used to wish animals could get revenge, that the dog could bite the man who was mercilessly beating him, that the horse bleeding under the whip could throw off the man tormenting him."[43] Had Michel examined the archive of working animals around her with a different lens, she might have located animal resistance if not revenge. Jason Hribal has detailed a menagerie of working animals' job actions and revolts, from cows refusing to be milked to zoo animals refusing to perform to horses resisting attempts to ride them.[44]

Michel was not slaughtered by the French state during the Commune's bloody denouement. She was arrested and, after daring the state to execute her at her trial, she was sentenced to penal transportation and sent off to New Caledonia, France's imperial possession in the South Pacific. In exile, in a penal colony, she remained determined to fight the terrors of the French state. Michel began organizing with the indigenous people of the island, the Kanak, and supporting their revolt against their colonizers.

In her letters back to Paris, however, her thoughts turned to her cat, whom she felt she had abandoned. A nurse looking after Michel's elderly mother had this to say in response to one of Michel's letters:

> *My Dear Louise,*
>
> *I ask you to stop sending such incredible letters about your cat to your poor mother immediately. . . . She is very frail at this time, but perhaps you wish her to become ill, with your insane letters. Do you know how many letters you write to her about your cat? You can't know. You should have given money stamps to unfortunate people instead. However, your cat is much more important than your sympathy for unfortunate people!*[45]

The sentiment of this letter is similar to one Paul Lafargue, Communard and Marx's son-in-law, expressed in his 1881 article, "Bourgeois Sentimentalism":

> When it comes to beasts the bourgeois have the tenderness of angels. They feel themselves to be closer relatives of beasts than of workers. In England, that official country of hypocrisy, everywhere there are societies for the protection of dogs, cats, sparrows, etc.[46]

Lafargue introduces one of Marx's central criticisms of "animal rights," one still with us today. Namely, how can a po-

PAUL LAFARGUE
LE DROIT
À LA PARESSE

EDITIONS ALLIA

FIGURE 6.9. *Le droit à la paresse* (*The Right to Be Lazy*), by
Paul Lafargue, Marx's son-in-law, with cat on the cover.

litical radical be a proponent of rights for animals when human rights already seem an impossibility? How can one defend cats, dogs, sparrows, and so on when workers the world over are defenseless, ever at the mercy of capitalism? What kind of Marxist soldier would include consideration of a cat in the defense of her military position?

There has long been suspicion—if not derision—of animal rights in Marxist circles. And, indeed, the language of "rights" should provoke concern; rights confer a limited conception of freedom regardless of the subject to whom they are accorded. Thus, many animal supporters now use a language of liberation in place of liberal enfranchisement. Still, many Marxists have continued in their dismissal of and pessimism about the emancipation of animals. At the same time, we have noted throughout our study Marxists' willingness to use animals and draft them into the cause, which we will see most powerfully in the next chapter's consideration of the wildcat strike. Even Lafargue's book has a cat on its cover!

The perspective that undergirds the Marxist position is one of competition and declining returns: somehow to be in favor of animal freedom and equality must entail a lessening of support for other freedoms and equalities, those properly intended for humans. But beware of the language of diminishing returns, of a scarcity of equality—this kind of analogizing represents a logic of capitalism in which there is never enough. To counteract such sentiments one could even go back to the philosophy of Socrates, a vegetarian, and remind critics that equality and peacefulness are not competitive virtues. Indeed, they are the opposite, or should be: loving others makes others easier to love. These truths of animal love, animal compassion, and cat comradeship were certainly cultivated and strengthened by many members of the Paris Commune. After its destruction, the remaining Communards took them on their travels to London, Switzerland, the South Pacific, and Russia.

Returned from exile, Louise Michel, for example, attended the 1890 International Vegetarian Congress in England.[47]

Radical geographer and Communard Élisée Reclus went on to publish *On Vegetarianism*, in which he wrote of the domination of Porkopolis in North America, as both Cincinnati and Chicago were once known. His writing was republished in England in *The Meat Fetish*, whose title borrowed one of Marx's most important concepts, the commodity fetish. Reclus's title suggests the fetish structure might be a way to understand animal eating. Operating under the spell of the commodity fetish, humans are unable to refuse to participate in the suffering that their extractive consumerist lives entail. They know that what they buy and how they live is destructive to human flourishing but they proceed nonetheless. Reclus understood a similar construction to be at work in the consumption of meat. He notes how people

> often praise bloody flesh as a source of health, strength, and intelligence. And without disgust they go into butcher shops with slippery reddish pavement and breathe the sickly sweet odor of blood! How much difference is there between the dead carcass of a cow and that of a man? Their severed limbs and entrails mixed in with one another look quite similar.[48]

Reclus suggests we see animals differently, not as a collection of species to consume, but as a collection of beings with whom to share lives and build worlds. And it is there the cat appears in Reclus's thought. He writes:

> The horse and the cow, the wild rabbit and the cat, the deer and the hare—these are more valuable to us as friends than as meat. We are eager to have them either as respected fellow workers, or simply as companions in the joy of living and loving.... [They are] neither our servants nor our machines, but rather our true companions.[49]

The Paris Commune has had multiple lives. It has been discussed for its many successes and many failures. And indeed some Communards, like Michel and Reclus, ultimately deserted organized party politics for anarchism, perhaps because animals and their comrades were more welcome there. The feline context of the Commune poses questions still relevant for any workers' democracy today: Should not animals be considered "part of the working class," as Hribal contends?[50] Can animals lead us not only to interspecies equality but new forms of human equality, as disability theorist Sunaura Taylor suggests?[51] In the face of climate change caused by capitalists, do not we need not only communism but "vegan communism," as environmental historian Troy Vettese imagines?[52] Such questions might now be understood as a legacy of the Paris Commune, whose very existence Marx considered a political victory and whose multiple imaginings continue to inform Marxist thought and theory.

After the destruction of the Commune a different kind of feline radicalism took over Paris. It was a consumer radicalism, an avant-garde radicalism, a radicalism of style and image. And it, too, turned toward the cat. Le Chat Noir is thought to have been the first Parisian cabaret, and its famous feline iconography still resonates today. The location of this establishment was kitty-corner to the spot where the Communards were massacred in 1871. The cabaret opened its doors ten years later. Today these two juxtaposed historical sites and associations still stand in the Montmartre neighborhood, where they continue to commemorate the tension between workers' radicalism and bourgeois reactions to it. The first is the Square Louise Michel; the second a postcommune monument to the Catholic church, the saccharine Sacre Coeur basilica that one historian has called "the salt in the wound of the Paris Commune."[53]

In the face of the revanchism of white supremacy and racial capitalism in the postbellum United States, the ongoing expansion of the British Empire, and the defeat of the Paris Commune, Marx turned his attention to Russia and to accounts of peasant life and organization emerging there. He had learned enough Russian to read reports of communal activities and began to reevaluate his long-held belief that the historical path toward communism was through capitalism. In Russian collectivism he saw something different, another route to a freer future. Perhaps communism could arise anywhere through self-organization. Perhaps it could germinate in any society in which forms of nonhierarchical collectivity had already appeared.

It was then that Marx began to read the work of Louis Henry Morgan, whom we encountered in chapter 3 in our own consideration of the Euro-American colonization of indigenous nations and cats' roles therein. We remember that Marx studied Morgan's book *Ancient Society* and recounted passages from it in *Ethnological Notebooks.* Marx was particularly impressed by the Haudenosaunee confederation and its political equality. There is no evidence that Marx read Morgan's later books, including the idiosyncratically titled *The American Beaver and His Works*, but if he had, Marx would have seen a lament similar to those of Communards Reclus and Michel. For it was there that Morgan offered his own critique of imperialism, including that of humans over nonhuman animals. Morgan wondered, "Is it to be the prerogative of [humans] to uproot and destroy not only the masses of the animal kingdom numerically, but also the great body of the species?" He then considered that "we deny [other species] all rights, and ravage their ranks with wanton and unmerciful cruelty. The annual sacrifice of animal life to maintain human life is frightful."[54]

Marx read voraciously, and it's enough to recount what he did read without speculating on what he didn't. Yet his long turn away from animals and the problem of species-being deserves some context. During the last decade of his London years, indeed of his life, London emerged as not only the capital of capital but the capital of cats. London's Crystal Palace hosted the world's first well-documented cat show in 1871, shortly after the fall of the Paris Commune. Marx passed many of his London days in the reading rooms at the British Museum, where he likely encountered announcements for cat shows.

All breeds of domestic cats—many of them bearing imperial names such as Burmese, Siamese, Siberian, and so on—emerged as a bourgeois fascination, and the bourgeoisie continued to fixate with awe on British royalty, then led by Queen Victoria. The queen herself advocated for cats, noting their bad reputation had rendered them "generally misunderstood and grossly ill-treated."[55] Her own cat was called White Heather. Cats had treated Victoria well, as memorialized in a still well-known children's rhyme first printed in London in 1870.

> Pussy cat pussy cat, where have you been?
> I've been to London to see the queen
> Pussy cat pussy cat, what did you do there?
> I killed a mouse under her chair.[56]

Meanwhile, the British bourgeoisie were entertained with a cascade of imperialist feline tales that poured in from their ever-expanding empire. In 1802–1803 Captain Matthew Flinders circumnavigated the British Empire's newest conquest, a continent he named Australia, or unknown southern land. Abroad Flinders's ship was his cat, Trim, to whom he penned a eulogy after Trim disappeared while both parties were being held captive in Mauritius.

"The best and most illustrious of his race," Flinders wrote of Trim. "The most affectionate of friends, faithful of servants,

FIGURE 6.10.
Judith Holmes
Drewry's 1950
scupture of
imperialist
Matthew Flinders
with his "loyal
servant," Trim.
Market Place
installation,
Donington,
England.

and best of creatures. He made the tour of the globe, and a
voyage to Australia, which he circumnavigated, and was ever
the delight and pleasure of his fellow voyagers."[57] Unable to
imagine trans-species equality, or really any equality other than
with those whom they considered themselves already equal,
Flinders and a British public eager for cat dramas viewed Trim
as a servant.

   In one of the first printed books devoted exclusively to domestic cats, English cat fancier and organizer of the world's
first cat show, Harrison Weir, followed Flinders's language in
his 1889 book *Our Cats*. He noted, "The small or large dog

FIGURE 6.11. Regal and cheap: bourgeois mass advertising by English biscuit company MacFarlane Lang, 1930s.

may be regarded and petted, but is generally *useless*; the Cat, a pet or not, *is of service*."[58] Weir concluded, "Were it not for our Cats, rats and mice would overrun our house, buildings, cultivated and other lands."[59] Cats were servants, but they were also possessions; note in the book's title a favorite word of the bourgeoisie, *our*.

As the bourgeoisie gradually conquered England, felines were domesticated in more ways than one. By the end of the nineteenth century the domestic cat, once Satan incarnate, became a hard worker and trusty servant. The tiger was transformed from an evil revolutionary into a storybook character in imperialist Rudyard Kipling's *Jungle Book,* whose Shere Khan is presented as a lame yet arrogant feline. And the lion, the most noble creature of all, was, in keeping with bourgeois convention, now used to sell biscuits and crackers. The final bourgeois lesson in nineteenth-century England: delight the nation with commodities and commodified stories; make them regal and make them cheap.

As Marx neared his own end, he was reading widely in English and French literature and planning to undertake a study of the reactionary novelist Honoré de Balzac. A certain Marian Comyn had visited the salons for open discussions and Shakespeare readings that the Marx family frequently hosted in their London home. Author of one of the first biographies of Marx, Comyn remembers a house full of animals—dogs,

FIGURE 6.12. Black cat respect: Marx's grave at Highgate Cemetery, London. Photographer and date unknown.

each one named after an alcoholic beverage—visitors, and vivacious conversation. Marx and his wife, Jenny, had nicknamed their daughter, the socialist feminist cat lover Eleonor, Tussy, to rhyme with *pussy*.[60] As one of the final people present with Marx, Comyn recorded, "The last time I saw Dr. Marx he lay in his coffin, his hands folded over his breast—a warrior who had fought valiantly until his weapons were taken from him by a force greater than his own. A tranquil and majestic power remained."[61] Her recollection includes an attempt to offer Marx's daughter condolences, only to be "stopped . . . imperiously."

Tussy Marx explained to Comyn, "I want no condolences. If he had lingered during a long illness, and I had seen his mind and body decaying before my eyes, I should have stood in need of consolation. But it was not so. He died, in harness, with intellect untouched. He has earned his rest."[62]

Marx's last words had been, in keeping with his character, a critique of the very concept of last words. They were, indeed, dialectical: "Last words are for fools who haven't said enough!"[63]

Every Paw Can Be a Claw

REVOLUTIONS WITH CATS, REVOLUTIONS
AGAINST CAPITALISM, 1900–2000

PART IV

7

Sabo-Tabbies

"The fight is tough and you can't see through it?
Shut your traps and a cat will do it."

—RALPH CHAPLIN, "THAT SABO TABBY KITTEN,"
INTERNATIONAL WORKERS OF THE WORLD PROTEST SONG

ometime in June 1828, one of New York City's leading textile entrepreneurs, Alexander Knox, came into his office to find that a threatening note had been thrown through the window. By the late 1820s, labor organizing, agitating, and even striking had come to the city, which was on its way to becoming the most important global manufacturing center in the world, a distinction it would achieve by the 1850s. Yet handloom weaving was not as dominant in New York as in surrounding cities. Knox now sought to open such a factory. Before his enterprise could become established, however, workers had begun to unite against him.

Addressed to "Boss-Nox," the note was a warning from labor to capital:

Sir

I tak the chanc to let you no
Either Quit the Busness
Or else pay the price
You ought to for if you
dont you will be fixed
We will neither
lieve your house nor
house stade you mind
The Black Cat.[1]

Knox ignored the note. Soon enough, the Black Cat demonstrated the seriousness of its intent. Those operating under its signature destroyed some of Knox's weaving equipment and chased and beat his son. Knox then reported the note and actions to the authorities, thus generating a historical record.

Is this the first black cat to confront capitalism? Long a symbol of Satan, witchcraft, excessive sexuality, and bad luck, by the mid-twentieth century the black cat comes to represent organized labor, anarchism, and proletarian revolution. The revolutionary cat's twentieth century, however, begins in the nineteenth with the foregoing Black Cat of New York City's artisan weavers, the cat and animal lovers of the Paris Commune, Shelley's multitudinous lions, and now, as we will see, with the hymns of the Civil War, the great railroad strike of 1877, Russian woodcuts, German zoology, and African American folklore.

These nineteenth-century feline-tinted events helped to produce a class consciousness in twentieth-century proletarians who then confronted a fully developed, industrialized, globalized capitalism. Using their new understanding of—in part

derived from Marx—and their solidarity against their bourgeois antagonists, these proletarians began to undertake radical, redistributive—in a word, revolutionary—actions in the
United States, Mexico, Germany, and Russia. Some of these
events were staged locally, some nationally, and others worked
in concert to reorganize the world.

In the nineteenth century the bourgeoisie had rescued the
domestic cat from Satan's lair and turned it into their loyal servant, a creature with whom to pass a Sunday afternoon. The

FIGURE 7.1. Artist unknown, International Workers of the World
propaganda poster, 1916.

bourgeoisie had likewise expropriated the lion from the aristocracy and used that beast in new advertising schemes and to stock public zoos. Now, in the twentieth century, we will witness proletarians turn toward Marx's legacy as well as toward a heritage of feline power. Cats emerge as potent symbols against capitalist domination. They become interlocutors with whom a proletarian revolution may be planned and potential partners in carrying it out. Proletarians and theorists unite these forces—Marx and cats—to revolt against the bourgeoisie and revolutionize society yet again. In this chapter, *wildcat* morphs from a descriptor of banking to one of striking and insurrection. The failed German revolution of 1848 returns as another failed revolution in 1918–19, led in part by the Marxist Rosa Luxemburg and her cat, Mimi. In Russia a communist revolution succeeds; one of its leaders, Vladimir Lenin, had discussed the potential for communist liberation with Luxemburg and Mimi while in exile in Zurich. When he returned to Russia this cat lover helped to execute the first successful communist revolution at the state level (he helped to execute the Russian tsar, as well); the Union of Soviet Socialist Republics was formed.

Had the bourgeoisie scoured the historical record its members may have been more prepared for the emergence of the twentieth century's proletarian cat. They might have remembered Comte de Buffon's eighteenth-century assessment of cats as "faithless domestics," as he asserted in *Natural History*. He then explained why: they "possess an innate cunning," are "naturally inclined to theft," and "know how to conceal their intentions."[2]

As the twentieth century dawns, the contradictions of capitalism intensify. Capitalist forces of production have made the bourgeoisie rich through science, industry, and exploitation. Capitalist relations of production have consolidated and empowered proletarians. They see a world that they have made, one that is owned and operated by and for the bourgeoisie.

FIGURE 7.2. Vladimir Lenin and feline comrade, 1922.

Yet proletarians have been watching and studying. They have formed workers' associations, Marxist reading groups, and labor unions. They are hopeful and willful, and they are now prepared to undertake their own leap. Marx having passed, we now meet a new generation of Marxists who return to his journalism, philosophy, and political writings. As they study his thought, they amend and update his analysis of capitalism. Luxemburg does so through her work on imperialism and accumulation; Lenin through a study of the party and state; Leon Trotsky argues for a permanent revolution.

Through these critics and their comrades we will meet a new generation of proletarians and radicals who have identified capitalism as the source of their misery and constriction, and who now fight to destroy it: black proletarians, women, vegetarians, antifascists, communists, socialists, and anarchists, too. Proletarian actors sought to borrow from cats their power and stealth as well as their hostility to the bourgeoisie and their independence from that class. Felines have always been capitalist history's most radical animals, and we have seen that, for centuries, cats have been singled out and persecuted for their abilities to overturn social order and to leap from one place to another. We understand why proletarians would invite them into their expanding pantheon as they sought to make their own revolution.

Marxists have enrolled cats in all matters of political and theoretical endeavors. They have represented cats, mimicked them, borrowed their names and personalities, used them for motivation and for intimidation. By the twentieth century the class struggle truly had become a cat struggle, one whose long shadow continues to our own day. But under what conditions did cats and anticapitalists come together in the early days of the long twentieth century? What sort of political communities did these cats enter and how were they received? "As we fight together for a world free of exploitation, oppression, and bigotry, we have to be able to trust and count on each other. *Comrade* names this relation," writes Marxist political scientist and cat lover Jodi Dean.[3] In continuing to struggle toward a workers' democracy free from the imperatives of capitalist immiseration, we must address a question: Whom, exactly, do we consider a comrade?

If history tells us anything, it is that whenever Marxists have circumscribed their relations of comradeship, their abilities to critique social conditions and to transform those conditions from inequality to equality, from exploitation to cooperation, have suffered. W. E. B. Du Bois said Marxism had a "Negro problem"; as we will soon see, the German Social Democrats of the 1910s had a "nationalism problem"; generations of Marxists have had an "indigenous problem"; and, yes, most Marxists have also had a "cat problem," or an "animal problem" more generally.

And so the time has come to direct our bestiary toward a new question: Can Marxists become comrades with cats? Has an interspecies communism already appeared in our history and is now waiting to be rediscovered? Or perhaps such a coalition is on our collective horizon and on the verge of being made real through human and feline action and interaction? Conversely, we must also explore whether feline fellow travelers occupy a similar position for Marxists as for the bourgeoisie, one reflected in that class's possessive terminology of "our cats" and "our loyal servants." So we must also ask, Do cats dwell in history as what Marxist literary theorists have termed an empty signifier, a symbol passively waiting to be grabbed and put to work by whatever power takes hold of its furry paw? Or are they truly creatures of Marxist critique? That is the question that will bring us to this section's dialectic as the problem of cats and comradeship is considered anew.

THE SOFTEST PAW CAN BE A CLAW: BLACK CATS, FAT CATS, AND THE AMERICAN CENTURY

In 1877 a massive labor action spread across the newly re-United States, choking one of the country's most important, and most imperialist, new industries: the railroad. Seemingly meant for the transport of people and commodities, railroad companies also functioned as immense stockholding operations as well as powerful financial and political entities. Thus they were filled with scandal and swindle, much like the metropolises through which they snaked. After (another) few years of economic panic and depression that included the withholding of wages, in July 1877 workers across multiple railways, the country's largest employment sector, went on strike. Their action began in West Virginia and moved westward, to Pittsburgh and Chicago, and north, to Baltimore and New York, as workers in city after city undertook a coordinated refusal to work.

Striking workers were soon met with the reality that a strike against a company is always, necessarily, a strike against the state, as the state itself is "but a committee for managing the common affairs of the bourgeoisie," in Marx's words.[4] In 1877, before municipalities had regular police forces, railroads' own mercenaries and private soldiers were used to suppress the strike, and, when that failed, federal troops were sent in.

In St. Louis strikers went as far as to seize control of much of the city. Six years earlier workers had marched in New York and London in solidarity with the Paris Commune, and now, in St. Louis, authorities claimed a commune under worker's control had arrived stateside. One military historian wrote of St. Louis, "For the first time, property owners of the conservative middle and upper classes faced fears of revolution and equated the strike to the Paris Commune of 1871."[5] With reference again to France, *The Independent* newspaper claimed of the strikers that they "are worse than mad dogs.... Napoleon was right when he said that the way to deal with a mob is to exterminate it."[6]

The Napoleonic approach to social unrest accurately described the country's response to this, its first major industrial labor action. Workers were fired, imprisoned, and killed as the entire apparatus of the American state sought to force them back to work. Some sympathetic journalists took note of that, too. A different, more radical newspaper noted, "Presidents, judges, governors and legislators are but cats' paws nowadays in the interest of rings and corporations."[7]

The "cat's paw" of an ostensibly independent US state became a literal cat in the work of German American cartoonist Thomas Nast, who repeatedly employed various felines to symbolize the fraud, corruption, and entanglement that had become a regular part of American business in its relations with both municipalities and the federal government. Oil companies, railroad companies, and beef companies were all found to

GLEVELAND
SHIRT

THE
DEN
OF
CORRUPTION
AND
FRAUD.

THE CURIOUS EFFECT OF CLEAN LINEN UPON THE DEMOCRATIC PARTY.

FIGURE 7.3. Thomas Nast's depiction of a Tammany Hall tiger, 1862.

be involved in illicit activity, from monopoly price setting to embezzlement to bribery.

Yet the real radical cats of the late nineteenth and early twentieth centuries were found not in magazines and caricatures but in Chicago, a city whose connection to an emerging labor movement, industrial capitalism, and animals can hardly be overstated. It was in Chicago that the Haymarket Massacre took place in 1886. After union members' and labor activists' agitation for an eight-hour workday ended in more state-sponsored proletarian slaughter, some organizers began to realize that a structural confrontation with capitalism was necessary. Why call for an eight-hour working day when one could call for the end of work? The state's response to the initial Haymarket rally, on May 1, a day now devoted to labor, radicalized a new generation of anticapitalists (both socialist and anarchist), and part of their new radicalism took feline form. Anarchist Emma Goldman traced her own political awakening to the massacre and compared her personal determination to

FIGURE 7.4. Ralph Chaplin's sabo-tabby, created for Walker C. Smith's *Sabotage* pamphlet, 1913.

that of a cat: "As my friends always used to say, 'Emma is like a cat—throw her down from the highest point, and she will land on her paws.'"[8]

The most important union to emerge from Chicago was also the most feline: the International Workers of the World, or IWW. Lucy Parsons, who would become one of the founders of the IWW, lost her husband to execution during the fallout from the Haymarket Massacre. A woman of color, Parsons represents what was so radical about the IWW: unlike the staid American Federation of Labor, the IWW welcomed all races, all genders, and all trades into its effort to build "one big union." To symbolize its energy and power, the union adopted the icon of a black cat.

The fact that the city that grew the one big feline union of the IWW was one with an international reputation for animal slaughter must be considered. Chicago had earned the nickname "hog butcher to the world" for its development of mechanized animal killing, and many socialists as well as IWW members ventured through its novel stockyards. The most famous to do so was socialist journalist and novelist Upton Sinclair, whose novel *The Jungle* gave readers a taste of labor conditions in the industrial abattoir of capitalism.

Elizabeth Gurley Flynn, an IWW organizer, cited Sinclair's work in her own decision to abstain from eating meat. In her memoir, *Rebel Girl*, she noted that Sinclair "wrote this book in 1906 to expose the terrible conditions of the stockyard workers and to advocate socialism as a remedy."[9] But Flynn drew other conclusions. "After reading [*The Jungle*] I forthwith became a vegetarian!" she wrote. Flynn's interpretation of Sinclair's work was rather different than Sinclair's; while also a vegetarian, Sinclair maintained that "I have never had any sympathy with that 'humanitarianism' which tells us it is our duty to regard pigs and chickens as our brothers."[10] Flynn noted this odd discrepancy and wondered why "the public seized rather upon the horrible descriptions of filth, diseased cattle, floor sweepings and putrid meat packed in sausages and canned foods" to the neglect of the living and working conditions of the animals themselves.[11]

Yet another IWW organizer, Mary E. Marcy, also made her way through Chicago's stockyards. Marcy had a dual organizing mission: to expose stockyard labor conditions and to popularize the economics of Karl Marx, which she did through her illustrated book *Shop Talk Economics*. Yet it was a series of essays collected under the heading *The Letters of a Pork Packer's Stenographer* that garnered national attention.[12] Marcy wrote of the machinations of slaughterhouse legal departments, designed to indemnify corporations, quiet worker unrest, and coordinate price-fixing. Marcy revealed what Élisée Reclus and Louise Michel had prophesied in our last chapter: that human cruelty toward animals neatly segues into human cruelty toward humans. In Marcy's work this interspecies message came out in literary language—Marx himself loved the chiasmus— when Marcy declared, "In the hide department, men skin HOGS. In the legal department, hogs skin MEN."[13] When black Marxist poet Claude McKay composed his famous 1919 poem of worker longing and fear in the face of white supremacy and capitalism, he offered a porcine beginning: "If we must die, let it not be like hogs."[14] Alas, Marcy did not take the next step of calling for animal freedom from slaughter as part of her socialist politics.

It was not only capitalism's critics who passed through Chicago's storied stockyards. Indeed, one of the most important capitalists of the twentieth century, anti-Semite, cow hater, and soy enthusiast Henry Ford, was taken with these "vertical abattoirs," and they served as an inspiration for his Highland Park Ford plant.[15] In the velocity and scale of animal dismemberment, Ford saw the future of capitalism. He recollected, "The idea [of the automotive assembly line] came to me in general by the lift height that are used in the slaughterhouses of Chicago for meat processing."[16] Ford, along with engineer and prophet of scientific management Fredrick W. Taylor, retrofitted slaughterhouse design into automobile production plants to realize what some Marxists have designated as a new form of capitalist organization: Fordism, or high-wage, high-intensity factory work. Animal references predominated as they did so. Taylor understood workers to be "intelligent Gorillas," able to complete tasks with average dexterity and minimal creativity. It was Taylor who broke down the assembly line into ever smaller component actions and parts, designed to be executed at mass scale in as little time as possible. Ford and Taylor were interested in workers' domestic lives, too; Ford sent moral inspectors into his employees' homes to ensure proper conduct and garnished wages for infractions found therein. In Taylor's private musings he wondered whether he could arrange the lives of both his sons and his cat according to similar principles of scientific management.

In a series of letters that Taylor penned to his cat, Putmut, he encouraged reorganization, repetition, and order. "Dear Put," one epistle began, and proceeded to mention a neighborhood tomcat who had been visiting the Taylor property. "Have you taught him to catch rats?" Taylor wondered. "My advice to you is to make him useful or drive him away," he continued.[17] Indeed, Putmut's name also derived from the principles of minimal variation found in scientific management. In his "cat talk" to the feline, Taylor babbled "pretty putty, pretty mutty," over and over again until the name stuck. Using a collar and brute force, Taylor trained Putmut to surveil his domestic property, at one point congratulating the cat on "a scheme of ridding the place of rats" that has "worked perfectly."[18] A different feline emerged in Taylor's prose when the subject of workers' rights appeared, however. Taylor wrote to industrialist James M. Dodge to discourage any form of workers' democ-

FIGURE 7.5. Carousel figure of a cat, ca. 1910–14. From the collections of The Henry Ford.

racy on the shop floor. As for trying to negotiate with union organizers, Taylor urged, "I should not devote five minutes to that if I were you.... What they want is to get a grip on your men and anything short of that will be like throwing a mutton chop to a tiger."[19]

Ford was so entranced by cats that he installed a custom designed feline carousel on his property. Perhaps summoning the Norse god Freyja, Ford's creation was a radically different but no less fantastic form of mechanized animal movement than what was found in the stockyards. It was the latter that regularly hosted school children and tourists who would marvel at its engineering.

While Taylor and Ford saw in industrial capitalism the need for speed, the IWW had begun suggesting the opposite. "Slow down," one of the union's mottos famously advised;

"the job you save may be your own." The Wobblies, as IWW members had come to be known, began to advocate a strategy of sabotage, which Flynn defined as "the withdrawal of efficiency."[20] A black cat was tasked with delivering the message and subsequently became perhaps history's most famous (to some; infamous to others) proletarian feline.

That cat was conceived in part by commercial artist and IWW organizer Ralph Chaplin, also of Chicago. I qualify Chaplin's work with "in part," however, because black cats were already circulating as symbols of disinheritance and resistance to oppression in Chicago. Chaplin intercepted this feline; he did not create it.

For example, black cats had begun to feature in Chicago's burgeoning African American print culture as more and more black proletarians escaped the cauldron of the South and mi-

FIGURE 7.6. Ralph Chaplin, *Organizing the Harvest Hands*. Cartoon from *Solidarity*, September 30, 1916.

About Black Cats

' Oh, Laud a-mussy now on me! '
Cried Sam, ' an' on dis history! '
An' den Sam went an' killed de cat—
Swo'e he'd make an end o' dat;—
Burried him in de light o' de moon,
Wid a rabbit's foot an' a silver spoon.
But de Black Cat riz, an' swallered him whole—
Bu'nt his house an' took his soul! "

"Doc," said one of his hearers, "dat cat wuz a wahm chicken an' a movin' chile! "

"Yes," remarked another, "black cats is dead bad luck.   Dey's hoodooed me mo' den once."

Then the club adjourned, amid stories of experiences with black cats.

FIGURE 7.7. J. K. Bryans, illustration from Corrothers, *The Black Cat Club* (1902).

grated north. In 1902 James David Corrothers published his collection of stories and poems, *The Black Cat Club*, written entirely in "Negro dialect." Illustrated by J. K. Bryans, *The Black Cat Club* had medieval-like feline marginalia on most pages. It brought together folklore from throughout the South, all united under the sign of the black cat. Bad luck for some might mean good luck for others; either way, the black cat occasioned a story.

As Chaplin worked to build the IWW as well as to unionize commercial artists, he reached back into leonine history and Marxist thought and combined what he found there with Americans' increasingly beef-centered diet to design the sabo-tabby, or the sabotage cat.[21] In his memoir, *Wobbly: The Rough and Tumble Story of an American Radical*, Chaplin recalls this black cat's intellectual genesis. At a dinner that included steak and cigars, Chaplin listens to a visiting European cast doubt on the IWW plan for "one big union" working toward true economic equality. The European argues that America will have no socialism because it knows no true poverty. Chaplin quotes this visitor saying, "There will never be real poverty in America. . . . In Europe it is a real thing. . . . [But here it is different, for example], meat, who eats meat?"[22] A steak, then as now, symbolized affluence and power, and its seeming availability to some workers was enough for this European visitor to dismiss the potential of an American socialist revolution. Chaplin responds uneasily to this claim. He does see poverty in America—indeed, he lives in it. He has seen workers killed, including during the Pullman car workers strike of 1893. He reports in his memoir that after dinner he could not sleep. "I got out of bed and tried to read a chapter from *Value, Price and Profit*," one of Marx's speeches from 1865, which had been transcribed into pamphlet form and published in 1898.[23]

Of course a Wobbly would select that of all of Marx's texts. It was in *Value, Price and Profit* that Marx delivered the famous lines the IWW would adopt as their guiding philosophy: "Instead of the conservative motto: —A fair day's wage for a fair day's work! they ought to inscribe on their banner the revolutionary watchword: —Abolition of the wages system!" But also in that text Marx returns to the domestic cat, which he had not done since 1845 in *The German Ideology*. "What an immense amount of the necessaries themselves must be wasted upon flunkeys, horses, cats, and so forth," Marx writes, as he goes on to reject the (still popular) idea that goods trade at their worth and that necessities and luxuries somehow have prices that reflect inherent values.

It is then that a fascinating associative passage appears in Chaplin's memoir. As he had been unable to sleep, he now finds himself unable to concentrate on *Value, Price and Profit*. Marx himself had lamented toward the end of that text that he had penned a "very long and, I fear, tedious exposition, which I was obliged to enter into to do some justice to the subject matter."[24] At least Chaplin's thought was interrupted by a topical reminiscence. He reports "the face of a young striker came between me and the pages."[25]

Here, suddenly, dramatically, Chaplin's mind turns to felines. He has already told the reader that he carries a copy of Shelley's poem "The Masque of Anarchy" in his breast pocket, and now those famous lines echo through history, just as Shelley predicted in the poem that they would. We remember that Shelley's poem concludes

> And these words shall then become
> Like Oppression's thundered doom
> Ringing through each heart and brain,
> Heard again—again—again—

Chaplin continues, "Shelley's lines started to run through my mind:

Rise Like Lions After Slumber
In an unvanquishable number

That was it! That was the answer."

Readers will no doubt ask, What? What was the answer? In fact, it appears in both singular and plural forms: Marxism is the answer, but so are lions; poetry is the answer, but so is politics. Cumulatively, the answer is distilled: from Marx to cats. Chaplin reports that soon after this feline epiphany he began drawing his famous black cat and "using [it] rather freely in my cartoons."[26] He explains, "My 'Sab Cat' was supposed to symbolize 'the slow down' as a means of striking on the job." Before Shepard Fairy plastered his OBEY stickers the country over, Chaplin had done so with his sabo-tabby "stickerettes." Chaplin's cat campaign—SABOTAGE, we might call it—left a mark.

Radical cats advocating industrial sabotage began appearing in towns and cities throughout the United States. In one particularly violent confrontation, the IWW was organizing in Everett, Washington, in 1916. A local newspaper reported that the union "stoked the fears of the city's leaders with the unsettling image of a spooky black cat. With its back arched and hackles raised, the cat appeared large, menacing and feral." Members of the city's local Commercial Club "became careful readers of [the union's paper] the *Industrial Worker*. In its pages, they were teased with cryptic references to the cat." So terrified were authorities that they launched an outright military assault, resulting in multiple dead union members and soldiers (who, it seems, died from friendly fire). This particular event, now known as the Everett Massacre, showed the power of the Wobblies and their cat. Under the headline "Reign of Terror at Everett," the sabotage cat "was reported to have sharpened its claws."[27]

Chaplin also had a knack for artistic sampling. To the tune of the racist southern hymn "Dixie Land" he composed a new jingle called "That Sabo-Tabby Kitten," much as he had repurposed "The Battle Hymn of the Republic" into the union song, still sung today, "Solidarity Forever."

"THAT SABO-TABBY KITTEN"
(TO THE TUNE OF "DIXIE'S LAND")

You rotten rats, go hide your face;
I'm right here, so find your places.
Hurry now! Wonder how?
MEOW! Sabotage!
The tiger wild in its jungle sittin'
Never fights like this here kitten.
Hurry now! Wonder how?
MEOW! Sabotage!
O, the rats all hate and fear me.
Meow! MEOW!
The softest paw can be a claw;
They seldom venture near me.
Hurrah, they saw your Sabo-tabby kitten!
The boss has cream for his lordly dinner;
Feed him milk and make him thinner.
Hurry now! Wonder how?
MEOW! Sabotage!
If you are down and the boss is gloating,
Trust in me instead of voting.
Hurry now! Wonder how?
MEOW! Sabotage![28]

Calling out the cat's paw of electoral politics, "That Sabo-Tabby Kitten" asked crooners and listeners alike to turn away from bourgeois democracy and toward workers' direct action. The IWW emphasized that the state will never back workers unless it is a workers' state. Its cat's wail resonated, and the federal government set out to declaw this union.

Like its contemporaries Rosa Luxemburg and Vladimir Lenin, the IWW refused to support World War I. During a war, of course, even the measly political rights a bourgeois democracy doles out to its citizens are recalled. Anarchist and cat citer Emma Goldman had her citizenship revoked. Many IWW members, including Big Bill Haywood, fled for Russia, where a different kind of politics was leaping onto the historical scene. Chaplin was imprisoned for the duration of the war. During his sedition trial, images of black cats were introduced as state's evidence against him.

By that imperialist war's end in the United States, the radical cat was cohabiting with several new bourgeois ones: a modernist cat and a progressive cat. In 1920, New York journalist, man of letters, and Gertrude Stein aficionado Carl Van Vechten published his learned yet dilettantish book *The Tiger in the House*. A compendium of literary history's most famous cats, this text is a feline reckoning; it asks readers to consider cats as creatures of both joy and gravitas. Containing pictures and stories, poems and myths, all of them feline, Van Vechten's text, like so much of modernism, is smart and beautiful but lacking in a politics. Sabo-tabbies and sedition trials were blanketing the nation while Van Vechten wrote, but nary one radical cat appears in his text. Indeed, the reader can never be entirely sure whether she is reading a proper academic study or a farce. The book's cover lifts the ironic profile image of a noble cat we first encountered in prerevolutionary France, but that momentous event and the tiger's long transformation as a result of it remain absent.

Soon after the book's publication in 1924, Frank Kent, a reporter for the *Baltimore Sun*, coined the term *fat cat* in his essay, "Fat Cats and Free Rides."[29] Unlike the sabo-tabby, which has been slowly lost to history, the fat cat remained, and it has since then referred to wealthy people, particularly those who donate money to political parties. In that postwar moment the

fat cat confronted the black cat and initiated a century-long feline back-and-forth. The fat cat is "progressive" but not radical,
descriptive but not analytical; it names a problem but instills
no fear. Marxist revolutionaries and their cats would do things
differently.

While World War I had the effect of curtailing socialist activity in the United States and expanding the country's growing empire, in Russia, the same war toppled that empire and
helped to birth the first communist state; in Prussia, it ended
another empire and began a short-lived republic in Germany.
Taking advantage of pan-European distraction, the United
States invaded a country we first visited in chapter 4, Haiti,
where it reestablished slavery in 1915 and took control of the
economy. One American soldier, Smedley Butler, who led the
Haitian "expedition," saw the light in his small book *War Is a
Racket*.[30]

But communists and socialists had been saying for years
that war was an imperialist racket for years. They had realized the imperialist truth of war without participating in it,
but through studying Marx and watching the development of
imperialist powers and monopolistic companies. At a certain
point these entities began to poach on each other's preserves,
and thus a new war began. As cat lover Vladimir Lenin explained, "The war of 1914–18 was imperialist, that is, an an-
nexationist, predatory, war of plunder, on the part of both
sides; it was a war for the division of the world, for the par-
tition and repartition of colonies and spheres of influence of
finance capital."[31] Empires, chasing after ever more imperial
spoil, were faced with a choice of peace and self-preservation
or war and self-destruction. Their choice was clear: force the
poor of each of their countries to kill each other en masse by

making use of new capitalist technologies. Yet the spectacle of industrial slaughter on a world scale presented an opportunity for a new generation of Marxists to unite (or try to) across the boundaries of race, gender, and nationality.

Those devoted to ending empire and establishing a workers' state were Marxist theoreticians as well as actors. The most influential among them were devoted to cats. Marx himself had stressed, "The philosophers have interpreted the world; the point is to change it."[32] But how should that change happen and what role would cats have, both in and after a proletarian revolution? Such questions preoccupied Lenin, Luxemburg, and Leon Trotsky. Each of these theorists and revolutionaries traced their lineage to Marx, and each did so through a feline form. Ultimately, each met a different end for doing so: Lenin, still visible today, like so many taxidermied animals, lies in Moscow's Red Square; Trotsky, assassinated by Joseph Stalin in Mexico City, died surrounded by his beloved rabbits and the many cats of his lover, Frida Kahlo; Luxemburg is now memorialized on the embankment of Berlin's Landwehr canal, where cat-hating paramilitaries tossed her impaled body some hundred-plus years ago.

Lenin had advised revolutionaries to "convert the imperialist [world] war into civil war."[33] Through a civil war between proletarians and property owners a new society would be created, one that could finally deliver peace. "War cannot be abolished unless classes are abolished and socialism is created," Lenin argued.[34] His strategic comment has been repeated and celebrated by Marxists for generations. What few have noted, however, is that Lenin's advice was received as feline in certain quarters. C. L. R. James, whose *Tigersprung* method produced a new history of Haiti and new Marxist understandings of revolution, saw in Lenin's claim a leap. "Turn the imperialist War into Civil War," James quoted in *Notes on Dialectics*. "How many sincere opponents of imperialism recoiled in horror," he continued, assuming they had understood Lenin's advice as "too rash, too crude, not now. (Trotsky was among them.)"[35] But, James continues, "Lenin would not budge. The socialist movement against imperialism would establish itself on the concrete transition—the opposition to the monstrous evil of the war. He didn't have to wait to see anything. That was there. It would LEAP up."[36] Indeed, the leap from imperialist war to civil war occurred in both Germany and Russia but produced quite varied outcomes. James was partial to the outcome of the later.

Lenin turned to aspects of Marx's genealogy both literally and conceptually. He had met Marx's son in-law, animal rights critic and laziness advocate Paul Lafargue, in Paris while researching the legacy of that previous leap, the Paris Commune.[37] Lenin was impressed to be in the same company as Marx's last living relative, his daughter and Lafargue's wife, Laura, and Lenin understood the Commune to be an example of the kind of government by proletarians he hoped to establish. Tussy Marx had killed herself in 1898 at the behest of an abusive partner. Lafargue and Laura Marx would kill themselves as well, and Lenin would deliver a eulogy for them. Like Marx, in his early work Lenin introduced the cat in an attempt to settle his basic categories. Of course we note the strange, shared etymology here: cat*egory*, true in both Russian and German as well. To arrive at a category—the basic unit of abstract thought—one transits through a cat.

In his 1909 book *Materialism and Empiro-criticism* Lenin had set forth to defend a philosophy of materialism—the belief that our minds reflect the world—against a new onslaught of idealism—the belief that the world reflects our minds. "To the mouse no beast is stronger than the cat," Lenin wrote.[38] While true for the mouse, the proposition does not have a universal validity. Thus, later in the text, in his discussion of positivism, or a value-free conception of science, Lenin returns to this statement: "Mach's recent positivism has not travelled far from Schulze and Fichte! Let us note as a curiosity that on this question too for Bazarov there is no one but Plekhanov—there is no beast stronger than the cat."[39]

Lenin draws here on the old fable by folklorist Ivan Kyrlov, "The Mouse and the Rat."[40] The fable has an interesting title and an unusual one. In a world of cat and mouse, cat and rat, lion and lamb, and so on, "The Mouse and the Rat" contains two vermin and two felines: mouse and rat, lion and cat. A dialectic of each, two versions of an animal category, but not exactly the same. And from this clash of dualisms and opposites emerges a truth.

THE MOUSE AND THE RAT

A mouse in haste once ran unto a Rat:
"Say neighbour, has the good news reached thy ear,
Into the Lion's claws hath fallen the cat?
And now for us a time of rest is near!"
"Gossip, no cause for gladness"
Was answered by the Rat in sadness,
"Hope not for such an idle cause!
The lion's life won't last the longest,
If once it come to using claws:
The cat of all the beasts is strongest!"

Materialism and Empiro-criticism would begin, not end, Lenin's associations with cats.

By the time of the First World War, Lenin and the Bolsheviks had built these theories into an outline of a disciplined party whose task it was to suppress dissent and cultivate a revolutionary vanguard. This put him in competition with the Mensheviks, who sought to enact a parliamentary democracy and who, in a series of cartoons, portrayed Lenin as a cat outdone by mice, which calls forth another Russian fable. Lenin's critique of parliamentary democracy still holds: it is "a democracy only for the rich, for the minority." He contrasted such a democracy to "the dictatorship of the proletariat, the period of transition to communism, [which] will for the first time create democracy for the people, for the majority, along with the necessary suppression of the exploiters, of the minority."[41]

When the Bolsheviks seized power Lenin moved into the government house with several cats with whom today he is sometimes pictured. He claimed to have quit eating meat in favor of rice cakes, a comment probably made in jest; he referred to his own meals as pet food. The first governing communist state, the Bolshevik Soviet Union, contained the first woman in history to become a member of a governing cabinet, cat lover and Marxist feminist Alexandra Kollontai. In *The Autobiography of a Sexually Emancipated Communist Woman,* she advocated for a program of free love, at least for humans. She was more cautious when it came to her feline.

In a letter to one of her regular correspondents, Anglo-Russian writer Ivy Low Litvinov, Kollontai describes the neutering of her tomcat, Alexander. Kollontai seems divided on the procedure and its aftermath. Should Alexander not also partake in the pleasures of free love? Perhaps. But the effects of his sexual freedom were that the house "became rather full of little kittens" such that it began to cost Kollontai extra money in "ailments" to support his offspring.

Kollontai regularly corresponded with Lenin as well, and while their letters mention some animals, cats do not appear to the archive. Pigs, however, do. "What a swine this Trotsky is—Left phrases, and a bloc with the Right against the Zimmerwald Left!! He ought to be exposed (by you) if only in a brief letter to *Sotsial-Demokrat*!" Lenin advised Kollontai.[42] We will return to Trotsky in due course. But, for the moment, we follow the role of cats in Lenin's realization that personal example and even state power do not a revolution ensure. He ad-

FIGURE 7.8.
Still from Sergei
Eisenstein's cat-
oriented film,
Strike!

vocated for "achieving the prerequisites for that definite level of
culture in a revolutionary way."[43] A revolution needed the support of revolutionary novels, films, and designs. Here, again,
felines would participate. A popular Soviet children's primer
included the story "Lenin and the Tomcat Vaska" written by
Vladimir Bonch-Bruyevich.[44] Indeed, Vera Zasulich, now well-
known for her nineteenth-century correspondence with Marx
about communal and precapitalist social forms in Russia, had
a series of feline names for Lenin. She often referred to him as
"the big tom-cat" and, occasionally, "the wicked" or "cunning
tom-cat."[45]

Early Soviet culture remains known for its invention and
creativity. Cats entered into the aesthetics of the era, where
they became crucial content for radical new cinematic and
literary forms. Sergey Eisenstein, noted for the development
of filmic montage, turned to multiple cats in his first feature-
length film, the 1925 *Strike!* The clash of cats, from kittens to
calicos to black cats to dead cats, undergirds some of the film's
montage sequences.

Soviet literary theory, too, sought to bring the clash of dialectic opposites exemplified in montage into the analysis of
novels and language. Mikhail Bakhtin's influential notion of

heteroglossia, or the realization of many conflicting voices in any literary work, included those of cats. When he sat for interviews he would speak with his cat as part of the process.

Bakhtin's work drew on a long series of carnival traditions in which the voices of the poor and disinherited were imagined as suddenly powerful and agential. In Russia this tradition had long been associated with the saying "the mice bury the cat," as the Mensheviks had suggested they had done to the cat Lenin.[46]

The experimentalism of early Soviet culture was short-lived, however, and perhaps the most notable cat tale of the period concerns the repression of writing in a censorious Soviet state. The novel is Mikhail Bulgakov's *The Master and Margarita,* only published outside the Soviet Union and years after its author's death. The text moves between satire and allegory and has as its dark character a black cat who might as well have hailed from the European Middle Ages. The feline Behemoth is as large as his name would indicate, and he shape-shifts his way through Moscow, drinking, gaming and being as irreverent as anyone could expect from a satanic, satiric Soviet feline.

But the real feline behemoth of the Russian revolution was Trotsky. As in his name, Lev, which is Russian for *lion.* True to his etymology, Trotsky reports in his autobiography, *My Life,* that under his command the Soviet Red Army was commended for "fighting like lions."[47] Yet as the politics and alliances of competing factions developed within the Soviet Union, Trotsky was ostracized for not being lion enough as well as for his tiger-like ways.

The tiger accusation came after Trotsky suggested the Bolsheviks study fascist methods, that something of tactical value could be gleaned from analyzing one's enemies. The charge seems to have marked the beginning of his long exile from Soviet political life and power. Yet the tiger had been part of his analytical frame before he was accused of being one. In *The*

Third International after Lenin, written in 1928, he explained his concept of uneven capitalist development by reference to what he called "such tiger-leaps."[48] Trotsky writes:

> Imperialism links up incomparably more rapidly and more deeply the individual national and continental units into a single entity, bringing them into the closest and most vital dependence upon each other. . . . It attains this "goal" by such antagonistic methods, such tiger-leaps, and such raids upon backward countries and areas that the unification and leveling of world economy which it has effected, is upset by it even more violently and convulsively than in the preceding epochs.[49]

For Trotsky, the tiger leap is undertaken by capitalism. His feline leap is thus similar to Marx's generic leap of capital. "Only

FIGURE 7.9. V. I. Mezhlauk, *Trotsky and Kamenev*, illustration from the wonderful, and wonderfully titled, *Piggy Foxy and the Sword of Revolution: Bolshevik Self-Portraits*, edited by Alexander Vatlin and Larisa Malashenko.

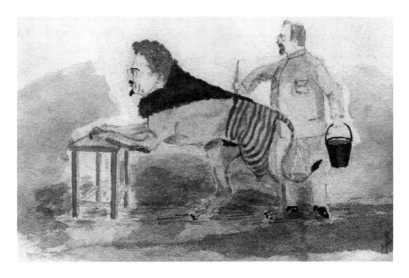

in the mind of economists does [capitalist technology] leap to the aid of individual workers," Marx writes in one passage.[50] "The difference between these various elements of commodity value ... leaps to the eye," he comments in another.[51] Marx is recalling Hegel's leap from quantity to quality, which we considered in chapters 2 and 4, and which both Lenin and James cited.

The year after introducing the tiger leap into Soviet political analysis, Trotsky was forced into exile. But he stayed a critic and analyst of world affairs, and he viewed with worry the rise of German fascism. He then turned to a different large cat as he wondered whether Hitler would be contained by Europe or whether Germany would break the Treaty of Versailles and realize its own imperial ambitions. In his essay "Hitler's 'Disarmament' and Prospects of War with Soviet Union," he notes that "only some 'fortunate' circumstances, in the form of complications between the heavily armed states of Europe, could permit National-Socialism, in the very next period, to execute a panther's leap."[52] Reader, those fortunate circumstances occurred. Germany's first so-called panther leap, or *Panthersprung,* had transpired in 1911, when the country lost its imperial possession of Morocco to France; a warship named the SMS *Panther* had participated in the military failure and generated this feline nomenclature. Its second attempt, which Trotsky predicts here, had its denouement in World War II.

Was it Trotsky, then, who first rendered the Marxist leap feline by drawing on the annals of German imperialism? Benjamin had been in Moscow in 1926–27 and had read Trotsky. Perhaps Benjamin's tiger leap was Soviet in derivation? For Trotsky, being called a tiger and then advocating for a communist overcoming of the tiger leaps of capitalism were both portents—the first of suspicions of his person and the second of suspicions of his approach to revolution. Trotsky went into exile, arriving and dying in Mexico among sometime *animaliers* Diego Rivera and Trotsky's lover (and Rivera's wife), Frida

Kahlo. In Mexico City, Trotsky met C. L. R. James shortly before he was assassinated by agents of Joseph Stalin. James had already published his tiger-focused *The Black Jacobins*, and after his meeting with Trotsky he would produce his LEAP-focused *Notes on Dialectics*. It seems, then, that origin cannot be our goal. More likely, this was a cat conjuncture, a kind of asynchronous synchronicity whose final overdetermination was feline.

Lenin refers to cats in his prose and poses with them in pictures; Trotsky's birth name and critique of imperialism were feline. Kollontai was a cat lover and critic of cats' love lives. Yet it is revolutionary and theoretician Rosa Luxemburg whose life bisects the utopian hope and dystopian despair of a Marxism that offers a feline critique of capitalism. She named her cat, found in 1905 in the workers' school where she taught political economy, Mimi, Hebrew for *rebellion* as well as *bitter*. As we first encountered in our introduction, Luxemburg carried both senses of the name with her. Utopian because cats—indeed many animals—appear in Luxemburg's work as potential revolutionary comrades. Utopian because when, in the smoldering ashes of World War I, workers in Germany revolted and declared a socialist republic, it was Luxemburg who stood atop the dais. And utopian because in a world of sexist, abusive communist men (including, unfortunately, her long-term lover, who, even more unfortunately, had the feline name of Leo), she led a radical life. But dystopian because her theorization never extended to the animals to whom she professed such devotion; dystopian because, unlike Russia's 1917 Revolution, Germany's 1918–19 effort ended without a workers' state; and dystopian, finally, because of the fascist ending she met.

Luxemburg's life parallels Lenin's in some ways: exile and jail, theory and revolution. She, too, was part of a Russian orbit; she hailed from its imperial backwater of Poland. Like him she plumbed the writings of radicals and progressives, insisting again and again that capitalism could not be resisted with compromise, but only with overturning. "Reform or revolution?" she asked.[53] And she consistently answered with the latter. Yet her revolutionary life was more pronounced in its relationship to cats and less rigid in its relation to party structure and discipline.

In her critique of a certain socialist newspaper's reluctance to support a mass strike, for example, she notes that its policy "goes around the whole problem of a mass strike like a cat around its milk."[54] Nor did she exclude Lenin from her feline deliberations. In one letter Luxemburg recollects an afternoon spent with him in Zurich, where they were both in exile.

> Yesterday Lenin came, and up to today he has been here four times already. . . . Mimi impressed Lenin tremendously. He said that only in Siberia had he seen such a magnificent creature, that she was a *barskii kot*—a majestic cat. She also flirted with him, rolled on her back and behaved enticingly toward him, but when he tried to approach her she whacked him with a paw and snarled like a tiger.[55]

Her magnum opus, *The Accumulation of Capital*, was composed with help from Mimi. There she diagnosed a lacuna in Marx's prose and solved a problem with his theory of accumulation that is still appreciated today. How, she wondered, does accumulation continue within a closed system, as Marx's *Capital* seems to propose? She understood the situation in feline terms: "We are led to believe that the market simply grows bigger and bigger. The logic is circular—like a cat chasing its tail."[56] Luxemburg's answer departed from the feline circularity she used in her analysis. She argued there must be an outside, and only if there are times and spaces of noncapitalism can capitalism continue its expansion, which it does through a combination of imperialism and forms of credit and debt.

Unsurprisingly, cats entered into the usual internecine party struggles as well. One comrade reprimanded Luxemburg

FIGURE 7.10. Cartoon of Rosa Luxemburg in conversation with Mimi. Source: Evans, *Red Rosa*, 107. Courtesy of Kate Evans.

for the victuals she purchased for Mimi, noting that the same money, the same meat, could have been used to feed the poor. She, in turn, retorted, "Why are you telling me this? Don't I do everything in my power to fight for all the poor? You shouldn't spoil my joy with Mimi."[57]

Plus ça change, as the French say. Even in the revolutionary moment of impending world war, animals and humans were turned against each other and placed in competition by Marxists. Even for these small moments of interspecies comradeship cat-loving communists were castigated. Luxemburg issued her own critiques of her comrades, not for their feline interactions but for their support of World War I. How, she wondered, could a socialist revolution transpire if workers in one country were willing to slaughter those of another at the behest of nationalist, capitalist accumulation? The German Social Democratic Party, given the power of the purse, had voted to fund World War I.

As the imperialist First World War raged, Luxemburg was imprisoned for insulting the kaiser. In prison—she had debated taking Mimi with her but decided against it—she found comradeship in a different suite of species, birds and the odd working animal brought inside the prison walls. She had become, in Marx's words, *vogelfrei,* or "bird free."[58] Marx uses this term to isolate the particular "double freedom" that capitalism delivers. In capitalism, one is free to do whatever one likes, but is likewise free of anything that might help one do it. Now, in prison, Luxemburg was freed from her daily life, her loves, her political problems, but also freed from the ability to realize political change. She turned to birds in her isolation and perhaps imagined flying over the walls that confined her. An amateur botanist, she made prints of the prison's plants.

It was with the prisons' working animals, however, that she shared her sense of captivity. In one letter she recounted watching a Romanian water buffalo being admonished and lacerated as it delivered a cartful of goods to the prison yard. Luxemburg describes how

> during the unloading, the animals stood completely still, exhausted, and one, the one that was bleeding, all the while looked ahead with an expression on its black face and in its soft black eyes like that of a weeping child ... who does not know how to escape the torment and brutality.... How far, how irretrievably lost, are the free, succulent, green pastures of Rumania! ... [We] stand here so powerless and spiritless and are united only in pain, in powerlessness and in longing.[59]

She fantasied about a life in which she could "paint and live on a little plot of land where I can feed and love the animals."[60] Still, as the years in prison, and World War I, dragged on, her thoughts returned to Mimi. She wondered in another letter, "Who is here to remind me of [basic goodness], since Mimi is not here? At home so many times she knew how to lead me onto the right road with her long, silent look, so that I always had to smother her with kisses ... and say to her: You're right, being kind and good is the main thing."[61]

The water buffalo, the birds, Mimi; these animals seem to have been Luxemburg's comrades. And yet her theory of accumulation and imperialism did not account for the ways in which other species have been swept up into capital accumulation and might desire to break free from it. She even quotes Engels's speciesist claim that "the final victory of the socialist proletariat [will be] a leap of humanity from the animal world into the realm of freedom."[62] In her citation of Engels she highlights the importance of the leap. Luxemburg writes, "This 'leap' is also an iron law of history bound to the thousands of seeds of a prior torment-filled and all-too-slow development."[63] But we must highlight a different aspect, a certain irony: a cat lover uses a feline term in expressing her hope of abandoning nonhuman animals in a quest for freedom. Luxemburg famously solved a lacuna in Marx's theory of accumulation, but this question of animal freedom, of who leaps where and from whom we take our cue to leap, constitutes a lacuna in her own life.

Amid the toxic rubble of World War I, the Central Powers were defeated, the Prussian Empire collapsed, the nation-state of Germany emerged, and Rosa Luxemburg was freed from prison. With Karl Liebknecht she founded the Spartacus League, an early iteration of the German Communist Party distinct from that country's war-supporting socialists. With the war over and Germany's politics suddenly flexible and contested, sailors began to mutiny in port after port, workers' councils seized control of key German cities, and a socialist republic was declared in Berlin. But, alas, if we have learned anything from our study of revolutions in modernity, it is that any revolution will need to overcome a counterrevolution. As Luxemburg called for a workers' state she was targeted for assassination, not only by the proto-Nazi militia, the German Freikorps, but by socialists. Reform or revolution became reform against revolution. It should be noted that the Freikorps, the group that did her in, had associated women, sex workers, communists, and cats into a seamless category. They targeted the "proletarian women [who] are whores and cats [and] communists who live in a 'cathouse.'"[64] Homosexuals, too, were on their list; Berlin's gay bar at the time was called Zur Katzenmutter: that is, The Mother Cat.

Nature-adoring communist playwright Bertolt Brecht's epitaphs for deceased comrades often contained animals; tigers, sharks, even bedbugs make appearances. He had considered the American Porkopolis in his play *Saint Joan of the Stock-*

yards. But for Luxemburg he stuck to a language of economic class:

> Red Rosa now has vanished too
> Where she lies is hid from view
> She told the poor what life's about
> And so the rich have rubbed her out[65]

THE CAT-COMRADE
DIALECTIC

We return to Lenin for the definition of a category that we have used repeatedly and must interrogate just as often. What, precisely, constitutes a dialectic, as a thought, as an action? Lenin explains, "*Dialectics* is the teaching which shows how *opposites* can be and how they happen to be (how they become) *identical*—under what conditions they are identical, becoming transformed into one another—why the human mind should grasp these opposites not as dead, rigid, but as living, conditional, mobile, becoming transformed into one another."[1]

Our second question: What is the relationship of identity and opposition between the cat and the comrade? When is a cat a cat and when is a cat a comrade? Can both identities be occupied simultaneously or is there too strong an opposition between them? As C. L. R. James presents Lenin, "Identity means difference. Difference means identity. And now with a leap we can get into it."[2]

FIGURE 14.1. "Chairman Meow," internet meme, 2018.

If any philosophical tradition is equipped to answer such questions, it is Marxism. Marxists should be able to understand how cats are both distinct from them—in that they are not human—and, in that distinction, also like them—cats are subject to and may be subjects of a proletarian revolution. Luxemburg's own dialectics provide an example of the interplay between opposition and identity. Take her famous conjoining of acts that are spontaneous with those that are organized. Luxemburg argued that "spontaneity and organization" should not be understood as separate activities but as different moments of a single political process. In their clashing opposition Luxemburg could see their continuous identity. And in her example of the fight she shows how the identical can also be a site of difference. She writes, "The working classes in every country only learn to fight in the course of their struggles ... in the middle of the fight, we learn how we must fight."[3] Distinction comes through repetition: one fights to fight, and, in fighting, the fight becomes a new fight.

Now, as applied to the tension between cats and comrades, we can clearly say that Marxists rely on cats; they share a sympathy with them and an appreciation, even love, of them. They repeatedly employ that famous feline gesture, the leap. But we can also say that Marxists lack the sense of identity with cats that would enable Marxists to consider cats as comrades.

One American socialist, Constance Webb—both a Trotsky supporter and the second wife of Marxist C. L. R. James— addressed the issue directly in her 2003 memoir, *Not without Love*. She recounts an evening of speeches at a California Socialist Party event in the 1930s, during which a demure Webb tells an "old revolutionary" that she enjoyed his talk. He responds, "Do you like cats?" "I was surprised," she explains, and proceeds to proclaim an enjoyment of all animals. But the old revolutionary is persistent. "Cats are remarkable animals," he asserts, "much more intelligent than dogs." He proceeds to list various feline superlatives. Webb begins to blush but says she does not know why. Then she adds, "Later I realized that I felt foolish talking about cats when my comrades were nearby."[4]

Webb's memoir offers a rare moment of feline-oriented reflection, one that contains a truth: Marxists both enjoy and distance themselves from cats. What prevents the cat-comrade dialectic from being realized in anything other than negative form, as it is above? Like so many communist revolutions, cats have been stillborn as comrades. They appear and disappear. They take multiple forms:

> They are radical—the black cat
> They are progressive—the fat cat
> They are fascistic—the tiger
> They are unpredictable—the wildcat
> They are regal—the lion
> They are civilized—the purebred
> They are fearsome—the panther
> They are frolicsome—the kitten
> They leap—all felines

Cats have been embraced by Marxists throughout history, but never as comrades, only as signs thereof. And now, in a sense, we come to the central question of *Marx for Cats*: Are cats only signs? Is this history of Marx and cats a random one? Could any animal suture together an archive of capitalism and its critique, if one were to dig deeply enough through the footnotes and marginalia? Or are cats somehow uniquely critical beings?

While Lenin and Luxemburg transited through Switzerland in exile and developed a dialectics of identity and opposition, Swiss linguist Ferdinand de Saussure was there as well, working on a new theory of signification that he would publish in 1916 in his *Course in General Linguistics*. Lenin wanted to know how opposites might be similar. Saussure wanted to know why one meaning adheres to one word and another meaning to another word. Why, for example, do the letters *c-a-t* signify one mammal and the letters *r-a-t* signify another?

Saussure argued that difference produces meaning but the content of the difference is random. *R-a-t* might signify that

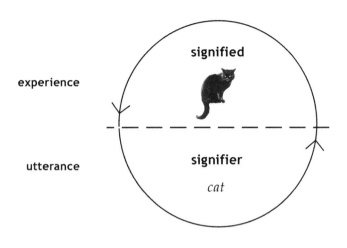

FIGURE 14.2. "Signifier, signified, cat," a popular structuralist pedagogical tool, creator and date unknown.

which is currently signified by *c-a-t*, or vice versa; the signifier will communicate meaning as long as there is some difference between it and other signifiers.

But wait—Saussure uses the example of a cat (*chat* in French, but it refers to the same thing) to argue that the evolution of language cannot be predicted over time; it, too, contains a certain randomness. Generations of Marxists interested in the relationship between language and political change have seized on this lesson of signification and, like Saussure, have used a cat to do it. Contemporary American Marxist literary critic Fredric Jameson follows this feline path in teasing out how meaning accrues in postmodernism. He writes of "the so-called 'referent,' the 'real' object in the 'real' world to which the sign refers—the real cat as opposed to the concept of a cat or the sound 'cat.'"[5]

British Marxist literary critic Terry Eagleton goes even further:

"Cat" may mean a furry four-legged creature, a malicious person, a knotted whip, an American, a horizontal beam for raising a ship's anchor, a six-legged tripod, a short tapered stick, and so on. But even when it just means a furry four-legged animal, this meaning will never quite stay the same from context to context: the signified will be altered by the various chains of signifiers in which it is entangled.[6]

In tarrying with why a word means one thing and not another, many Marxist literary theorists have offered feline examples. We may apply these literary lessons in signification in order to reach some resolution of the question at the heart of the cat-comrade dialectic.

On the one hand, no meaning is fixed, and that is as true of politics as it is of language. New possibilities always adhere to whatever present we find ourselves in. Who counts as comrade and under which conditions are states that can and must be updated and expanded.

On the other hand, meaning does find a certain stability, as does history itself. To change the stability of meaning and of history requires a dialectical disruption—what first Lenin and then James simply called a leap. While Marxists have theorized and instantiated disruptions of many of the forces and relations of production, they have not done so to the cat-comrade relationship. And yet that history already exists; it needs only to be exfoliated. Cats are both random examples and examples that have ceased to be random through each political-economic iteration of them. In the next chapter, the last of our bestiary, we turn to the group that sought to claim the cat as a comrade not in symbol but in fact.

8

Black Panthers

*"A man needs a black panther on his side when he
and his family must endure . . . loss of job, eviction, starvation
and sometimes death for political activity."*

— STOKELY CARMICHAEL, "WHAT WE WANT"

y the 1930s, collective striving toward a
communist workers' democracy whose
model emanated from the Soviet Union
could be found the world over, even in
Alabama. In the American Deep South,
where a system of sharecropper farming
trapped African Americans in a perpetual cycle of forced labor
and debt, and where Black organizing against this economy
brought violence from the state as well as extra-state groups like
the Ku Klux Klan, a communist party nonetheless took root.
Black communists organized for higher wages, better housing,
and education. A few of them traveled to New York and Moscow, and many of them understood Russians as "the new Yan-
kees," Stalin as "the new Lincoln," and the "Soviet Union as the

IS THIS THE PARTY YOU WANT?

DEMOCRATIC PARTY

OF ALABAMA

or

IS THIS ?

LOWNDES COUNTY FREEDOM ORGANIZATION

ONE MAN -- ONE VOTE

FIGURE 8.1. White supremacist rooster or Black Panther power is the choice presented in this political education pamphlet. Student Nonviolent Coordinating Committee, 1966.

new Ethiopia."[1] In 1935 the communist-influenced sharecroppers' union launched a strike in multiple locales in Alabama for a one-dollar-a-day wage. In some the strikers prevailed, while in others, including Lowndes County, they were met with brutal violence.

Still, collective organizing against a racist, capitalist state continued in Lowndes County, and some thirty years later a new organization for racial and economic justice took root. The Lowndes Country Freedom Organization sought to build a political party for African Americans, to run Black candidates in elections, and to contest the racism of the Democratic Party. Due to widespread illiteracy, the Democrats used a white rooster on the ballot to indicate where to mark; for those who could read, the party's motto was "White Supremacy/For the Right." The Lowndes Country Freedom Organization used an animal, too: a black panther. Chairperson of the organization, John Hulett, explained the choice of feline in a 1966 interview: "The black panther is an animal that when it is pressured it moves back until it is cornered, then it comes out fighting for life or death. We felt we had been pushed back long enough and that it was time for Negroes to come out and take over."[2]

This chapter is framed by our bestiary's final cat, the black panther, under whose guidance it becomes possible to narrate a mid- to late twentieth century of anticapitalist cats whether those felines are queer, communist, Black, vegan, or, more likely, a combination thereof. Black Panthers reached out to participate in a post–World War II, anti-imperialist global solidarity network. A different kind of black cat was present at the first gay uprising, and a Black Panther was there to invite those queer felines into a larger political world. One of the most forceful calls for a Marxism that takes not only cats but all animals seriously as comrades likewise comes from a Black Panther. Other cats continue their presence, of course. Lions return to herald in new technologies for a new era, not waterwheels or railroads but mutual funds; tigers are transformed again, into mascots of anti-inflationary monetary policies and signs of financial prowess; cats of all colors enter the lesbian rights movement and remain firmly entrenched there even today; and, finally, a new crop of philosophers begins to consider the problem of the animal. Among that group are a few Marxists, but more of them are ethicists predisposed toward utilitarianism and poststructuralists predisposed against Marxism.

The era from the 1930s to the 1990s spans Fordism, fascism, and finance. To develop within such varied historical terrain, Marxism would need to be made anew and certainly cats would have a role. As the twentieth century proceeded, European Marxists surveyed their own legacy and noted that communism had emerged and continued to emerge where it wasn't expected, in Russia, China, Vietnam, and Cuba; meanwhile, fascism had emerged where Communism was supposed to, in Western Europe. Marxist Antonio Gramsci examined the scene from the confines of a fascist prison in Italy and noted that the work of the Marxist revolutionary would need to be updated. He struggled to locate exactly what was required. "Something has changed, fundamentally. This is evident. What is it?" He asked in his voluminous *Prison Notebooks*.[3] Gramsci soon turned his attention to what he called "the manure of history." That was the pasture where Marxists would have to toil—hadn't they always? Gramsci then turned feline. "There is not even the choice between living for a day like a lion, or a hundred years as a sheep," he wrote, citing one of Mussolini's favorite aphorisms.[4] "You don't live as a lion, even for a minute, far from it: you live like something far lower than a sheep for years and years and know that you have to live like that."[5] Perhaps in Western Europe. But in Asia, tigers of communist revolution emerged; in the United States, the Black Panthers roared; and in a revolutionary and decolonizing Caribbean, the Cuban Revolution was victorious and Fidel Castro included cats in the effort.

Many of the felines of history and of our bestiary return in the late twentieth century: lions, wildcats, tigers, domestics both long-haired and short. "Capitalism is a motley painting of everything that has ever been believed," explain self-identified

Marxists Gilles Deleuze and Félix Guattari.[6] Their claim reveals a certain truth of capitalist effluvia: it never disappears. No fact or object is ever truly obsolete once the capitalist mode of production has taken hold. Rather, what seems to have been discarded is placed in the dustbin of history so that someone might retrieve it in the future and sell it for a buck—an old term for animal skins whose meaning was transmuted during the mid- to late nineteenth-century wildcat craze to refer to money.[7] Marxists began to dig through the rubble. They turned to painting, literature, film, fairs, and spectacles—what we know simply as culture—to look for clues as to what had gone wrong with their political project and to locate what could be retrieved from it. In the world of culture they saw the power of capitalist productivity; in their reading of Marx, however, they continued to see that capitalism was doomed, though now they believed its final eclipse might take longer to arrive. Things might get worse before they got better. "History puts its worst foot forward," suggested Jameson.[8] Dialectics should be understood as the "ontology for the wrong state of affairs," according to Theodor Adorno, one of the Marxists we'll soon meet. A dialectician can find hope where there is none and despair in a sea of bounty.

That ability to see otherwise is crucial for a world in which, as the cat-comrade dialectic suggests, meaning itself might be random. If that is the case, then cats are emancipated into a kind of symbolic freedom in which they can stand in for anything and become open to anyone. Indeed, such a state of affairs represented an opening for a group of economic conservatives, including Ayn Rand, Friedrich Hayek, and Milton Friedman, each of whom emerged as an influential proponent of capitalism and each of whom made a claim on a feline to support his or her novel economic theories. As we saw briefly in this bestiary's introduction and will return to in this chapter, French poststructuralist Jacques Derrida celebrated this possibility of

untethered meaning with his cat. But if cats are open to anyone and can stand for anything, what special role might they
offer Marxists? And if Marxism is a theory of culture and not
just one of political economy, what might it offer to or retrieve
from the culture of cats? The Black Panthers refused to compromise on the meaning of liberation. Facing down the force of
the American empire, they continued to advocate for a material
reorganization of social life as the only way to end racism and
poverty. As a result, many were threatened or killed by the US
government. Many of the culturally oriented Marxists, however, and some of the standouts of part IV of this bestiary—
Gilles Deleuze, Guy Debord, Walter Benjamin—killed themselves. Was it too much to see in *Hello Kitty* a glimpse of utopia? To forestall action in place of contemplation, even if a cat
sat on one's desk while doing so? There was another path, and
there still is.

NEGATIVE CATS: THE FRANKFURT SCHOOL
AND THEIR CRITIQUE OF ANIMALS

If any group of Marxists could have developed a theory of feline Marxism, it would have been the Frankfurt School—the
bourgeois Marxists who first turned toward music, image, and
literature as a site to undercover the truths and possibilities
latent in a capitalist society. This group of thinkers rose from
the ashes of the failed 1918–19 revolution in Germany. After
the destruction of the Paris Commune a new cultural liberti-
nism had appeared in France, complete with cabarets, surreal-
ism, and so on. Such a moment was also found in the United
States after World War I, where the Roaring Twenties constituted an era of progressive politics and new art forms. Likewise, in Germany, after the assassination of Rosa Luxemburg
and with the end of World War I, a new and short-lived era
of political and cultural transformation developed during the

Weimar Republic. A new Marxism emerged as well. It had its base at the Institute for Social Research in Frankfurt, hence its name. Mirroring the spirit of Weimar Germany, the Frankfurt School turned away from revolution and toward culture. It's not that its members did not appreciate the revolutionary efforts of comrades like Luxemburg and Lenin, but they believed the time for such revolution was not quite right—and the facts of Nazism in Germany and fascism in Italy and Spain would do little to convince them otherwise. What fascism and World War II did do, however, was exile most of their Jewish members to the United States, save Walter Benjamin, who killed himself in Spain while trying to flee there.

Benjamin had left behind a baggy manuscript full of nineteenth-century vignettes, quotations, and incomplete thoughts, all of which strove to combine a Marxist analysis of capitalism with a capitalist past of discarded consumer objects and stories, some of them animalic. There was the man who walked his turtle in order to experience a slower time. There were Grandville's many animal characters and Fourier's utopian beasts, all of which added to Benjamin's textual *Tigersprung*. Indeed, Benjamin's method of reading history was a tigerlike series of leaps from one moment and one subject to another. Leonine references, never completely worked out, dot the text. One standalone quotation reads, "The lion likes nothing better than having its nails trimmed, provided it's a pretty girl that wields the scissors"; another claims that "every animal is a sphynx."[9] Benjamin referred to this project, which was posthumously called *The Arcades Project*, in animalic terms, and claimed it came "howling like some small beastie in my night whenever I don't let it drink from the most remote sources during the day."[10]

Benjamin was the most fanciful of the group and animals contributed to his effort. But his colleagues Theodor Adorno and Herbert Marcuse likewise reached into the animal kingdom as they set out to understand what had gone wrong in a postwar world. How had the Germanic culture that had given history Hegel and Marx also given it Hitler? Adorno's book *Minima Moralia: Reflections on a Damaged Life* offers a series of short essays on living in the aftermath of European fascism. For Adorno, this was a depleted world in which there could be no politics. "Even solidarity, the most honourable mode of conduct of socialism, is sick," he lamented. Adorno chose a feline to deliver this news. "Katze aus dem Sack," his essay on political sickness was titled: cat out of the bag.[11]

Adorno considered the place of animals in an era of monopoly capitalism in its fascist variety where, unsurprisingly, the lion makes an appearance: "When industrial magnates and Fascist leaders want to have pets around them, their choice falls not on terriers but on Great Danes and lion cubs."[12] So as lions represent fascism, for Adorno, humans' treatment of animals reveals a fascistic possibility in all of us: "The possibility of pogroms is decided in the moment when the gaze of a fatally wounded animal falls on a human being. The defiance with which [the human] repels this gaze — 'after all, it's only an animal' — reappears irresistibly in cruelties done to human beings, the perpetrators having again and again to reassure themselves that it is 'only an animal.'"[13]

For Adorno, capitalism itself instructs people to turn away with indifference from animals, the poor, those who suffer. Blame the commodity. When exchange value dominates, most things and most people are rendered equivalent — able to be exchanged for something else at the right price. Adorno understands that such equivalence may easily become indifference. Who cares if this person suffers; there's someone else who may be suffering more or less. This is capitalism's ideology. Adorno chooses a cat to explain it: "If the lion had a consciousness, his rage at the antelope he wants to eat would be ideology," Adorno writes in *Negative Dialectics*.

Love you will find only where you may show yourself weak without provoking strength.

Theodor W. Adorno, Minima Moralia

FIGURE 8.2. Adorno aphorism with kittens. Source: Defunct "Adorno Cats" Tumblr site.

Still, in a world made ill by capitalism, for Adorno animals modeled another life where moments of redemption might appear. "Human beings have not succeeded in so thoroughly repressing their likeness to animals that they are unable in an instant to recapture it and be flooded with joy."[14] For the analytical Adorno, the draw of certain animals remained inexplicable. When this composer and student of music set out to write an operatic adaptation of cat lover Mark Twain's novel *Tom Sawyer*, he named one of his librettos "Death Song to the Tomcat." The animalic aspect of Adorno's opera was so pronounced that one colleague inquired about it. Adorno responded in a letter, "The consistent symbolism of the dog and cat, for which I have no theory yet, is the most puzzling thing."[15] It is this sense of irony and puzzlement amid ruin and hopelessness that motivated the Adorno Cats Tumblr page and that continues to populate the internet with Adorno cat memes.[16]

Adorno's feline ambivalence indicates a larger issue, however, which critics of the Frankfurt School have long seized on: What is the appropriate balance between hope and despair? If some hope is to be found in animals, why not in politics? Why can't one turn one's gaze to the wounded animal and hold it there? Reach out and take its paw, even? Adorno offered a singular answer: the "wrong life cannot be lived rightly."[17] His most famous student offered a different one. We now meet scholar and activist Angela Davis, who hailed from the panther state of Alabama and who traveled to Europe in the 1960s to study with members of the Frankfurt School. Her vision sought to combine Marxist theory with Black radical practice, to risk living the right life wrongly, and to involve animals in doing so. Davis confronted her teacher. She reports, "During one of my last meetings with [Adorno] ... he suggested that my desire to work directly in the radical movements of that period was akin to a media studies scholar deciding to become a radio technician."[18]

She chose another teacher, Frankfurt School member Herbert Marcuse, who believed in the possibility of radical politics, who had a menagerie of philosophical qualms regarding animals, and who had relocated to California to teach. Davis would soon go there, too, and would join the Los Angeles branch of the Black Panther Party. Like Adorno, Marcuse critiqued the fact of domination and the problem of freedom in a post-Holocaust world. He included in his exploration "the unrelenting exploitation of the animal kingdom in our days." As a cat sat atop his desk Marcuse wondered, "Can the human appropriation of nature ever achieve the elimination of violence, cruelty and brutality in the daily sacrifice of animal life. . . . ?"[19] Then, unlike his colleague, he proceeded to the next conceptual step: if human domination of nature causes suffering, might that suffering be abated by a different relationship to nature? Marcuse both hesitated and wondered, "In the face of suffering inflicted upon man it seems terribly premature to call for universal vegetarianism . . . and yet, no free society is imaginable . . . which does not make a concerted effort to reduce animal suffering."[20] It does not seem that Marcuse moved beyond equivocation on the question of animal comradeship and vegetarianism as a form of social liberation. But Davis did.

ARMED CATS AGAINST CAPITALISM

The Black Panther Party for Self-Defense had been founded in 1966, in Oakland, California, in a Marxist reading group. These cats sought to replace a capitalist ideology with a communist one that specifically attended to the experience of African Americans in the United States. As one Panther put it, "The ideology of the Black Panther Party is the historical experiences of Black people in America translated through Marxism-Leninism."[21] John Hulett, the chairperson of the Lowndes County Freedom Organization, had first used the panther symbol while organizing Black communities in Alabama. The organization and the image caught the attention of Stokely Carmichael, chairperson and national organizer for the Student Nonviolent Coordinating Committee, who adopted and helped to circulate the mascot. "A man needs a black panther on his side when he and his family must endure . . . loss of job, eviction, starvation and sometimes death for political activity," Carmichael explained.[22] Carmichael ventured to California to participate in a Black Power rally, and there Huey P. Newton and Bobby Seale adopted the name and logo to become the Black Panther Party for Self-Defense.

The organization was run by black activists and worked in predominately black communities. But the Black Panthers understood what Marxist Stuart Hall would later explain with such clarity: that in a late twentieth-century capitalist society "race is the modality in which class is lived."[23] Thus Panther cofounder Bobby Seale stressed, "Working class people of all col-

**An Attack Against One
Is An Attack Against All**

**The Slaughter of Black
People Must Be Stopped!
By Any Means Necessary!**

FIGURE 8.3. Black Panther power: *An Attack against One Is an
Attack against All*. Poster distributed by Robert Brown Elliot League,
ca. 1970.

ors must unite against the exploitative, oppressive ruling class.
Let me emphasize again—we believe our fight is a class struggle, not a race struggle."[24] Theirs was a revolutionary struggle
whose ten-point program called for "an end to the robbery by
the capitalists of our black and oppressed communities" and
demanded "an immediate end to POLICE BRUTALITY and
MURDER of Black people."[25] The Panthers fought for a mate-

rial transformation of society in which people of color could live and flourish. "We want land, bread, housing, education, clothing, justice and peace," they articulated. The party's power and organization earned it a terrifying accolade from the FBI: "The Black Panthers are the greatest threat to the internal security of the country," commented the agency's director, J. Edgar Hoover.[26] When Hoover rendered this judgment on the susceptibility of the country to a radical Marxist group, the United States was supposedly doing quite well economically. After World War II it had emerged as a political and economic leader of the world's capitalist countries.

Indeed, the period from the 1940s through the mid-1970s has been labeled by economic historians "the Golden age of Capitalism."[27] These years remain defined by high wages, unionized work, steady accumulation across multiple industries, and government coordination of supply and demand. One notices that all the drama of scandal and depression, financial shock and currency manipulation are missing from this list. Under conditions of state coordination and a lack of competition, working on the massive undertaking of rebuilding a destroyed Europe and suburbanizing the United States with ample federal subsidies, capitalism finally ran smoothly—for a few years, at least, and not for everyone, of course. In the United States, African Americans, women, farm workers, domestic workers, and queers were left out of the arrangement, as were Marxists. In exchange for steady wage increases and continuing union recognition in growing industries, many leading labor unions agreed to excise socialists and communists from their ranks. They were rewarded for doing so. Unions received government contracts worth billions of dollars to build armaments destined for Korea and Vietnam, and many unions got on board with the project of American imperialism.

This is the economic reality in which the Black Panthers formed and the one that they confronted. Like the IWW, the radical feline organization of chapter 7, the Black Panthers were unapologetic in their belief that force must be used to overthrow capitalist oppression. They were likewise emphatic that any war launched by a capitalist state was an imperialist war. Thus the Panthers understood themselves as fighting an empire. They followed an anti-imperial path of feline solidarity that stretched from Mao's China to Ho Chi Min's Vietnam. When the United States threatened any country that would follow the Chinese example of a peasant-led communist revolution, Mao explained that revolutions could not be undone by the "paper tiger" of the United States, which possessed a fearmongering exterior, to be sure, but an ultimately hollow core. "Mao" translates as "cat" in Cantonese, as the famous "Chairman Meow" meme (figure 14.1) continues to remind us. Vietnam successfully fought off both a colonial presence and a capitalist invasion; communist leader Ho Chi Minh said the Vietnamese were "tigers" compared to the invading and colonizing presence of the Franco-American elephant. The North Vietnamese offered to free their American prisoners of war in exchange for the American state freeing Black Panthers from prison, which the United States refused. The Panthers reached out to Cuba, where they were given a training ground to prepare for their armed insurrection. Fidel Castro under-

FIGURE 8.4. Mao Zedong repeatedly referred to the United States as a "'Paper Tiger,' loud but hollow." Source: *China Pictorial*, 1950.

stood multiple felines as part of his struggle. After his party's revolution in Cuba, Castro had claimed he wanted to abolish a standing army and replace it with "a peoples' militia, amusingly adding he was prepared to distribute arms 'even to cats'!"[28]

The Panthers armed themselves, displayed their weapons publicly, and followed police as officers harangued and terrorized Black communities. Their feline name extended to their tactics. Police patrols would now have "panther patrols" surveilling them in order to protect neighborhoods of color. Living in what they called "panther pads," they provided free food and other forms of aid to Black communities. As with the IWW, the Panthers' black cat symbol was widely considered part of its force. The IWW had artist Ralph Chaplin; the Panthers had Emory Douglas, an artist who became the Black Panther Minister of Culture and set out to design the visual presence of the Panthers in posters, flyers, and Panther newspapers.[29]

While the images of panthers did not seem to inspire the fear that Chaplin's sabo-tabby had, the Panthers themselves were a terrifying presence for a state organized by racism and capitalism. Thus the United States government assassinated of many of them, including Panther organizers Fred Hampton and George Jackson. For a time the Panthers persisted and their organization grew nationally and maintained its revolutionary ambitions. As historian Joshua Bloom noted in 2013, "Not since the Civil War almost a hundred and fifty years ago have so many people taken up arms in revolutionary struggle in the United States."[30] W. E. B. Du Bois had said that nineteenth-century enslaved African Americans would "turn like uncaged tigers on the rebel hordes."[31] In the 1960s many black communists became Panthers and set upon the American empire. In doing so they recruited "many thousands of young black people, despite the potentially fatal outcome of their actions, [to] join the Black Panther Party and dedicat[e] their lives to revolutionary struggle."[32]

One of them was the student of Adorno and then Marcuse, Angela Davis. She was already a member of the Communist Party of the United States when she became a Panther. She recounts her membership in and relationship to the Panthers in a collection of her writings and interviews, *Freedom Is a Constant Struggle*.

> I was studying in Europe in 1966, the year that the BPP was founded. After I joined the Communist Party in 1968, I also became a member of the Black Panther Party and worked with a branch of the organization in Los Angeles, where I was in charge of political education. However, at one point the leadership decided that members of the BPP could not be affiliated with other parties, at which point I chose to retain my affiliation with the Communist Party.

FIGURE 8.5. Angela Davis on covers of the weekly *Black Panther* Intercommunal News Service publication, March 4, 1972, and March 11, 1972.

However, I continued to support and to work with the BPP. When I went to jail, the Black Panther Party was a major force advocating for my freedom.[33]

Unlike Panthers Hampton and Jackson, Davis was not assassinated by the American state. But it wasn't for lack of trying. The state sought to kill her not by furtive assassination but by legal procedure. She was put on trial and charged with capital crimes. While awaiting trial in prison, this Panther became a vegetarian. In the 1990s she came out as a queer woman. The Panthers have been criticized for their misogyny and heteronormativity, but in fact they reached out to both feminist and queer organizations. Panther leader Huey Newton argued in 1970, "Whatever your personal opinions and your insecurities about homosexuality and the various liberation movements among homosexuals and women (and I speak of the homosexuals and women as oppressed groups), we should try to unite with them in a revolutionary fashion."[34]

Felines were present for one of the first queer uprisings. In 1967 a gay bar called the Black Cat Tavern in Los Angeles was raided. Police raids of gay spaces were common. What was different about this one was that the queers fought back. Before Stonewall, this feline-named bar launched one of the first rebellions of the gay rights movement.

There was a mutual sympathy and political identification, as Black and homosexual Americans were ostracized, surveilled, and attacked by the state. But perhaps there was also a feline identification as well. The Panthers had philosophical crossovers and working alliances with the League of Black Revolutionary Workers, where, again, we find a feline trace.[35] With American labor unions becoming more conservative and with many of them supporting the project of what black Marxist Cedric Robinson would name "racial capitalism," movements such as DRUM, or the Dodge Revolutionary Union Movement,

FIGURE 8.6. Queer cats staged one of the first gay anti-police actions in Los Angeles, 1966.

produced their own radical histories in the 1970s when they launched a series of wildcat strikes against some of the major corporations of the Fordist order. Wildcat strikes refer to actions conducted without union support; here they were conducted by coalitions of union radicals. Labor historian Martin Glaberman studied their tactics, interracial coalitions, and feline insistence in his article "Black Cats, White Cats, Wild

Cats." The organizations memorialized and publicized their efforts in their own print cultures, too.

It is fitting to conclude that the 1960s were a decade of feline radicalism. Perhaps unsurprisingly, when avant-garde French filmmaker Chris Marker sought to capture the history of the most famous political decade of the century, he turned to a cat to do so. In his 1977 film *A Grin without a Cat* [*Le fond de l'air est rouge*], he details the triumphs and failures of political and economic radicalism the world over.

Like so many in our archive, Marker signified and was signified by a cat. "When asked for a picture of himself, [Marker] usually offered a photograph of a cat instead," reports one colleague. "For example, Marker was represented in famed French filmmaker Agnes Varda's 2008 documentary *The Beaches of Agnes* by a cartoon drawing of a cat, speaking in a technologically altered voice."[36] Marker had good reason to select a feline avatar; Varda had herself made a documentary about the Black

FIGURE 8.7. *A Grin without a Cat* (*Le fond de l'air est rouge*). Still from the 1977 film by Chris Marker.

Panthers in 1968. As cats dominate the title and Marker's public persona, they appear in the film's visuals and narration, too. Describing war criminal and petty thief Richard Nixon as he attends a diplomatic summit in France, the film's voice-over notes, "Nixon looks unwell on the steps of Notre Dame, troubled. In fact, this whole collection of chiefs of state looks pretty sickly. Power must be bad for the health: just look at them. Compare their expressions with the clear eyes of a cat. That's the ultimate test. A cat is never on the side of power."[37]

If only that were true.

OBJECTIVIST AND NEOLIBERAL FELINES

In 1966 the Russian-born American philosopher Ayn Rand engaged in a correspondence with *Cat Fancy* magazine. Rand was already well-known for her work as a novelist; she had published *The Fountainhead* in 1943 and her magnum opus, *Atlas Shrugged*, in 1959. She had also begun to release her economic speculations in the form of essay collections including *The Virtues of Selfishness* and *Capitalism: The Unknown Ideal*. Now she turned her attention to cats, and they, seemingly, to her.

While the Black Panthers were organizing for collective betterment through overcoming capitalism, Rand advocated for increased selfishness in individuals and for capitalist exchange to permeate all aspects of society. When *Cat Fancy* magazine was launched in 1965, Rand purchased a subscription. The editors took note of their famous new customer and inquired in a letter about the relationship between Rand's objectivist philosophy of self-interestedness and her connection to cats. Rand responded, "You ask whether I own cats or simply enjoy them, or both. The answer is: both. I love cats in general and own two in particular." *Cat Fancy* was a magazine for cat owners; Rand owned cats; for her, pleasure and ownership were co-constitutive. Rand used the occasion of her correspondence to elaborate in a feline idiom precisely how objectivism should be understood. She quotes the question posed by *Cat Fancy* editor Leslie S. Smith, "We are assuming that you have an interest in cats, or was your subscription strictly objective?" Rand responds:

> My subscription was strictly objective *because* I have an interest in cats. I can demonstrate *objectively* that cats are of a great value, and the charter issue of *Cat Fancy* magazine can serve as part of the evidence. ("Objective" does not mean "disinterested" or indifferent; it means corresponding to the facts of reality and applies both to knowledge and to values.) I subscribed to *Cat Fancy* primarily for the sake of the pictures, and found the charter issue very interesting and enjoyable.[38]

How differently had cats appeared in the political economy of John Maynard Keynes, one of the economic architects of the postwar capitalist world. Keynes, too, had turned toward a feline, and he, too, wanted to live in a capitalist world. But Rand and Keynes had opposing philosophies of how best to ensure capitalism's continuation. Rand thought to extol selfishness. Keynes sought to limit it. Keynes's message to advanced capitalist countries after the worldwide Great Depression of the 1930s was forceful and direct. For capitalism to work, Keynes insisted, it must be tempered.

Humans are guided by what Keynes called "animal spirits," which he believed lead economic actors to make less rational and more emotional economic decisions, particularly in moments of crisis. Keynes suggested corralling everyone's animal spirits for the greater good.

He had written of the neurotic "purposive man" who is "always trying to secure a spurious and delusive immortality for his acts by pushing his interest in them forward into time." Then Keynes turned directly to felines. He continued by asserting that the purposive man "does not love his cat, but his cat's kittens; nor, in truth, the kittens, but only the kittens' kittens, and so on forward forever to the end of cat-dom."[39] How could capitalism persist in such a state? Cat lovers' aims would need to be redirected; animal spirits would need to be tamed. Keynes advised capitalist countries to limit dramatic economic fluctuation and provide at least the appearance of basic fairness and possibility within their own borders. He suggested that fiscal cycles could be managed and adjusted in response to the events of the world and that such management could provide more people with decent wages.

The difference between these two feline-trained economic philosophers alerts us to a historical change, one not limited to cats but one that would affect them. Cats had become sites of contest. The meaning of *cat* had been detached from its referent such that for every radical cat we find we can just as easily locate a reactionary one. The CIA, for example, participated in the American government's attempts to excise the Black Panthers, but it also made use of domestic cats when it launched Operation Acoustic Kitty to spy on communists in the mid-1960s. CIA agents implanted microphones in cats' necks and placed them around the Soviet embassy in Washington, DC, with the hope that the felines would manage to enter the building and perhaps take up residency there.[40]

But it seems the wired cats had their own political designs, and Operation Acoustic Kitty was deemed a failure, as were the agency's many attempts to pick off Castro and its imperialist misadventures in Vietnam. But the emancipation of cats into agents seemingly available to anyone introduces a larger problem into our bestiary—a certain unmooring that unites finance, philosophy, and felines.

We have already addressed linguist Saussure and his turn to a cat to contextualize the breaking of the sign-signifier chain. Why does c-a-t refer to a cat and r-a-t to a rat and not the reverse? Saussure's concerns were neatly located in pairs: x and y, y and z, and

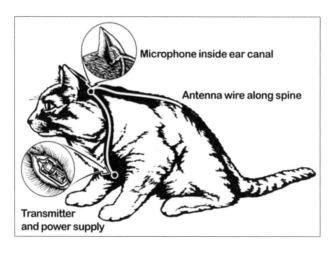

FIGURE 8.8. Diagram from the CIA Operation Acoustic Kitty's Soviet stealth project. Source: National Security Archive.

so on. French semiotician Roland Barthes, too, offered a feline explanation of the double nature of meaning in 1957.

> I am a fifth [year] student...I open my Latin grammar book and read the following sentence...*quia ego nominor leo*. I stop and think: there is something ambiguous about this proposition...its words have clear enough meaning, *my name is lion*, [yet] the sentence is obviously there to convey something else....I am an example of grammar.[41]

For Barthes in the 1950s, meaning was dichotomized. But in the 1970s a new problem emerged, and a single break in the chain of meaning was now understood by some philosophers as indicative of multiple breaks: a break within a break within a break and so on, a kind of infinite regress. If there's no necessary connection between x and y, then there's none between x and z, either. That first philosophical recognition of the break had been termed structuralism to note that meaning ping-ponged around within a given structure. Now, in the late sixties and early seventies, the poststructuralists claimed meaning was free floating; it bounced around, but not within any kind of structure. Barthes was only one of many philosophers who included a cat in pursuing the ultimate rupture of signification.[42]

The French pioneered this philosophy, but US president Richard Nixon joined the chorus in a different form. He essentially removed the United States from the general capitalist agreement of the postwar era, the Bretton Woods accords, by announcing that the US dollar, by then the world's most dominant currency, would no longer be indexed to gold. Like linguistic signs, the dollar would be detached from its material referent. The dollar would now be valuable not because it could be exchanged for specie, or gold, but because it was said to be valuable. French philosophers and US economic policy makers may not be the most intuitive set of interlocutors but in the 1970s they had two things in common: a displeasure with Marxism and a certain set of feline habits. It is thus cats who will lead us through that strange end of the long twentieth century, when conservative neoliberals, centrist Keynesians, and French poststructuralists found themselves in conversation about the relationship between meaning and money. Each brought a feline into their corner to garner support.

We begin with American neoliberal economist Milton Friedman, who laid out his approach to the government regulation of economic activity in an editorial titled "Barking Cats."[43] "What would you think of someone who said, 'I would like to have a cat, provided it barked'?" Friedman began. His particular locus of concern in "Barking Cats" was the US Food and Drug Administration and that agency's mission to ensure the safety of substances that Americans ingest. Friedman was opposed to the FDA, not because it did not possess a noble mission but because regulation could not work. It's not enough to mean well, Friedman argued. Rather, he maintained, a government regulatory agency is fundamentally misguided by virtue of

> its constitution in precisely the same way that a meow is related to the constitution of a cat. As a natural scientist, you recognize that you cannot assign characteristics at will to chemical and biological entities, cannot demand that cats bark or water burn. Why do you suppose that the situation is different in the social sciences?[44]

Cats cannot be changed from creatures who meow to ones who bark. From that feline proposition Friedman argues for a general law: market activities cannot be regulated, certainly not by governments. Friedman and his barking cats were beginning their intellectual and policy oriented dismantling of the Keynesian United States in which, simply put, some of the working class and socially vulnerable had been somewhat protected from the ravages of the market. Here is famous Keynesian economist Paul Samuelson in 1948 explaining why such regulation is necessary. In a world of unchecked capitalism, Samuelson wrote, "a rich man's cat may drink the milk that a poor boy needs to remain healthy."[45] Such a state of affairs is problematic for the poor boy, but—here is the basic Keynesian point—it's problematic for the rich man, too, because capitalism cannot be sustained in such an environment.

Keynesian buffers to capitalism's necessary inequalities were hardly palatable to neoliberals during the 1950s and 60s. But at least for developed capitalist nations there was enough money to go around. It was a time when, as Marxist David Harvey put it, "There [were] evidently, more ways to make a profit than there [were] to skin a cat."[46] But that was not the case by the 1970s, when the golden age of capitalism began to tarnish. Keynesian and cat lover Paul Krugman noted this diminution in his book *The Return of Depression Economics*. "In the early 1970s, for reasons that are still somewhat mysterious, growth slowed throughout the advanced world," he writes.[47] Like Marx said of William Cobbett so many years ago, Krugman did not see, could not see, "the modern bourgeoisie, he saw the machine but not the hidden power motive."[48] Keynesians remain baffled over the long economic decline that began in the 1970s and continues into our own day. But for Marxists, the reason for the slowdown was and remains quite clear. Marxist economist Robert Brenner explains, "Between 1970 and 1990, the manufacturing rate of profit for the G-7 economies taken together was, on average, about 40 per cent lower than between 1950 and 1970."[49] Capitalism, measured by its rate of profit, was beginning to reach its productive limit. We have made Brenner's acquaintance before in the "Brenner debate" of the 1970s, which sought to explain how capitalism emerged from feudalism. In an age of a slowing rate of profit, perhaps something else will emerge from capitalism. But, as always, what emerges will be contested.

The neoliberals had been organizing intellectually and institutionally, and an economic slowdown provided them the opening they needed to make their case—Rand against society; Friedman against regulations. Austrian economist Friedrich A. von Hayek, the most intellectual of the bunch, focused his critique on the centerpiece of Keynesian economic policy, an acceptance of some amount of inflation. Here he stepped in with his own feline concerns. In a speech in 1969 he explained, "We have inflation borne prosperity which depends for its continuation on continued inflation. . . . It has taken 25 years to reach the state [we are in now in, which] to slow down inflation produces recession. We now have a tiger by the tail: how long can inflation continue? If the tiger [of inflation] is freed, he will eat us up. Yet if he runs faster and faster while we hold on, we are still finished!"[50] Hayek saw the golden age of capitalism as a false coin, doomed to failure. Marxist Ernest Mandel

A TIGER
BY THE TAIL
THE KEYNESIAN LEGACY OF INFLATION

FRIEDRICH A. VON HAYEK
COMPILED BY SUDHA R. SHENOY

FIGURE 8.9. Neoliberal book cover with tiger, from Hayek's third
edition, copublished by the Mises Institute (2009).

agreed with him that capitalism is doomed and cited Hayek's *A Tiger by the Tail* in his famous book, *Late Capitalism*.[51] In order to combat the ruthless tiger of inflation, neoliberals advocated for an austerity state. Mandel offered a different approach and argued for a socialist revolution.

Hayek, Friedman, and their neoliberal cohort were visionaries as well as activists, and their reshaping of global economies has affected workers from the United States to the United Kingdom to Chile. They seem to have had certain effects on philosophy, too, particularly the French kind. We now turn again to the poststructuralists whom we first considered in our bestiary's introduction. Recall that my own feline companion, The Mitten, and I spent months trying to parse the opportunities and problems of this group of philosophers who, in the wake of the dissolution of the Bretton Woods accords, turned away from Marxism and toward cats. Whether it was the Marxist conception of class, the promise of a workers' democracy, the revolutionary seizure of state power, or the singular importance of the economy, poststructuralists suggested that meaning was simply too elastic and therefore conditions too contradictory to focus on one goal like that of overcoming capitalism.

It was Jacques Derrida who claimed that the signifying chain of meaning was so open as to never require an actual referent. To insist on linguistic stability, he said, was to be a prisoner of an order he named *phallogocentrism*. That order is tied to too stable a meaning, whether it be found in psychoanalysis and its dominant symbol of the phallus or in Western philosophy and its order of logic. In Derrida's *vie quotidienne*, the man named his cat Logos and made reference to his penis in discussion with said feline. In his philosophy, however, he followed the path of the author of "Barking Cats," neoliberal economist Milton Friedman: no regulations. Thus literary scholar Michael Tratner notes that "Derrida's arguments . . . come closest to those of one of the most important anti-Keynesians, Mil-

FIGURE 8.10. Jacques Derrida and Logos. Photo by Sophie Bassouls/
Sygma/Corbis.

ton Friedman." He explains the link: "Friedman argues that
money plays an important role in the economy precisely because it is a system for distributing signifiers which have no
referent ... [and] the policies which Friedman advocates bear
similarity to some of what Derrida explores."[52] Tratner calls
this similarity "Derrida's Debt to Milton Friedman," and he
"suggest[s] that the economic developments that made inflation a powerful political buzzword [in the 1970s and '80s] contributed to the plausibility of theories such as Derrida's."[53]

It was his "debt to Friedman" that set Derrida on a path
toward animals. To turn away from meaning is to turn away
from Marx and from humanism but, it seems, to turn toward
cats. Multiple scholars now cite Derrida's article "The Animal
That Therefore I Am" as one of the foundational texts of animal studies—I did so myself in this bestiary's introduction.[54] A
few years after the article appeared, Derrida restated his claims
in book form, where cats are similarly showcased. Readers soon
find themselves in the primal scene of animal studies, in which
they encounter a naked Derrida and his feline.

The cat that looks at me in my bedroom or bathroom, this cat that is perhaps not my cat or "my pussycat" does not appear here to represent, like an ambassador, the immense symbolic responsibility with which our culture has always charged the feline race, from La Fontaine to Tieck (author of "Puss in Boots"), from Baudelaire to Rilke, Buber and many others.[55]

He goes on, but we will stop. Because even as he tries to use cats to separate himself from Marx, he cannot. Ludwig Tieck is not the author of "Puss in Boots"; Giovanni Francesco Straparola is. He wrote that generative feline story while in Venice in the sixteenth century, at the same time as Marx's ninth-great-grandfather, Meir Ben Isaac Katzenellenbogen, was there. There's another hidden Marxist reference in this passage: philosopher Martin Buber was related to Katzenellenbogen, and thus also related to Marx.

Part of the project of poststructuralism has been to employ animals to steer theory away from Marx. But announcing that one is moving on from Marx does not equate to a world that does not need Marxists. Marx himself said that the Middle Ages could not live on Catholicism alone. The capitalist economies of the 1970s, '80s, and '90s couldn't live on poststructuralism. Meaning may have been up for grabs, but the distribution of money certainly was not. By the 1980s a new age of finance capital had dawned, led by cats, as had been the haute finance of the late nineteenth-century British Empire. The growing economies of the East were called the Asian Tigers. The roaring economy of neoliberal Ireland was dubbed the Celtic Tiger. The pioneer of mutual funds baptized himself "the lion of Wall Street" in his autobiography of the same name, *The Lion of Wall Street: The Two Lives of Jack Dreyfus*.[56]

When times are good, investors are led to riches by big cats. But when markets head south, investors are told to be wary

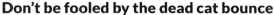

Don't be fooled by the dead cat bounce
– S&P 500

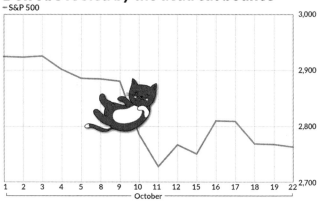

FIGURE 8.11. Stock market crests and troughs: the dreaded dead cat bounce. *MarketWatch*, October 23, 2018.

of a "dead cat bounce," or a momentary rise in an asset that will continue to fall. From bulls to bears, animals dominate the stock market—originally a term for cows.

FELINES IN RETROSPECT

Poststructuralists weren't the only philosophers to turn toward animals. In 1970 the term *speciesism* was introduced, and in 1974 Peter Singer published his problematic but nonetheless important book *Animal Liberation,* in which he suggests that an ethical life requires the avoidance of animal products.[57] But while Singer argued for a utilitarian ethics, Marxists would argue otherwise. First, however, they had to confront their own tradition's legacy. Beginning in the 1990s a new generation of ecologically oriented Marxists started to criticize the "species narcissism" of Marx's writing; they began to wonder if Marx's theory of labor was "predicated on a division between human and nonhuman animals," or if Marx himself did not commit "ideological violence against animals."[58] There certainly exists some real truth to these concerns. But there also exists the possibility for a new narration of Marxism. The best guide to that other understanding of Marxism remains a cat, namely sometime Black Panther Angela Davis.

Davis's fundamental political impulse—liberation for the poor, for people of color, for those who suffer under the domination of an other—led her to receive the Soviet Union's Lenin Peace Prize; it also led her to veganism. Yet she did not arrive there through a utilitarian ethics of the greatest good for the greatest number as Singer had. Rather, she turned to Marx and one of his most central ideas (which, in our bestiary, was addressed through the wildcat in chapter 5): use value and exchange value.

The dichotomy between these two forms of value is found at the beginning of Marx's most famous text, *Capital*. Use value and exchange value undergird the core of Marx's understanding of how value, the ultimate condition for and goal of a capitalist society, is structured. As capitalism comes to predominate in a certain historical moment, people stop viewing objects and subjects in terms of their use, or for what they are and how they are incorporated into an individual life. Instead, people begin to view them as potential sites of exchange—what can I trade this for?—and thus of profit.

Davis recounts the experience of seeing farm animals penned in alongside a road. How, she wonders, do we come to see these incarcerated cows as food? She explains, "the lack of critical engagement with the food that we eat demonstrates the extent to which the commodity form has become the primary way in which we perceive the world." In a world structured by the commodity form, one privileges exchange value over use value. After all, no one makes money by consuming something oneself; to make money, something must circulate. Davis continues, "We don't go further than what Marx called the exchange value of the object, we don't think about the relations that that object embodies.... That would be quite revolutionary to develop a habit of imagining the human relations and the non-human relations behind all of the objects that constitute our environment."[59] Davis then suggests, Why not see livestock as agents of pleasure and suffering? As designers of their societies and cultures as well as participants in and critics of human social forms? Why not see them, and all animals, in the words of our last dialectic, as our comrades? Why not realize they have already been our comrades? They structure our

FIGURE 8.12. Lenin and cat, in contemporary Belarus.

political-economic landscape. They orient our imagination. An entire history of capitalism can be narrated through them, with them, and perhaps for them.

And then this former Panther gets personal: "I usually don't mention that I'm vegan ... [but] it is a part of a revolutionary perspective. How can we not only discover more compassionate relationships with human beings but how can we develop more compassionate relationships with the other creatures with whom we share this planet?"[60]

Cats have been our symbolic and philosophical comrades. We must consider them our comrades in a more robust sense, too, as friends, equals, teachers, and students. They offer us a conceptual and material invitation to meet their own comrades (and enemies) and to chart a different understanding of the bestiary that is nature. Maybe not yet. But as Jodi Dean explains, "Comrade is a carrier of utopian longing."[61] We work toward comradeship, and once located, we must strive to maintain it. Perhaps that's what the erectors of this contemporary statue in Belarus had in mind: two comrades gesture toward an open future, which they will shape together.

EPILOGUE

Pussy Cats

*"Hunger is hunger; but the hunger that is satisfied by cooked
meat eaten with a knife and fork differs from hunger that
devours raw meat with the help of hands, nails and teeth."*

— KARL MARX, *GRUNDRISSE*

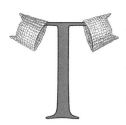his book was largely written during the
SARS-COVID-19 pandemic of 2020–21.
After twenty-some years of zoonotic respiratory infections providing a kind
of rehearsal—swine flu, bird flu, SARS,
MERS—it was this coronavirus, derived
from animal agriculture, that birthed a global pandemic. In
the United States a particular mix of anti-Asian racism and
overattachment to animal agriculture informed early responses
to the COVID-19 crisis. Concern with Chinese consumption
of strange and exotic animals structured public discourse for
the first months of the pandemic as commentators of various
political stripes wondered what kind of culture hosts and pa-
tronizes so-called wet markets. Such questions were an exten-

sion of previous racist concerns with Chinese food that had focused on the consumption of certain mammals such as dogs and civet cats.

But, as multiple scholars have argued, global capitalist animal agriculture has become a recipe for environmental destruction and for human as well as animal suffering, and this kind of pandemic was not only possible but likely.[1] Lands are deforested; methane is produced; excessive energy is required for the generation, transport, and refrigeration of animal products; and, finally, places of animal production are transformed into sites for the evolution and transmission of new diseases, from local bacterial infections to global viral ones.

When the intensity of the COVID-19 pandemic mushroomed and its morbid potential became known and accepted in the spring of 2020, much of American public life and many of its organizations and institutions, from schools to transportation, were shuttered as a first wave of viral infections took root. Other institutions were declared essential and allowed to remain open, such as grocery stores and medical facilities. Still others were required to remain open, including slaughterhouses. President Donald Trump may not have been prepared to use the Defense Production Act to require the production of lifesaving face masks or ventilators, but he did use the power of that law to declare meat production an essential infrastructure. The virus derived from animals, and slaughterhouses throughout the country functioned as hot spots of viral transmission throughout much of the pandemic. Yet few socialists, Marxists, or fellow travelers stood in solidarity with cows, pigs, and chickens or the largely immigrant labor force that dismembers them as Trump ordered that these places of death and disease continue operations.

But if nonhuman animals were one cause of the pandemic, they were also a source of comfort during it. Unsurprisingly, cats played a role. Netflix's breakout pandemic hit, *Tiger King*, offered a true menagerie of feline and human suffering as Joe Exotic, a gun-toting gay man, was on view presiding over his Oklahoma animal compound of low-wage workers and starving, caged felines. Offering an explanation of the docuseries' success that any feudal noble would have agreed with, a critic for the *New York Times* wrote, "The root [of the show's popularity] is the luscious regality of these big cats—it is difficult not to be transfixed by them."[2]

When homebound workers and critics were not watching big cats, they were likely interacting with diminutive ones, either in real life or on Zoom and other digital platforms. Here the breakout domestic feline was the "Zoom cat," a cat meme produced after a Texas judge was unable to change his zoom profile picture from that of a domestic shorthair and had to announce to the colleagues with whom he was meeting, "I am not a cat." The internet, as everyone knows and as Jodi Berland has demonstrated in *Virtual Menageries*, teems with animals—the cat is only the most cited of these beasts.

Are cats over-cited on digital platforms because they represent freedom from strictures of work and routinized play, as Oxana Timofeena contends?[3] We now know that the genre of cats as sites for and representations of social disorganization is centuries old. It is a genre that not only diagnoses a particular feature of capitalist overwork but was present at that feature's inception. Slavoj Žižek inadvertently confirmed this feline association when he claimed that "cats are lazy, evil, exploitative . . . so if I were to be in government, I would tax having a cat, tax it really heavy."[4] Whether cats' well-recognized refusal to work for others is a beacon of a postwork world or a hindrance to reaching one is surely one of the central questions of this book. It remains unanswered not for archival reasons but for experiential ones—such investigations are not possible to answer in advance, nor individually. They can be explored, in part, retrospectively; understanding the ambition and am-

FIGURE E.I. Abira Ali, *Pussy Hat*, 2017. One of many pussyhats worn in protest of Donald Trump's presidential inauguration.

bivalence of "the manifold uses of things is," as Marx says, "the work of history."[5]

History's work closed on Trump's presidency in 2020 with a pandemic derived from animal agriculture; it had greeted the beginning of that presidential era with a pussy protest. When Trump assumed the office of the president in January 2017—after receiving roughly three million fewer votes than his opponent—the United States erupted in demonstrations and agitations at airports, in schools, and in the streets. Before his election as president, Trump had been recorded bragging to an associate that, as a famous rich man, he could assault without consequence any woman he desired. He could "just start kissing them. Just kiss—I don't even wait. And when you're a star they let you do it. You can do anything. Whatever you want. Grab them by the pussy. You can do anything."[6] During his many decades in American public life Trump has provided a true compendium of racist, misogynistic, and xenophobic comments. But in 2017, the pussy comment sent millions into the streets, and it was the pussy cat with her pussy hat that become the sign of anti-Trump resistance.

As cis and trans women donned homemade pink caps with feline ears and took to the streets, some carried signs that advised Trump that "this pussy won't be grabbed." Drawing on a long history of associating violence against women and sex workers with cats—one that spans the Middle Ages, the early modern period, Nazi Germany, and into the late capitalist United States—these protesting pussies refused to endure another violent attack by a capitalist man. Vegan and former Black Panther Angela Davis was an honorary cochair of the formal event, known as the January 21, 2017, Women's March on Washington. Months later, the Russian punk band Pussy Riot stormed the New York–based Trump Tower building. "We believe that political prisoners are more important than sexist bullshit," the group claimed, initiating their own pussy protest.[7]

His presidency bookended between the feudal-like events of a pandemic and feline resistance, Trump took refuge in the power of the lion in his failed electoral bid of 2020. He tweeted the insignia of the southern white supremacist group VDARE, whose leonine image had been borrowed from a Dutch neofascist group, the Lion's Guard, and transformed into a Trump slogan. According to *Hyperallergic,* "The shadowy Lion's Guard takes its name from a quote from Italian Fascist Benito Mussolini. The dictator once said, 'It is better to live one day as a lion than 100 years as a sheep.'"[8] Indeed, Trump had cited this leonine Mussolini quotation in 2016 when he retweeted a certain @ilduce2016. When pressed by media outlets for seeming to have endorsed Mussolini, Trump explained, "It's OK to know it's Mussolini. Look, Mussolini was Mussolini. It's OK to—it's a very good quote, it's a very interesting quote."[9]

We remember that Italian Marxist Antonio Gramsci offered a critique of Mussolini's animal aphorism. The choice between lion and sheep had been foreclosed, Gramsci argued in the 1930s. It was time, rather, "to toil in the manure of history."[10] There are multiple ways to read Gramsci here. Perhaps after the coming of fascism, history has changed course? Perhaps the arc of progress has ruptured and the scope of human agency and possibility need to be reexamined? These are plausible interpretations. But in the context of *Marx for Cats* another reading is warranted, one that suggests humans no longer need to choose among nonhuman animals for their own temporary habitation, whether for pets, aphorism, or fantasy, as though such animals were so many commodities waiting to be selected and retrieved from a shelf. Perhaps "the manure of history" invites us to examine where our own course of human-animal relationality has led over a span of the longue durée and where it is destined to continue. This question leads us to our last dialectic.

THE CATS FOR MARX DIALECTIC

The first sentence of Marx's sprawling three-volume study, *Capital*, appears straightforward: "The wealth of societies in which the capitalist mode of production predominates presents itself as an 'immense collection of commodities,' its unit being the single commodity." *Commodity* seems a simple word. In fact, few things in in Marx's work are what they first appear, and *commodity* becomes the conceptual key to understanding the whole text, if not the whole of Marx's thought.

But not until nine hundred pages later do we understand what a commodity actually is. Both material and abstract, the commodity holds all of capitalism's relations and possibilities. To become a critic of capitalism is necessarily to understand the commodity in myriad ways, and to be a reader of Marx is to meet his concepts at the beginning of *Capital* as well as at the end. In structuring his book Marx confronted the crux of so much of philosophical writing, namely, the temporal unfolding of a thought and the necessary moments of suspension and assumption such an unfolding requires. Only at the end does the beginning make sense. Yet one starts any book at the beginning, and there must be enough conceptual force to carry the reader to their final comprehension. Søren Kierkegaard, a thinker closely associated with the phrase "leap of faith," said something similar about the awareness of our own human being: "Life can only be understood backwards; but it must be lived forwards." That is true for our collective life as well, a collectivity otherwise known as history.

In this book we have encountered multiple Marxes, Marxists, and Marxisms as they intersect with a similarly diverse constituency of felines. But we have yet to encounter the narrative Marx, the one for whom conceptual scaffolding was a first principle. Marx himself reflected on the structure of his masterwork, *Capital*, and noted that

> of course the method of presentation must differ in form from that of inquiry. The latter has to appropriate the material in detail, to analyze its different forms of development and to track down their inner connection. Only after this work has been done can the real movement be appropriately presented.[11]

This methodology, whereby the end is apparent at the beginning but the reasons for its appearance are only fully comprehensible at the end, manifests at every level of *Capital* and also, I hope, at every level of *Marx for Cats*, including that of the reading process itself. "There is no royal road to science," Marx said, "and only those who do not dread the fatiguing climb of its steep paths have a chance of gaining its luminous summits."[12] I hope our incline has been made somewhat easier by following the well-trod trails of bobcats and mountain lions.

Yet, have we actually arrived at a Marx for cats, or has this book been mistitled, and have we in fact been reading cats for Marx? We have seen how the longue durée of history may train its focus on cat as object. We have noted how Marx made use of cats in his discussion of revolution, abstraction, and value. And we have realized how generations of Marxists, from Rosa Luxemburg to Angela Davis, as well as generations before Marx whose emancipatory spirit Marxists nonetheless claim, from Gracchus Babeuf to Thomas Paine, have been fellow feline travelers. But we have not seen how Marx or Marxism might be presented *to cats* or how Marx's work or Marxism writ large might become *for cats*.

It is here that we realize that "Marx for cats" is itself a dialectical term; it represents the not yet arrived at end of a dialectical tension and anticipates the moment of resolution, the moment in which cats for Marx must be, and must always have been, *Marx for Cats*. Marx, Marxism, historical materialism; these habits of thought cannot be divorced from their feline proclivities—although critics have tried. They have attempted to discount feline work while allying themselves with feline power; they have ridiculed concern for animals as a form of bourgeois sentimentality; and yet, as this book has demonstrated, cats have been present from capital's first exchanges, for its imperialist journeys and racist seizures, for slavery and struggle, but also for calls to freedom and deliverance from this capitalist world.

We don't know what Marx for cats is, exactly, and we cannot know. Thus the process of reading both *Capital* and *Marx for Cats* contains a structural similarity to the process of producing a new and different world. As we plan collectively to materialize a future society that is more free and equal than our capitalist present, we must accept a certain amount of openness, unknowing, and indeterminacy. "It's easier to imagine the end of the world than the end of capitalism," goes the nihilistic jingle so popular among Marxists today. It's wrong on so many levels. One doesn't imagine postcapitalism; one materializes it, and through the act of materializing, the imagination changes. As the imagination changes, new relationships become possible. Nowhere is this promise more true than in the specter of an interspecies Communism. We don't know what form it will take; indeed, we cannot know until we collectively build and inhabit that form together. But we do know that a world of factory farms, global warming, and zoonotic pandemics alongside untold human and animal suffering *is not it*.

What would egalitarian pet ownership look like? It would likely not be *ownership* at all. What about an egalitarian zoo? It would be unrecognizable. How would a bountiful world of interspecies equality where everyone "could develop to their fullest species potential" appear in historical form? Can we look at animals differently? Can we move away from the twin logics of dominance and sentimentality? To look forward we must retrieve from the past, so the last moment of this bestiary returns to that medieval genre's allegorical structure to behold our own moment of symbolic revelation: this bestiary, too, was always about something else, namely, a different political economy of animality for which Marx has been a stand-in for the former and cats for the latter. The question of how to transform allegorical impulse into material manifestation is not one that anyone—reader, writer, or cat—can answer before the fact. It may only be answered in egalitarian and interspecies form, collectively, practically, and repeatedly.

Thus we take another leap. It will not be a *salto mortale*, as Marx called the leap of value as it travels from commodity to gold. Nor is our final leap the kind where the capitalist "mode of production acquires an elasticity, a capacity for sudden extension by leaps and bounds" and "can leap over the natural limit" of individual humans.[13] Nor is our final leap exactly a Benjaminian *Tigersprung*, which, of course, is a leap into the past, even if an unknown one. Rather, ours will be a *salto utopico*, a leap into some yet to be realized utopia, one Thomas Spence envisioned in the eighteenth century, in which "lisping infants shall tame tygers lead."[14]

To arrive there we must leap over a certain kind of Marxism. That is the Marxism that Ted Benton has labeled a kind of "species-narcissism," an approach that Renzo Llortente argues was "constitutive of Marx's thinking."[15] We must also leap over a certain liberalism that invites us to save the "wild animals" while 60 percent of the earth's mammalian biomass is constituted by farmed cattle destined to become first-world food.

I've made my own leap, too, both forward and backward, and no Marxist endeavor, whether a political campaign or a bestiary, can be completed without a self-criticism. A better bestiary would not have been chronological—chronology assumes and reproduces too facile a notion of history, one in which, as Marx so rightly said, "all cats are grey"; it would have been global, not provincially trained on the Euro-American West and that entity's dominion; and, finally, a better bestiary author would not have abandoned her vegetarianism for some fifteen years of her early adulthood. It was a cat who brought me back, The Mitten, to whose memory this book is dedicated. He came to me in a dream and instructed me that my feelings of love and devotion for him could be, and should be, extrapolated to all animals. This is a lesson I had known but had forgotten. It took a cat to remind me.

NOTES

INTRODUCTION

Epigraph: Perry Anderson, *Passages from Antiquity to Feudalism* (London: New Left, 1974), 8

1 Luxemburg, *Letters of Rosa Luxemburg*, 143.
2 See Dean, *Comrade*, for the term's longer genealogy.
3 Luxemburg, *Letters of Rosa Luxemburg* , 143.
4 Benjamin, "Theses on the Philosophy," 261.
5 Marx, *Capital*, 1:454.
6 Avrich and Avrich, *Sasha and Emma*, 381.
7 Marx and Engels, *German Ideology*, 177.
8 Adorno, *Minima Moralia*, 82.
9 For the emergence of this field in the literary in terms of Derrida, see Wolfe, "Human, All Too Human."
10 Derrida, *Animal That Therefore I Am*, 6.
11 Marx, *Critique of Political Economy*, 206.
12 Marx, *Critique of Political Economy*, 206.
13 Marx, *Eighteenth Brumaire*, chap. 1, trans. Padover.
14 Marx and Engels, *Manifesto of the Communist Party*, 481.
15 Marx, *Eighteenth Brumaire*, 6.
16 Marx and Engels, *Manifesto of the Communist Party*, 487.
17 Marx, *Eighteenth Brumaire*, chap. 1, trans. Padover.

18 For a good overview of these concerns, see Benton, "Marx, Ani-
    mals, and Humans." For the most sophisticated rendering of an
    eco-Marxism, see Kōhei Saitō's *Karl Marx's Ecosocialism.*

19 Arrighi, *Long Twentieth Century,* ix.

20 Arrighi, *Long Twentieth Century,* x.

21 Job 12:7–10 (New International Version).

22 Marx, *Capital,* 3:801.

23 Jameson, *Political Unconscious,* 1.

24 Marx, *Critique of Hegel's Philosophy,* 182.

25 *A Declaration by the Representatives of the United States of Amer-
    ica, in General Congress Assembled* (Philadelphia, 1776), https://
    www.archives.gov/founding-docs/declaration-transcript.

26 James, *Black Jacobins,* 43.

27 C. Jones, "French Crossings."

28 Marx and Engels, *Manifesto of the Communist Party,* 486.

29 Hobson, *Imperialism,* 63.

30 Ralph Chaplin, "That Sabo-Tabby Kitten," Antiwar Songs, last
    modified May 22, 2014, https://www.antiwarsongs.org/canzone
    .php?id=47398&lang=en.

31 Guevara, "Socialism and Man in Cuba," 225.

32 Angela Davis, "Angela Davis on the Struggle for Socialist Interna-
    tionalism and a Real Democracy," interview by Astra Taylor, *Jaco-
    bin,* October 21, 2020, https://www.jacobinmag.com/2020/10
    /angela-davis-socialist-internationalism-democracy.

33 Grace Lee Boggs and Angela Davis, "On Revolution: A Conver-
    sation between Grace Lee Boggs and Angela Davis," 27th Empow-
    ering Women of Color Conference, March 2, 2012, https://www
    .radioproject.org/2012/02/grace-lee-boggs-berkeley/.

CHAPTER ONE. LION KINGS

Epigraph: *The Etymologies of Isidore of Seville,* trans. Stephen A.
Barney, W. J. Lewis, J. A. Beach, and Oliver Berghof (Cambridge:
Cambridge University Press, 2006), 251.

1 The details of this story come from Dutton, *Charlemagne's Mustache,* 47.

2 Marx, *Capital,* 1:706.

3 Marx, *Critique of Hegel's "Philosophy of Right,"* 82.

4 Petrarch, *Apologia cuiusdam anonymi Galli calumnias*, 108.

5 Braudel, *Civilization and Capitalism*.

6 Daston and Park, *Order of Nature*, 173.

7 See Aston and Philpin, *Brenner Debate*.

8 Marx, *Capital*, 1:878n3.

9 Brown, "No Barbarians Necessary."

10 Scott, *Art of Not Being Governed*.

11 Marx, *Capital*, 1:708.

12 Marx and Engels, *German Ideology*, 85; Marx, *Capital*, 1:716n5.

13 P. Anderson, *Passages from Antiquity*, 139.

14 Sheehan, *German History*, 97.

15 Marx and Engels, *Manifesto of the Communist Party*, 484–85.

16 Dutton, *Charlemagne's Mustache*, 43.

17 Heng, *Invention of Race*, 151.

18 P. Anderson, *Passages from Antiquity*, 137.

19 Van Renswoude, "Art of Disputation," 49.

20 P. Anderson, *Passages from Antiquity*, 142.

21 Vitalis, *Ecclesiastical History of Orderic Vitalis*, 4:94–95.

22 B. Burke, *Genealogical and Heraldic Dictionary*, 852.

23 Marx, *Capital,* 1:338.

24 Engels, *Peasant War in Germany*, 572.

25 Quoted in Heng, *Invention of Race*, 38.

26 Quoted in Thompson, *Making of the English*, 89.

27 Machiavelli, *Prince*, 60.

28 Marx, *Critique of Political Economy*, 389. See also Marx, *Grundrisse*, 508.

29 Andrew Latham, "Medieval Geopolitics: Marxism and Medieval War," Medievalists.net, February 2020, https://www.medievalists.net/2020/02/marxism-medieval-war/.

30 Engels, *Peasant War in Germany*, 412.

31 I thank Jason Hannan for this story. Glassé, *New Encyclopedia of Islam*, 102.

32 Lipton, *Images of Intolerance*, 89.

33 Ruth Schuster, "This Day in Jewish History, 1189: Richard I Is Crowned and London's Jews Are Massacred," *Haaretz*, September 4, 2013, https://www.haaretz.com/jewish/.premium-1189-long-live-the-king-death-to-jews-1.5329011.

34 Hosler, *Siege of Acre*, 55.

35 Baldwin, *Raymond III of Tripolis*, 119.

36 Kuhns, "Bestiaries and Lapidaries," 1854.

37 Anglicus, *Medieval Lore*, 134–35.

38 Fossier, *Axe and the Oath*, 197.

39 See Heng, *Invention of Race*, 230.

40 The Aberdeen Bestiary, Aberdeen University Library, MS 24, fol. 23v, https://www.abdn.ac.uk/bestiary/ms24/f23v.

41 Jameson, "Beyond the Cave," 13.

42 Althusser, "Contradiction and Overdetermination," 115.

INTERMEZZO ONE. THE LION-CAT DIALECTIC

1 Quoted in Cole, *Birth of Theory*, 24.

2 Hegel, *Aesthetics*, 187.

3 Quoted in Cole, *Birth of Theory*, 11.

4 Hegel, *Phenomenology of Spirit*, 219.

5 Hegel, *Science of Logic*, 320.

6 The phrasing is, in fact, Marx's.

7 Hegel, *Phenomenology of Spirit*, 219.

8 Hegel, *Phenomenology of Spirit*, 111.

CHAPTER TWO. THE DEVIL'S CATS

Epigraph: Quoted in Irina Metzler, "Heretical Cats: Animal Symbolism in Religious Discourse," *Medium Aevum Quotidianum* 59 (2009): 16–32.

1 Translation quoted from Baroja, *World of the Witches*, 76.

2 Polo, *Travels of Marco Polo*, 287.

3 Famously attributed to both Fredric Jameson and Slavoj Žižek. See Jameson, *Seeds of Time*, xii; Jameson, "Future City," 76; Žižek, "Spectre of Ideology," 1.

4 Marx, *Capital*, 1:170.

5 Marx, *Capital*, 1:88.

6 *Oxford English Dictionary Online*, s.v. "mortgage"; "finance," accessed September 8, 2021.

7 Daston and Park, *Order of Nature*, 173.

8 Marx, *Capital*, 1:235.

9 Engels, *Peasant War in Germany*, 412–13.

10 Hilton, *Bond Men Made Free*, 109.

11 Marx, *Capital*, 1:176.

12 Fossier, *Axe and the Oath*, 195.

13 Oeser, *Katze und Mensch*, 87, quoted in Metzler, "Heretical Cats," 23.

14 Quoted in Lipton, *Images of Intolerance*, 89.

15 Quoted in Metzler, "Heretical Cats."

16 Quoted in M. Jones, *Secret Middle Ages*, 39.

17 Lipton, *Images of Intolerance*, 88.

18 Marx, *Manifesto of the Communist Party*, 486–87.

19 Marx and Engels, *Manifesto of the Communist Party*, 486–87.

20 For the gruesome history and the town's attempt to make amends, see Patrick J. Lyons, "The Wrong Day to Be a Cat in Belgium," *New York Times*, May 10, 2016, https://www.nytimes.com/2016 /05/11/world/what-in-the-world/belgium-cat-thrown-tower -ypres.html.

21 Federici, *Caliban and the Witch*, 36.

22 See Lea's magisterial *History of the Inquisition*, vol. 3.

23 Federici, *Caliban and the Witch*, 194.

24 Federici, *Caliban and the Witch*, 37.

25 Mills, *Seeing Sodomy*, 267.

26 Mills, *Seeing Sodomy*, 34

27 See Costagliola, "Fires in History."

28 Hilton, *Bond Men Made Free*, 103.

29 Metzler, "Heretical Cats," 23–24.

30 Hilton, *Bond Men Made Free*, 106.

31 Mark, "Cats in the Middle Ages."

32 Federici, *Caliban and the Witch*, 33.

33 Lipton, *Images of Intolerance*, 90.

34 Lipton, *Images of Intolerance*, 95.

35 Lipton, *Images of Intolerance*, 97.

36 Lipton, *Images of Intolerance*, 99.

37 Irina Metzler, "Why Cats Were Hated in Medieval Europe," Medievalists.net, October 2013, https://www.medievalists.net/2013 /10/why-cats-were-hated-in-medieval-europe/.

38 Rogers, *Cat*.

39 Hilton, *Bond Men Made Free*, 53.

40 Hilton, *Bond Men Made Free*, 70.

41 Tuchman, *Distant Mirror*, 95.

42 Marx, *Manifesto of the Communist Party*, 482.

43 Russell, *Kett's Rebellion in Norfolk*, 51.

44 Marx, *Critique of Hegel's "Philosophy of Right,"* 17.

45 Barker, *1381*, ix.

46 Barker, *1381*, 86.

47 Translated from Middle English. For both versions, see the side-by-side translation of "The Manciple's Prologue and Tale" at https://chaucer.fas.harvard.edu/pages/manciples-prologue-and-tale, accessed January 30, 2023.

48 Linebaugh, *London Hanged*, 29.

49 It's unclear when the cat was placed at the prison's door. See Linebaugh, *London Hanged*, for this and many other references to cats and crime.

50 Müntzer, *Hochverursachte Schutzrede*, 149.

51 Quoted in Gritsch, *Thomas Müntzer*, 23.

52 Kilgour, *Evolution of the Book*, 93.

53 This story hails from Weinstock Netanel's wonderful article "Maharam of Padua."

54 Marx, *Capital*, 1:919.

55 Marx, *Capital*, 1:742.

56 Marx, *Capital*, 1:534.

57 Marx, *Capital*, 1:742.

58 Marx, *Capital*, 1:739.

59 Choron, Choron, and Moore, *Planet Cat*, 54.

60 Hegel, *Dokumente zu Hegel's Entwicklung*, 352.

CHAPTER THREE. DIVINE LYNXES

Epigraph: Barbara Alice Mann, *The Land of the Three Miamis: A Traditional Narrative of the Iroquois in Ohio* (Toledo, OH: University of Toledo Urban Affairs Center Press, 2006), 22.

1 Hannah-Jones, "Arrival," 4.

2 Cronon, *Changes in the Land*, 24.

3 E. Morgan, "Slavery and Freedom."

4 Marx and Engels, *Manifesto of the Communist Party*, 485.

5 Marx, *Class Struggles in France, 1848–1850*, 122.

6 Marx and Engels, *Manifesto of the Communist Party*, 485.

7   See Cronon, *Changes in the Land*.

8   Braudel, *Civilization and Capitalism*, 2:230.

9   Dewdney and Kidd, *Indian Rock Paintings*, 14, 114; Rajnovich, *Reading Rock*, 102; Mallery, "Picture-Writing of the American Indians," 481.

10 Mann, "Lynx in Time," 433.

11 Mann, "Lynx in Time," 433.

12 Mann, *Land of the Three Miamis*, 22.

13 Rosemont, "Karl Marx and the Iroquois," 207.

14 Rosemont, "Karl Marx and the Iroquois," 207.

15 For a genealogy of the Cat Nation, see Pendergast, "Kakouagoga or Kahkwas."

16 Mann, "Lynx in Time," 426.

17 Marx, *Ethnological Notebooks*.

18 V. Anderson, *Creatures of Empire*.

19 V. Anderson, *Creatures of Empire*, 1.

20 Agarwal, "Yellowing the Logarithm."

21 Stacy Schiff, "The Witches of Salem," *The New Yorker*, September 7, 2015, https://www.newyorker.com/magazine/2015/09/07/the-witches-of-salem.

22 Maggie Gordon, "Haunted Stamford: 1692 Witch Trial," *Stamford Advocate*, October 30, 2013, https://www.stamfordadvocate.com/news/article/Haunted-Stamford-1692-witch-trial-4941025.php.

23 Gordon, "Haunted Stamford."

24 Marx and Engels, *Manifesto of the Communist Party*, 487.

25 Morais, "Marx and Engels on America," 5.

26 Davidson, *How Revolutionary*, 101.

27 Davidson, *How Revolutionary*, 101.

28 Marx, *Capital*, 1:704.

29 Edward Redmond, "Washington as Land Speculator," George Washington Papers, Articles and Essays, Library of Congress, accessed May 12, 2023, https://www.loc.gov/collections/george-washington-papers/articles-and-essays/george-washington-survey-and-mapmaker/washington-as-land-speculator/.

30 Eric Foner and Matt Karp, *The Mass Politics of Antislavery,* YouTube video, December 3, 2019, https://www.youtube.com/watch?v=xqRyQRM9yuQ. Adams's quotations found in Greg Grandin,

"Slavery and American Racism were Born in Genocide," *Nation,* January 20, 2020.

31 Marx, *Economic Manuscripts of 1857–58*, 263.

32 Marx and Engels, *Manifesto of the Communist Party*, 485.

33 Marx, *Capital*, 1:519.

34 Weber, *Protestant Ethic*, 36.

35 Carlyle, *Essays on Literature*, 33.

36 Du Bartas, *Divine Weeks*, 299.

37 For the treatment of Washington's slaves, see Mary V. Thompson, "The Only Unavoidable Subject of Regret," Mount Vernon updated November 1999, https://www.mountvernon.org/george -washington/slavery/the-only-unavoidable-subject-of-regret/.

38 For the story of Washington's dogs, see Lesley Kennedy, "George Washington: Founding Father—and Passionate Dog Breeder," History.com, updated February 4, 2020, https://www.history .com/news/george-washington-dogs.

39 Marx, *Eighteenth Brumaire*.

40 Marx, *Eighteenth Brumaire*.

41 *A Declaration by the Representatives of the United States of America, In General Congress Assembled* (Philadelphia, 1776), https:// www.archives.gov/founding-docs/declaration-transcript.

42 *Declaration by the Representatives*.

43 Marx and Engels, "Address of the Central Committee," 316.

44 Thomas Jefferson to John Holmes, April 22, 1820, manuscript/ mixed material, Library of Congress, https://www.loc.gov/item /mtjbib023795/.

45 "Memoir on the Megalonyx, [10 February 1797]," Founders Online, National Archives, https://founders.archives.gov /documents/Jefferson/01-29-02-0232.

46 Marx, *Capital*, 1:742.

47 The tomcat story is included in multiple biographies of Hamilton, including the Ron Chernow book that the musical *Hamilton* is based on.

48 Adams, *Diary of John Adams*, April 26, 1779.

49 Marx and Engels, *Manifesto of the Communist Party*, 486.

50 For the history, see "History of the Old State House," Revolutionary Spaces, accessed September 20, 2021, https://www .revolutionaryspaces.org/osh/history-osh/.

51 Paine, *Rights of Man*, 158.

52 Paine, quoted in Thompson, *English Working Class*, 91.

53 Paine, *Rights of Man*, 158.

54 Quoted in Nelson, *Thomas Paine*, 9.

55 Paine, *Collected Writings*, 718.

56 Thomas Paine, "Cruelty to Animals Exposed," *Pennsylvania Magazine*, May 1775, International Vegetarian Union, accessed May 12, 2023, https://ivu.org/history/northam18/paine.html.

57 Paine, "Agrarian Justice," in *Rights of Man*, 425.

58 See, for example, Karl Widerquist, "Was Thomas Paine a Proponent of Universal Basic Income? Short Answer: Yes," Basic Income European Network, January 14, 2020, https://basicincome.org/news/2020/01/was-thomas-paine-a-proponent-of-universal-basic-income/.

59 Nelson, *Thomas Paine*, 203–4.

60 Monahan, "Reading Paine from the Left," *Jacobin*, March 6, 2015, https://www.jacobinmag.com/2015/03/thomas-paine-american-revolution-common-sense/.

61 Image and text taken from Trinity College, Cambridge. See "Tokens of Revolution: The Propaganda Coins of Thomas Spence and His Contemporaries," Fitzwilliam Museum, Cambridge, accessed May 12, 2023, https://www.fitzmuseum.cam.ac.uk/dept/coins/exhibitions/spence/index2.html.

62 Thomas Spence, *Rights of Infants*.

63 Marx and Engels, *German Ideology*, 460–61.

64 For a wonderful discussion of Spence, see Linebaugh, *Red Round Globe*.

INTERMEZZO TWO. THE TIGER-TYGER DIALECTIC

1   Benjamin, "Philosophy of History," 255.

2   Benjamin, "Philosophy of History," 255.

3   Benjamin, "Philosophy of History," 261.

4   Anatoly Liberman, "The Oddest English Spellings, Part 20: The Letter 'y,'" *OUPblog*, May 15, 2013, https://blog.oup.com/2013/05/oddest-english-spellings-part-20-letter-y/.

1   Clark, *Farewell to an Idea*, 21.

2   Beal, *English Pronunciation*, 2.

3   *Times* (London), July 13, 1793.

4   *Courier de Londres*, July 30, 1793. Cited in Pedley, "Blake's 'Tyger' and Contemporary Journalism," 45.

5   Marx and Engels, *German Ideology*, 193.

6   Marx and Engels, *German Ideology*, 193.

7   Montaigne, "Apology for Raymond Sebond," 331.

8   P. Anderson, *Lineages of the Absolutist State,* 52.

9   P. Anderson, *Lineages of the Absolutist State*, 52.

10 Landrin, *Le chat*, 93.

11 Sahlins, *1668*, 229.

12 Sahlins, *1688*, 230.

13 Sahlins, *1688*, 240.

14 Buffon, *Natural History*, 6:1–2.

15 Buffon, *Natural History*, 208.

16 Engels, "Preface," xvii.

17 Freund and Yonan, "Cats."

18 Freund and Yonan, "Cats."

19 Darnton, *Great Cat Massacre*.

20 Darnton, *Great Cat Massacre*, 75–76.

21 Darnton, *Great Cat Massacre*, 77.

22 Hribal, *Fear of the Animal Planet*, 1.

23 J. P. Evans's 1906 book, *The Criminal Prosecution and Capital Punishment of Animals,* provides a compendium of animals in various juridical states; this story comes from that text.

24 Freund and Yonan, "Cats."

25 Rousseau, *Social Contract*, 41.

26 Freund and Yonan, "Cats."

27 Rousseau, *Emile*, 118.

28 Marx, "Bourgeoisie and the Counter-Revolution," 192–93.

29 Lefebvre, *Coming of the French Revolution*, x.

30 Hobsbawm, *Age of Revolution*, 23.

31 Buffon, *Natural History*, 7:57.

32 Bingley, *Animal Biography*, 225.

33 Quoted in Robbins, *Elephant Slaves and Pampered Parrots*, 218.

34 Marx, *Poverty of Philosophy*, 177–78.

35 *Adieu Bastille*, Illustration, 1789, Library of Congress, Prints and Photographs Division, https://www.loc.gov/pictures/item /2004679080/.

36 Engels, "On the History," 317.

37 De Goncourt, *Catalogue raisonné*, 153–54.

38 Quoted in Hicks, *Explaining Postmodernism*, 101.

39 Marx and Engels, *German Ideology*, 178.

40 Hobsbawm, *Age of Revolution*, 70.

41 Robespierre, "Réponse de Maximilien Robespierre," 89.

42 Marx and Engels, *German Ideology*, 53.

43 C. Jones, "French Crossings."

44 Buffon, *Natural History*, 9:129.

45 C. Jones, "French Crossings."

46 Quoted in Pedley, "Blake's 'Tyger' and Contemporary Journalism," 48.

47 Benjamin, "Philosophy of History," 261.

48 I thank Benjamin Kohlmann for this explanation of Benjamin's use of the word.

49 Susan Buck-Morss, personal communication with the author, July 26, 2021.

50 Marx, "Speech at the Anniversary," 656.

51 Saint-Just, *Oeuvres Complètes*, 430.

52 Romilly, *Life of Sir Samuel Romilly*, 351.

53 Quoted in Pedley, "Blake's 'Tyger' and Contemporary Journalism," 46.

54 Arendt, *On Revolution*, 67–68.

55 Huot, *Les massacres à Versailles*, 25–26. See "The Menagerie in the Revolution," *Rodama: A Blog of 18th Century and Revolutionary French Trivia*, December 10, 2015, http://rodama1789.blogspot. com/2015/12/the-menagerie-in-revolution.html.

56 Oswald, *Cry of Nature*, 7.

57 Birchall, *Spectre of Babeuf*, 136.

58 Quoted in Jenson, "Living by Metaphor," 74.

59 Fischer, *Modernity Disavowed*, 4

60 James, *Black Jacobins*, x.

61 James, *Black Jacobins*, 282.

62 Jenson, "Living by Metaphor," 74–75.

63 Jenson, "Living by Metaphor," 75.

64 James, *Notes on Dialectics*, 99 (capitalization and spacing in original).

65 James, *Notes on Dialectics*, 100 (capitalization in original).

66 Jenson, "Living by Metaphor," 78.

67 This is how Peter Linebaugh reads it in *The Many-Headed Hydra*.

68 Blake, *Descriptive Catalogue*, E543.

69 Spence, *Rights of Infants*.

CHAPTER FIVE. WILDCATS

Epigraph: Mary Clavers [Caroline Matilda Kirkland], *A New Home—Who'll Follow? Or, Glimpses of Western Life*, 4th ed. (New York: C. S. Francis, 1850), 192.

1 Douglass, *Narrative*, 60.

2 Douglass, *Narrative*, xiii.

3 Marx and Engels, *Manifesto of the Communist Party*, 487.

4 Marx and Engels, *Manifesto of the Communist Party*, 487.

5 Morais, "Marx and Engels on America," 5.

6 Dillistin, *Bank Note Reporters*.

7 Marx, *Capital*, 1:591.

8 The Minneapolis Federal Reserve offers a wonderful history of wildcat banking. Rolnick and Weber, "Free Banking," 10–19.

9 Clavers, *Settler's New Home*, 176.

10 Brecht, *Threepenny Opera*, 76.

11 Marx, *Capital*, 1:275.

12 *Set to between Old Hickory and Bully Nick*, 1834, lithograph by Anthony Imbert, Catalog record, Library of Congress, Prints and Photographs Division, http://www.loc.gov/pictures/item/2008661767/.

13 For this fascinating history, see Baumgartner, *South to Freedom*.

14 Wilder, *Little Town on the Prairie*.

15 "Exotic Animals and the Hunt for Gold," UNM News Room, University of New Mexico, January 8, 2018, http://news.unm.edu/news/exotic-animals-and-the-hunt-for-gold.

16 "The Black Cat," *The Poe Encyclopedia*, comp. Frederick S. Frank and Anthony Magistrale (Westport, CT: Greenwood, 1997).

17 Thoreau, quoted in Cronon, *Changes in the Land*, 4.

18 Thoreau, *A Year in Thoreau's Journal, 1851*, 184.

19 Emerson, "Experience," 489.

20 Thoreau, *Concord and Merrimack Rivers*, 181–82.

21 See Kotin, *Utopias of One*.

22 Marx and Engels, *Manifesto of the Communist Party*, 513.

23 Marx, *Capital*, 1:187.

24 Quoted in Foster, "Marx as a Food Theorist."

25 Marx, quoted in Edward Marx-Aveling and Eleanor Marx-Aveling, "Shelley and Socialism," *To-Day*, April 1888, https://www.marxists.org/archive/eleanor-marx/1888/04/shelley-socialism.htm.

26 Marx, *Eighteenth Brumaire*, 106.

27 The BBC reports, "In 27 October 1825, Farnham's most famous resident, the farmer, writer, and political commentator William Cobbett, reported seeing 'a big grey cat, the size of a medium-sized spaniel' whilst on a rural ride, at the ruins of Waverley Abbey. Little did he know, that his sighting would start a rumour mill which is still grinding on 200 years later." Heather Driscoll-Woodford, "The Surrey Puma: Fact or Fiction?," BBC Surrey, February 17, 2010, http://news.bbc.co.uk/local/surrey/hi/people_and_places/nature/newsid_8520000/8520071.stm.

28 E. Burke, *Reflections on the Revolution*, 117.

29 Castellano, "William Cobbett, 'Resurrection Man,'" 184.

30 Benjamin, "Philosophy of History," 257.

31 Quoted in Castellano, "William Cobbett, 'Resurrection Man,'" 196.

32 Heather Thomas, "The Bones of Thomas Paine," *Headlines and Heroes: Newspapers, Comics and More Fine Print* (blog), Library of Congress, April 2, 2019, https://blogs.loc.gov/headlinesandheroes/2019/04/the-bones-of-thomas-paine.

33 Marx, "Layard's Inquiry," 323.

34 Engels, *Condition of the Working Class*, 302.

35 Thomas C. Jones, "Karl Marx's London," *Migration Museum* (blog), January 10, 2019, https://www.migrationmuseum.org/karl-marxs-london/.

36 Marx, *Capital,* 1:290.

37 Marx, *Capital*, 1:174n34.

1 Marx, *Economic and Philosophic Manuscripts of 1844*, 276.
2 Engels, *Dialectics of Nature*, 457–58.
3 Engels, *Dialectic of Nature*, 458.
4 Marx and Engels, *German Ideology*, 481.
5 For this fascinating history, see Poovey, *History of the Modern Fact*.
6 Marx and Engels, *German Ideology*, 481.
7 Hegel, *Phenomenology of Spirit*, 9.
8 Marx, "Afterword to the Second German Edition of *Capital*," in Marx, *Capital*, 1:103.
9 Marx, *Capital*, 1:219.
10 The dialogue between Smith and Marx over the animals, and the quotations found therein, are found in Hribal, "Animals Are Part of the Working Class." Marx, *Capital*, 2:260, 2:292.
11 Engels, "Part Played by Labour."
12 Haraway, *When Species Meet*, 72.

<h3 style="text-align:center">CHAPTER SIX. DOMESTIC CATS,
COMMUNAL AND SERVILE</h3>

Epigraph: Élisée Reclus, *Anarchy, Geography, Modernity: Selected Writings of Élisée Reclus*, edited by John Clark and Camille Martin (Oakland, CA: PM Press, 2013), 160.
1 Warner, "Calvin."
2 Marx and Engels, *Manifesto of the Communist Party*, 487.
3 Marx and Engels, *Manifesto of the Communist Party*, 488.
4 Marx, *Capital*, 1:186.
5 Marx, *Capital*, 1:275.
6 Marx, *Capital*, 1:86.
7 Marx to Carl Klings, October 4, 1864, reprinted in Marx, *Letters on Capital*, 93.
8 Marx and Engels, *Manifesto of the Communist Party*, 488.
9 Harvey, *Paris*, 84–85.
10 Stahl, *Public and Private Life of Animals*, 7.
11 Benjamin, *Arcades Project*, 7.
12 Benjamin, *Arcades Project*, 18.

13 Fourier, quoted in Pettman, "Get Thee to a Phalanstery."

14 Pettman, "Get Thee to a Phalanstery."

15 Engels, "Fragment of Fourier's on Trade," 615.

16 Rancière, *Proletarian Nights*, 17. (Previously published in English as *Nights of Labor: The Workers' Dream in Nineteenth Century France*, translated by John Drury [Philadelphia: Temple University Press, 1989].)

17 Séguin, *Louis Napoléon le Grand*, 21–24.

18 Marx, *Eighteenth Brumaire*, 103.

19 Marx, *Eighteenth Brumaire*, 61.

20 Marx, *Eighteenth Brumaire*, 47.

21 Marx, *Eighteenth Brumaire*, 106.

22 Marx, *Eighteenth Brumaire*, 4.

23 Marx, *Eighteenth Brumaire*, 106.

24 Benjamin, "Paris," in *The Arcades Project*, 13.

25 Robin Blackburn, "Lincoln and Marx: The Transatlantic Convergence of Two Revolutionaries," *Jacobin*, August 28, 2012, https://jacobinmag.com/2012/08/lincoln-and-marx.

26 As translated in Marx, *On America*, 275; Marx, *Capital*, 1:305.

27 Weld and Grimke, *American Slavery as It Is*, 21.

28 Elliott, *Cotton Is King*, 718.

29 Quoted in Genovese, *Roll, Jordan, Roll*, 363.

30 Marx to Engels, January 11, 1860, in *Karl Marx, Frederick Engels: Collected Works*, 41:4.

31 Marx, "North American Civil War," 37.

32 Marx to P. V. Annenkov, December 28, 1846, in *Karl Marx Frederick Engels: Collected Works*, 41:14.

33 Marx and Engels, *Manifesto of the Communist Party*, 487.

34 See Marx and Engels, *Civil War in the United States*.

35 Du Bois, "Marxism and the Negro Problem," 103–4, 118; Du Bois, *Black Reconstruction in America,* 120.

36 Marx to Lion Philips, May 6, 1861, in *Karl Marx, Frederick Engels: Collected Works*, 41:277.

37 Marx to Lion Phillips, May 6, 1861.

38 Marx, *Capital* 1:305.

39 Quoted in Ross, *Communal Luxury*, 39.

40 Edwards, *Paris Commune*, 365.

41 Marx, *Critique of the Gotha Programme*, 87.

42 Marx, *Civil War in France*.

43 Quoted in Jon Hochschartner, "Was Communard Louise Michel a Vegetarian?," *Counterpunch*, January 10, 2014, https://www .counterpunch.org/2014/01/10/was-communard-louise-michel -a-vegetarian/.

44 See any of the marvelous work of Jason Hribal, especially *Fear of the Animal Planet*.

45 F. Chantraine to Louise Michel, October 15, 1883, International Institute for Social History, Louise Michel inventory, no. 155, http://www.iisg.nl/collections/louisemichel/inventory155a.php #translation.

46 Paul Lafargue, "Bourgeois Sentimentalism," *L'Egalité*, December 25, 1881, https://www.marxists.org/archive/lafargue/1881 /12/25.htm.

47 "The International Vegetarian Congress," *Vegetarian* (London), September 20, 1890, https://ivu.org/congress/1890/report.html.

48 Reclus, *Anarchy, Geography, Modernity*, 159.

49 Reclus, *Anarchy, Geography, Modernity*, 136.

50 Hribal, *Fear of the Animal Planet*.

51 Taylor, *Beasts of Burden*.

52 Troy Vettese, "The Political Economy of Half-Earth," *Bullet* (blog), *Socialist Project*, January 30, 2019, https://socialistproject .ca/2019/01/the-political-economy-of-half-earth/.

53 Molly Nolan, quoted in personal conversation, 2006.

54 H. Morgan, *American Beaver*, 283.

55 Fairholme and Pain, *Century of Work for Animals*, 94–95.

56 Elliott, *National Nursery Rhymes*, 9.

57 Stephen Gibbs, "'Affectionate friend, faithful servant and best of creatures': The touching tale of Trim, the humble ship's cat who made maritime history by helping Captain Matthew Flinders sail around Australia," *Daily Mail*, October 26, 2019, https://www .dailymail.co.uk/news/article-7497701/The-incredible-story -Trim-noble-ships-cat-sailed-Australia-Matthew-Flinders.html.

58 Weir, *Our Cats*, preface.

59 Weir, *Our Cats*, preface.

60 Rachel Holmes, "The Making of a Marx: The Life of Eleanor Marx, the Mother of Socialist Feminism," *Independent*, May 4, 2014, https://www.independent.co.uk/arts-entertainment/books

/features/the-making-of-a-marx-the-life-of-eleanor-marx-the
-mother-of-socialist-feminism-9317068.html. See also Harrison
Fluss and Sam Miller, "The Legacy of Eleanor Marx," *Jacobin*,
January 16, 2017, https://www.jacobinmag.com/2017/01/eleanor
-marx-legacy-labor-rights-socialist-feminism.

61 Comyn, "My Recollections."
62 Comyn, "My Recollections."
63 Quoted in Morson, *Words of Others*, 174.

CHAPTER SEVEN. SABO-TABBIES

Epigraph: Joyce L. Kornblug, ed., *Rebel Voices: An IWW Anthology*
(Oakland, CA: PM Press, 2011), 59, http://politicalfolkmusic.org
/blog/ralph-chaplin/sabo-tabby-kitten/.

1   Wilentz, *Chants Democratic*, 169–70.
2   Buffon, *Natural History,* 1–2.
3   Dean, *Comrade*, 15.
4   Marx, *Manifesto of the Communist Party*, 486.
5   Laurie and Cole, *Role of Federal Military Forces*, 32.
6   Quoted in Foner, *Great Labor Uprising*, 192.
7   Foner, *Great Labor Uprising*, 192.
8   Avrich and Avrich, *Sasha and Emma*, 381.
9   Flynn, *Rebel Girl*, 48–49.
10 Baker, *Animal Rights and Welfare*, 111.
11 Flynn, *Rebel Girl*, 48–49.
12 See, for example, *St. Louis Post-Dispatch*, May 14, 1905, 55.
13 Marcy, "Letters," 175 (capitalization in the original).
14 McKay, "If We Must Die," 177.
15 Grandin, *Fordlandia*, 34.
16 Quoted in "Disassembly Line: Workers' Conditions," Vegan Be-
    ings, March 1, 2013, https://veganbeings.wordpress.com/tag
    /assembly-line/.
17 Copley, *Frederick W. Taylor*, 230.
18 Copley, *Frederick W. Taylor*, 230.
19 Copley, *Frederick W. Taylor*, 429.
20 Flynn, *Sabotage*.
21 See Specht, *Red Meat Republic*.
22 Chaplin, *Wobbly*, 74.

23 Chaplin, *Wobbly*, 75.

24 Marx, *Value, Price and Profit*, 149.

25 Chaplin, *Wobbly,* 75.

26 Chaplin, *Wobbly*, 206.

27 Eric Stevick and Julie Muhlstein, "100 Years after Everett Massacre We're Still Learning More," *Daily Herald* (Everett, WA), November 3, 2016, https://www.heraldnet.com/news/100-years-after-the-everett-massacre-were-still-learning-more/.

28 Kornblug, *Rebel Voices*, 59.

29 Frank R. Kent, "Fat Cats and Free Rides," *American Mercury*, June 1928.

30 Butler, *War Is a Racket*.

31 Lenin, "Preface to the French and German Editions."

32 Marx, "Theses on Feuerbach," 5.

33 Lenin, *Socialism and War*, 21.

34 Lenin, *Socialism and War*, 11.

35 James, *Notes on Dialectics*, 100.

36 James, *Notes on Dialectics*, 100.

37 Read, *Lenin*, 26.

38 Lenin, *Materialism and Empiro-criticism*, 86.

39 Lenin, *Materialism and Empiro-criticism*, 141.

40 *Kriloff's Original Fables*, 112.

41 Lenin, *State and Revolution*, 468.

42 Lenin to Alexandra Kollontai, February 17, 1917, reprinted in *Collected Works*, 35:285–87.

43 Lenin, "On Revolution," *Pravda*, no. 117 (May 30, 1923).

44 Noa Rodman, "Lenin Cat," Libcom, March 15, 2018, https://libcom.org/forums/general/lenin-cat-08042011?page=2.

45 See Getzler, *Martov*, 90.

46 Bob Gould, "Reclaim Lenin from 'Leninists' and 'Leninism,' Part II," Ozleft, May 6, 2004, https://ozleft.wordpress.com/2004/05/06/reclaimleninpart2/.

47 Trotsky, *My Life*, 434.

48 Davidson, *How Revolutionary*, 295.

49 Trotsky, *Third International after Lenin*, 20.

50 Marx, *Grundrisse*, 702.

51 Marx, *Capital* 3:32.

52 Leon Trotsky, "Hitler's 'Disarmament' and Prospects of War with Soviet Union," *Militant* 6, no. 41 (September 2, 1933), https://www.marxists.org/archive/trotsky/1933/06/hitler1.htm.

53 Luxemburg, *Reform or Revolution*.

54 Nettl, *Rosa Luxemburg*, 1:365.

55 Le Blanc, "Lenin and Luxemburg."

56 Luxemburg, "Questions at Issue."

57 Quoted in Sparrow, "Mimi and Rosa."

58 Marx, *Capital,* 1:723.

59 Luxemburg to Sonja Liebknecht, December 1917, reprinted in Bronner, *Letters of Rosa Luxemburg*, 241.

60 Sparrow, "Mimi and Rosa."

61 Paul Le Blanc, "Revolutionary Letters," *Socialist Worker*, March 23, 2011, https://www.versobooks.com/blogs/439-revolutionary-letters-paul-le-blanc-on-rosa-luxemburg.

62 Luxemburg, *Junius Pamphlet*, 320.

63 Luxemburg, *Junius Pamphlet*, 320.

64 Theweleit, *Male Fantasies*, 68–69.

65 Brecht, "Epitaph, 1919," 176.

INTERMEZZO FOUR. THE CAT-COMRADE DIALECTIC

1 Lenin, "Conspectus," 109.

2 James, *Notes on Dialectics*, 84.

3 Luxemburg, "In a Revolutionary Hour," 554.

4 Webb, *Not without Love*, 23.

5 Jameson, "Postmodernism and Consumer Society," 549.

6 Eagleton, *Literary Theory*, 112.

CHAPTER EIGHT. BLACK PANTHERS

Epigraph: Stokely Carmichael, "What We Want." *New York Review of Books*, September 22, 1966.

1 Kelley, *Hammer and Hoe*, 161–68, 100.

2 Quoted in Bloom and Martin, *Black against Empire*, 42.

3 Gramsci, *Prison Notebooks*, xciii.

4 Gramsci, *Prison Notebooks*, 125.

5 Gramsci, *Prison Notebooks*, xciii.

6 Deleuze and Guattari, *Anti-Oedipus*, 34.

7 First usage in 1856, according to the *Oxford English Dictionary*.

8 Jameson, *Valences of the Dialectic*, 287.

9 Benjamin, *Arcades Project*, 634, 241.

10 Quoted in Buck-Morss, *Dialectics of Seeing*, 5.

11 Adorno, *Minima Moralia*, 82.

12 Adorno and Horkheimer, *Dialectic of Enlightenment*, 253.

13 Adorno, *Minima Moralia*, trans. Jephcott, 105.

14 Adorno, *Aesthetic Theory*, 165.

15 Quoted in Wipplinger, *Jazz Republic*, 208.

16 That Tumblr site is now defunct, but for a nice gloss, see Jordan Alexander Stein's essay, "Silly Theory," *LA Review of Books*, November 20, 2012, https://avidly.lareviewofbooks.org/2012/11/20/silly-theory/#:~:text=The%20silliness%20of%20theory%20makes,to%20put%20the%20pieces%20together.

17 Adorno, *Minima Moralia*, 39.

18 Davis, "Marcuse's Legacies," 47.

19 Marcuse, *Counterrevolution and Revolt*, 68.

20 Quoted in Young, "Herbert's Herbivore," 551.

21 Hilliard, "Ideology of the Black Panther Party," 122.

22 Quoted in Bloom and Martin, *Black against Empire*, 43.

23 Hall et al., *Policing the Crisis*, 386.

24 Seale, *Seize the Time*, 72.

25 "The Ten-Point Program," Marxists.org, accessed February 16, 2023, https://www.marxists.org/history/usa/workers/black-panthers/1966/10/15.htm.

26 "FBI Brands Black Panthers Most Dangerous of Extremists," *New York Times*, July 14, 1970.

27 Marglin and Schor, *Golden Age of Capitalism*.

28 Dolgoff, "Structure of Power in Cuba."

29 Douglas did not come up with the original design, however. For the full story, see Lincoln Cushing, "The Women Behind the Black Panther Party Logo," Stansbury Forum, February 18, 2018, https://stansburyforum.com/2018/02/18/the-women-behind-the-black-panther-party-logo.

30 Bloom and Martin, *Black against Empire,* 2.

31 Du Bois, *Black Reconstruction*, 120.

32 Bloom and Martin, *Black against Empire*, 2.

33 Davis, *Freedom Is a Constant Struggle*, 8.

34 Newton, "Women's Liberation and Gay Liberation," 157.

35 A. Muhammad Ahmad, "The League of Revolutionary Black Workers: A Historical Study," *History Is a Weapon*, accessed November 9, 2021, https://www.historyisaweapon.com/defcon1/rbwstudy.html.

36 See "Chris Marker Collection," Reel Suspects, accessed May 12, 2023, https://www.reelsuspects.com/portfolio-item/chris-marker-collection/.

37 Mark Sinker and Rob White, "Polcats: Debating Chris Marker's 'A Grin without a Cat,'" *Film Quarterly*, October 10, 2012, https://filmquarterly.org/2012/10/10/polcats-debating-chris-markers-a-grin-without-a-cat/.

38 Rand to Smith, 1966, reprinted in Berlinger, *Letters of Ayn Rand*, 638.

39 Keynes, *Essays in Persuasion*, 330.

40 Anthes, *Frankenstein's Cat*, 143–44.

41 Barthes, *Mythologies*, 114.

42 Ladsaria and Singh, "Semiotic Animal," 24–34.

43 Milton Friedman, "Barking Cats," *Newsweek*, February 19, 1973, https://miltonfriedman.hoover.org/friedman_images/Collections/2016c21/NW_02_19_1973.pdf.

44 Friedman, "Barking Cats."

45 Samuelson and Nordhaus, *Economics*, 49.

46 Harvey, *Limits to Capital*, 116.

47 Krugman, *Return of Depression*, 58.

48 Marx, "Layard's Inquiry," 189.

49 Brenner, *Economics of Global Turbulence*, 6.

50 Hayek, *Tiger by the Tail*, 126.

51 Mandel, *Late Capitalism*, 415n23.

52 Tratner, "Derrida's Debt to Milton Friedman," 798.

53 Tratner, "Derrida's Debt to Milton Friedman," 798.

54 Derrida, "Animal That Therefore I Am."

55 Derrida, *Animal That Therefore I Am*, 9.

56 Dreyfus, *Lion of Wall Street*.

57 Richard D. Ryder, *Speciesism* (privately printed leaflet, Oxford, 1970); Singer, *Animal Liberation*.

58 Benton, "Marxism and the Moral Status," 73–79; Benton, "Marx, Animals, and Humans," 40–44.

59 "Angela Davis on Veganism as Part of a Revolutionary Perspective," discussion with Grace Lee Boggs, Films for Action, January 5, 2016, https://www.filmsforaction.org/watch/angela-davis -on-veganism-as-part-of-a-revolutionary-perspective/.

60 Angela Davis, speech at "27th Empowering Women of Color Conference," cited in *Counterpunch*, https://www.counterpunch .org/2014/01/24/vegan-angela-davis-connects-human-and -animal-liberation/.

61 Dean, *Comrade*, 10.

EPILOGUE. PUSSY CATS

Epigraph: "Introduction to a Contribution to the Critique of Political Economy," in *Karl Marx, Frederick Engels: Collected Works,* 28:29.

1 See Wallace, *Dead Epidemiologists*.

2 Jon Caramanica, "The Alternate Aesthetic Realities of 'Tiger King,'" *New York Times*, June 2, 2020, https://www.nytimes.com /2020/04/02/arts/television/tiger-king-style.html.

3 Timofeena, *History of Animals*.

4 John Merrick, "'I'd Tax Cats. Heavily'—Slavoj Žižek," *Verso Books* (blog), October 13, 2014, https://www.versobooks.com/blogs /1726-i-d-tax-cats-heavily-slavoj-zizek.

5 Marx, *Capital* 1:45.

6 "Transcript: Donald Trump's Taped Comments about Women," *New York Times*, October 8, 2016, https://www.nytimes.com /2016/10/08/us/donald-trump-tape-transcript.html.

7 "Pussy Riot Stages Protest at Trump Tower," *Artforum*, October 25, 2017, https://www.artforum.com/news/-71880.

8 Zachary Small, "Trump Tweets Out Promotional Campaign Logo Using White Supremacist Symbol," *Hyperallergic*, August 29, 2019, https://hyperallergic.com/515238/ trump-tweets-out-promotional-campaign-logo-using-white- supremacist-symbol/.

9   Elena Schneider, "Trump Explains Tweeting Mussolini Quote," *Politico*, February 28, 2016, https://www.politico.com/story /2016/02/trump-tweets-interesting-mussolini-quote-219932.

10   Gramsci, *Prison Notebooks*, xciii.

11   Marx, *Capital*, 1:19.

12   Marx, *Capital*, 1:23.

13   Marx, *Capital*, 1:454; Marx, "The Chapter on Capital (continuation)," *Grundrisse*.

14   Spence, *Important Trial of Thomas Spence*, 93.

15   Foster and Clark, "Marx and Alienated Speciesism."

BIBLIOGRAPHY

Abromeit, John, and W. Mark Cobb, eds. *Herbert Marcuse: A Critical Reader*. New York: Routledge, 2004.

Adams, John. *Diary of John Adams*, vol. 1. Massachusetts Historical Society. https://www.masshist.org/jqadiaries/php/diaries#2.

Adorno, Theodor. *Aesthetic Theory*. Edited by Gretel Adorno and Rolf Tiedemann. Translated by Robert Hullot-Kentor. London: Bloomsbury, 2013.

Adorno, Theodor W. *Minima Moralia: Reflexionen aus dem beschädigten Leben*. Vol. 4 of *Gesammelte Schriften*. Edited by Rolf Tiedemann. Frankfurt am Main: Suhrkamp, 1980.

Adorno, Theodor. *Minima Moralia: Reflections on a Damaged Life*. Translated by E. F. N. Jephcott. New York: Verso, 2005.

Adorno, Theodor, and Max Horkheimer. *The Dialectic of Enlightenment*. New York: Continuum, 1993.

Agarwal, Neil S. "Yellowing the Logarithm: How Money Solved the Problem of Freedom." Ph.D. diss., CUNY Graduate Center, 2017. https://academicworks.cuny.edu/cgi/viewcontent.cgi?article=3350&context=gc_etds.

Althusser, Louis. "Contradiction and Overdetermination." In *For Marx*, translated by Ben Brewster, 87–128. London: Verso, 2005.

Anderson, Perry. *Lineages of the Absolutist State*. London: New Left, 1974.

Anderson, Perry. *Passages from Antiquity to Feudalism*. London: New Left, 1974.

Anderson, Virginia Dejohn. *Creatures of Empire: How Domestic Animals Transformed Early America*. New York: Oxford, 2004.

Anglicus, Bartholomew. *Medieval Lore: An Epitome of the Science, Geography, Animal and Plant Folk-Lore and Myth of the Middle Age, Being Classified Gleanings from the Encyclopedia of Bartholomew Anglicus on the Properties of Things*. Edited by Robert Steele. London: Elliot Stock, 1893.

Anthes, Emily. *Frankenstein's Cat: Cuddling Up to Biotech's Brave New Beasts*. London: Oneworld, 2013.

Arendt, Hannah. *On Revolution*. London: Penguin, 1990.

Arrighi, Giovanni. *The Long Twentieth Century: Money, Power, and the Origin of Our Times*. 2nd ed. London: Verso, 2010.

Aston, T. H., and C. H. E. Philpin, eds. *The Brenner Debate: Agrarian Class Structure and Economic Development in Pre-industrial Europe*. Cambridge: Cambridge University Press, 1985.

Avrich, Paul, and Karen Avrich. *Sasha and Emma: The Anarchist Odyssey of Alexander Berkman and Emma Goldman*. Cambridge, MA: Belknap Press of Harvard University Press, 2012.

Baker, Lawrence W. *Animal Rights and Welfare: A Documentary Labor Guide*. Santa Barbara, CA: Greenwood, 2015.

Baldwin, Marshall Whithed. *Raymond III of Tripolis and the Fall of Jerusalem (1140–1187)*. Princeton, NJ: Princeton University Press, 1936.

Barker, Juliet. *1381: The Year of the Peasants' Revolt*. Cambridge, MA: Harvard University Press, 2014.

Baroja, Julio Caro. *The World of the Witches*. Translated by O. N. V. Glendinning. Chicago: University of Chicago Press, 1964.

Barthes, Roland. *Mythologies*. Translated by Annette Lavers. New York: Noonday, 1972.

Baumgartner, Alice. *South to Freedom: Runaway Slaves to Mexico and the Road to the Civil War*. New York: Basic Books, 2020.

Beal, Joan C. *English Pronunciation in the Eighteenth Century: Thomas Spence's Grand Repository of the English Language*. Oxford: Oxford University Press, 2002.

Benjamin, Walter. *The Arcades Project*. Translated by Howard Eiland and Kevin McLaughlin. Cambridge, MA: Belknap Press of Harvard University Press, 1999.

Benjamin, Walter. "Theses on the Philosophy of History." In *Illumina-tions*. Edited by Hannah Arendt. Translated by Harry Zohn. New York: Schocken, 1968.

Benton, Ted. "Marx, Animals, and Humans: A Reply to My Critics." *Monthly Review* 71, no. 1 (May 2019): 40–44.

Benton, Ted. "Marxism and the Moral Status of Animals." *Society and Animals* 11, no. 1 (Jan. 2003): 73–79.

Berland, Jody. *Virtual Menageries: Animals as Mediators in Network Cultures*. Cambridge, MA: MIT Press, 2019.

Berliner, Michael S., ed. *Letters of Ayn Rand*. New York: Plume, 1997.

Bingley, W. *Animal Biography, or, Popular Zoology*. Vol. 1, *Mammifer-ous Animals*. London, 1820.

Birchall, Ian H. *The Spectre of Babeuf*. Basingstoke, UK: Macmillan, 1997.

Blake, William. *A Descriptive Catalogue*. In *The Complete Poetry and Prose of William Blake*, edited by David Erdman, 526–52. Garden City, NY: Anchor, 1988.

Bloom, Joshua, and Waldo E. Martin Jr. *Black against Empire: The His-tory and Politics of the Black Panther Party*. Berkeley: University of California Press, 2013.

Braudel, Fernand. *The Structures of Everyday Life*. Vol. 1 of *Civilization and Capitalism, 15th–18th Century*. Translated by Siân Reynolds. Berkeley: University of California Press, 1992.

Braudel, Fernand. *The Wheels of Commerce*. Vol. 2 of *Civilization and Capitalism, 15th–18th Century*. Translated by Siân Reynolds. Berkeley: University of California Press, 1992.

Brecht, Bertolt. "Epitaph, 1919." In *Poems, 1913–1956*, edited by John Willett and Ralph Manheim, 175–76. London: Eyre Methuen, 1976.

Brecht, Bertolt. *The Threepenny Opera*. Translated by Ralph Manheim and John Willet. London: Bloomsbury, 1979.

Brenner, Robert. *The Economics of Global Turbulence: The Advanced Capitalist Economies from Long Boom to Long Downturn, 1945–2005*. London: Verso, 2006.

Bronner, Stephen Eric, ed. *The Letters of Rosa Luxemburg*. Boulder, CO: Westview, 1978.

Buck-Morss, Susan. *The Dialectics of Seeing*. Cambridge, MA: MIT Press, 1989.

Buffon, Georges-Louis Leclerc. *Natural History, General and Particu-*

lar, with the Description of the King's Cabinet, 10 vols. Edited by
    James Smith Barr. London, 1797–1807.
Burke, Bernard. *A Genealogical and Heraldic Dictionary of the Peerage
    and Baronetage*. London: Harrison, 1885.
Burke, Edmund. *Reflections on the Revolution in France*. New York:
    Penguin, 1982.
Butler, Smedley. *War Is a Racket*. N.p: Dauphin Publications, 2018.
Carlyle, Thomas. *Essays on Literature*. Edited by Chris R. Vanden
    Bossche. Oakland: University of California Press, 2020.
Carmichael, Stokely. "What We Want." *New York Review of Books*, Sep-
    tember 22, 1966.
Castellano, Katey. "William Cobbett, 'Resurrection Man': The
    Peterloo Massacre and the Bones of Tom Paine." In *Commemo-
    rating Peterloo: Violence, Resilience, and Claim-Making during
    the Romantic Era*, edited by Michael Demson and Regina
    Hewitt, 183–204. Edinburgh: Edinburgh University Press, 2019.
Chambers, Robert. *The Book of Days: A Miscellany of Popular Antiqui-
    ties in Connection with the Calendar, Including Anecdote, Biogra-
    phy and History, Curiosities of Literature, and Oddities of Human
    Life and Character*. London: W. and R. Chambers, 1869.
Chaplin, Ralph. *Wobbly: The Rough and Tumble Story of an American
    Radical*. Chicago: University of Chicago Press, 1948.
Choron, Sandra, Harry Choron, and Arden Moore. *Planet Cat: A Cat-
    alog*. Boston: Houghton Mifflin, 2007.
Clark, T. J. *Farewell to an Idea: Episodes from a History of Modernism*.
    New Haven, CT: Yale University Press, 2001.
Clavers, Mary [Caroline Matilda Kirkland, pseud.]. *A New
    Home—Who'll Follow? Or, Glimpses of Western Life*, 4th ed. New
    York: C. S. Francis, 1850.
Cole, Andrew. *The Birth of Theory*. Chicago: University of Chicago
    Press, 2014.
Comyn, Marian. "My Recollections of Karl Marx." *Nineteenth Century
    and After* 91 (Jan. 1922). https://www.marxists.org/subject
    /women/authors/comyn/marx.htm.
Copley, Frank Barkley. *Frederick W. Taylor: Father of Scientific Manage-
    ment*, vol. 2. New York: Harper and Brothers.
Corrothers, James David. *The Black Cat Club*. Illustrated by J. K. Bryans.
    New York: Funk and Wagnalls, 1902.
Costagliola, Michel. "Fires in History: The Cathar Heresy, the Inquisi-

tion and Brulology." *Annals of Burns and Fire Disasters* 28, no. 3 (Sept. 2015): 230–34. https://www.ncbi.nlm.nih.gov/pmc/articles/PMC4883611/.

Cronon, William. *Changes in the Land: Indians, Colonists, and the Ecology of New England*. New York: Hill and Wang, 1983.

Darnton, Robert. *The Great Cat Massacre and Other Episodes in French Cultural History*. New York: Penguin, 1984.

Daston, Lorraine, and Katherine Park. *Wonders and the Orders of Nature, 1150–1750*. New York: Zone, 2009.

Davidson, Neil. *How Revolutionary Were the Bourgeois Revolutions?* Chicago: Haymarket, 2012.

Davis, Angela Y. *Freedom Is a Constant Struggle: Ferguson, Palestine, and the Foundations of a Movement*. Chicago: Haymarket, 2016.

Davis, Angela Y. "Marcuse's Legacies." In *Herbert Marcuse: A Critical Reader*, edited by John Abromeit and W. Mark Cobb, 43–50. New York: Routledge, 2004.

Dean, Jodi. *Comrade*. New York: Verso, 2019.

Deleuze, Gilles, and Félix Guattari. *Anti-Oedipus*. Minneapolis: University of Press, 1994.

Derrida, Jacques. "The Animal That Therefore I Am (More to Follow)." *Critical Inquiry* 28, no. 2 (Winter 2002): 369–418.

Derrida, Jacques. *The Animal That Therefore I Am*. Edited by Marie Luise-Mallet. Translated by David Wills. New York: Fordham University Press, 2008.

Dewdney, Selwyn, and Kenneth E. Kidd. *Indian Rock Paintings of the Great Lakes*. Toronto: University of Toronto Press, 1962.

Dillistin, William H. *Bank Note Reporters and Counterfeit Detectors*. New York: American Numismatic Society, 1949. http://numismatics.org/digitallibrary/ark:/53695/nnan78163.

Dolgoff, Sam. "Structure of Power in Cuba." In *The Cuban Revolution: A Critical Perspective*, chap. 13. https://archive.iww.org/history/library/Dolgoff/cuba/13/.

Douglass, Frederick. *Narrative of the Life Frederick Douglass, An American Slave*. Boston: Anti-Slavery Office, 1845.

Dreyfus, Jack. *The Lion of Wall Street: The Two Lives of Jack Dreyfus*. Washington, DC: Regnery Publishing, 1996.

Du Bartas, Guillaume de Salluste. *The Divine Weeks and Works of Guillaume de Saluste, Sieur du Bartas*, vol. 1. Edited by Susan Snyder. Translated by Josuah Sylvester. Oxford: Clarendon Press, 1979.

Du Bois, W. E. B. *Black Reconstruction in America: An Essay toward a History of the Part Which Black Folk Played in the Attempt to Reconstruct Democracy in America, 1860–1880*. Vol. 6 of *The Oxford W. E. B. Du Bois*, edited by Henry Louis Gates Jr. New York: Oxford University Press, 2007.

Du Bois, W. E. B. "Marxism and the Negro Problem." *Crisis* 40, no. 5 (May 1933): 103–4.

Dutton, Paul Edward. *Charlemagne's Mustache: And Other Cultural Clusters of a Dark Age*. London: Palgrave, 2004.

Eagleton, Terry. *Literary Theory: An Introduction*. London: Blackwell, 2003.

Edward, Second Duke of York. *The Master of Game*. Edited by Wm. A. Baillie-Grohman and F. Baillie-Grohman. London: Chatto and Windus, 1909.

Edwards, Stewart. *The Paris Commune of 1871*. London: Eyre and Spottiswoode, 1971.

Elliott, E. N. *Cotton Is King and the Pro-slavery Arguments Comprising the Writings of Hammond, Harper, Christy, Stringfellow, Hodge, Bledsoe, and Cartwright on This Important Subject*. Augusta, GA: Pritchard, Abbott and Loomis, 1860.

Elliott, J. W. *National Nursery Rhymes and Nursery Songs Set to Music*. London: George Routledge, 1871.

Emerson, Ralph Waldo. "Experience." In *Essays and Lectures*. New York: Library of America, 1983.

Engels, Frederick. *Condition of the Working Class in England*. In *Marx and Engels, 1844–1845*, 295–596. Vol. 4 of *Karl Marx, Frederick Engels: Collected Works*. Translated by Richard Dixon et al. New York: International Publishers, 1987.

Engels, Frederick. *Dialectics of Nature*. In *Engels* [1873–1883], 313–588. Vol. 25 of *Karl Marx, Frederick Engels: Collected Works*. Translated by Richard Dixon et al. New York: International Publishers, 1987.

Engels, Frederick. "A Fragment of Fourier's on Trade." In *Marx and Engels, 1844–1845*, 613. Vol. 4 of *Karl Marx, Frederick Engels: Collected Works*. Translated by Richard Dixon et al. New York: International Publishers, 1975.

Engels, Frederick. "On the History of the Communist League." In *Frederick Engels, 1882–1889*, 312–34. Vol. 26 of *Karl Marx, Frederick Engels: Collected Works*. Translated by Richard Dixon et al. New York: International Publishers, 1987.

Engels, Frederick. "The Part Played by Labour in the Transition from Ape to Man." In *Engels* [1873–1883], 452–64. Vol. 25 of *Karl Marx, Frederick Engels: Collected Works*. Translated by Richard Dixon et al. New York: International Publishers, 1987.

Engels, Frederick. *The Peasant War in Germany*. In *Marx and Engels, 1849–1851*, 397–482. Vol. 10 of *Karl Marx, Frederick Engels: Collected Works*. Translated by Richard Dixon et al. New York: International Publishers, 1978.

Engels, Frederick. "Preface to the Third German Edition of the *Eighteenth Brumaire of Louis Bonaparte*." In *Engels, 1882–1889*, 302–3. Vol. 26 of *Karl Marx, Frederick Engels: Collected Works*. Translated by Richard Dixon et al. New York: International Publishers, 1987.

Evans, J. P. *The Criminal Prosecution and Capital Punishment of Animals*. London: William Heinemann, 1906.

Evans, Kate. *Red Rosa: A Graphic Biography of Rosa Luxemburg*. New York: Verso, 2015.

Fairholme, Edward G., and Wellesley Pain. *A Century of Work for Animals: The History of the RSPCA, 1824–1924*. London: John Murray, 1924.

Federici, Silvia. *Caliban and the Witch: Women, the Body and Primitive Accumulation*. Brooklyn, NY: Autonomedia, 2004.

Fischer, Sibylle. *Modernity Disavowed: Haiti and the Cultures of Slavery in the Age of Revolution*. Durham, NC: Duke University Press, 2004.

Flynn, Elizabeth Gurley. *Rebel Girl: An Autobiography*. New York: International Publishers, 1973.

Flynn, Elizabeth Gurley. *Sabotage, the Conscious Withdrawal of the Workers' Industrial Efficiency*. Cleveland, OH: IWW Publishing Bureau, 1916.

Foner, Philip S. *The Great Labor Uprising of 1877*. New York: Pathfinder, 1977.

Fossier, Robert. *The Axe and the Oath: Ordinary Life in the Middle Ages*. Princeton, NJ: Princeton University Press, 2010.

Foster, John Bellamy. "Marx as a Food Theorist." *Monthly Review* 68, no. 7 (Dec. 2016). https://monthlyreview.org/2016/12/01/marx-as-a-food-theorist/.

Foster, John Bellamy, and Brett Clark. "Marx and Alienated Speciesism." *Monthly Review* 70, no. 7 (Dec. 2018). https://monthlyreview.org/2018/12/01/marx-and-alienated-speciesism/.

Freund, Amy, and Michael Yonan. "Cats: The Soft Underbelly of the Enlightenment." *Journal18*, no. 7 (Spring 2019). https://www .journal18.org/3778.

Genovese, Eugene D. *Roll, Jordan, Roll: The World the Slaves Made.* New York: Vintage, 1976.

Getzler, Israel. *Martov: A Political Biography of a Russian Social Democrat.* Cambridge: Cambridge University Press, 1967.

Glaberman, Martin. "Black Cats, White Cats, Wildcats: Auto Workers in Detroit." *Radical America* 8 (Jan.–Feb. 1975): 25–29.

Glassé, Cyril. *The New Encyclopedia of Islam.* Walnut Creek, CA: AltaMira Press: 2001.

Goncourt, Edmond de. *Catalogue raisonné de l'oeuvre peint, dessiné et gravé de P.-P. Prud'hon.* Paris: Rapilly, 1876.

Gramsci, Antonio. *Selections from the Prison Notebooks of Antonio Gramsci.* Edited by Geoffrey Nowell-Smith and Quintin Hoare. London: Lawrence and Wishart, 1971.

Grandin, Greg. *Fordlandia: The Rise and Fall of Henry Ford's Forgotten Jungle City.* New York: Metropolitan, 2009.

Gritsch, Eric W. *Thomas Müntzer: A Tragedy of Errors.* Minneapolis, MN: Fortress Press, 2006.

Guevara, Che. "Socialism and Man in Cuba." In *Che Guevara Reader,* edited by David Deutschmann, 212–30. Melbourne: Ocean Press, 2003.

Hall, Stuart, Chas Critcher, Tony Jefferson, John Clarke, and Brian Roberts. *Policing the Crisis: Mugging, the State and Law and Order.* Basingstoke: Palgrave Macmillan, 2013.

Hannah-Jones, Nikole. "Arrival." In *Four Hundred Souls: A Community History of African America, 1619–2019,* edited by Ibram X. Kendi and Keisha N. Blain, 28–34. New York: One World, 2021.

Haraway, Donna. *When Species Meet.* Minneapolis: University of Minnesota Press, 2003.

Harvey, David. *The Limits to Capital.* London: Verso, 1999.

Harvey, David. *Paris, Capital of Modernity.* New York: Routledge, 2006.

Hayek, F. A. *A Tiger by the Tail: The Keynesian Legacy of Inflation.* 3rd ed. Edited by Sudha R. Shenoy. London: Institute of Economic Affairs and Ludwig von Mises Institute, 2009.

Hegel, G. W. F. *Aesthetics: Lectures on Fine Art.* Translated by T. M. Knox. Oxford: Clarendon Press, 1975.

Hegel, G. W. F. *Dokumente zu Hegel's Entwicklung.* Edited by Johannes

Hoffmeister. Stuttgart–Bad Cannstatt: Frommann-Holzboog, 1974.

Hegel, G. W. F. *The Phenomenology of Spirit*. Translated by A. V. Miller. Oxford: Oxford University Press, 1977.

Hegel, G. W. F. *The Science of Logic*. Translated by George di Giovanni. Cambridge: Cambridge University Press, 2010.

Heng, Geraldine. *The Invention of Race in the European Middle Ages*. Cambridge: Cambridge University Press, 2018.

Hicks, Stephen. *Explaining Postmodernism: Skepticism and Socialism from Rousseau to Foucault*. Milwaukee, WI: Scholarly Publishing, 2004.

Hilliard, David. "The Ideology of the Black Panther Party." In *The Black Panthers Speak*, edited by Philip S. Foner, 122–23. Chicago: Haymarket, 2014.

Hilton, Rodney. *Bond Men Made Free: Medieval Peasant Movements and the English Rising of 1381*. London: Routledge, 2003.

Hobson, J. A. *Imperialism: A Study*. London: James Nisbet, 1902.

Hobsbawm, Eric. *The Age of Revolution, 1789–1848*. New York: Vintage, 1996.

Hosler, John D. *Siege of Acre, 1189–1191: Saladin, Richard the Lionheart, and the Battle That Decided the Third Crusade*. New Haven, CT: Yale University Press, 2018.

Hribal, Jason. "'Animals Are Part of the Working Class': A Challenge to Labor History." *Labor History* 44, no. 4 (2003): 435–53.

Hribal, Jason. *Fear of the Animal Planet: The Hidden History of Animal Resistance*. New York: AK Press, 2010.

Huot, Paul. *Les Massacres a Versailles en 1792. Eclaircissements historiques et documents nouveaux*. Paris: Challamel Aine, 1869.

Isidore of Seville. *The Etymologies of Isidore of Seville*. Translated by Stephen A. Barney, W. J. Lewis, J. A. Beach, and Oliver Berghof. Cambridge: Cambridge University Press, 2006.

James, C. L. R. *The Black Jacobins: Toussaint L'Ouverture and the San Domingo Revolution*. New York: Vintage, 1989.

James, C. L. R. *Notes on Dialectics: Hegel, Marx, Lenin*. London: Allison and Busby, 1980.

Jameson, Fredric. "Beyond the Cave: Demystifying the Ideology of Modernism." *Bulletin of the Midwest Modern Language Association* 18, no. 1 (Spring 1975): 1–20.

Jameson, Fredric. "Future City." *New Left Review* 21 (May–June 2003): 65–79.

Jameson, Fredric. *The Political Unconscious: Narrative as Socially Symbolic Act*. Ithaca, NY: Cornell University Press, 1981.

Jameson, Fredric. "Postmodernism and Consumer Society." In *The Anti-aesthetic: Essays on Postmodern Culture,* edited by Hal Foster, 111–25. Seattle, WA: Bay Press, 1987.

Jameson, Fredric. *The Seeds of Time*. New York: Columbia University Press, 1994.

Jameson, Fredric. *Valences of the Dialectic*. London: Verso, 2009.

Jenson, Deborah. "Living by Metaphor in the Haitian Declaration of Independence: Tigers and Cognitive Theory." In *The Haitian Declaration of Independence,* edited by Julia Gaffield, 72–91. Charlottesville: University of Virginia Press, 2019.

Jones, Colin. "French Crossings: III. The Smile of the Tiger." *Transactions of the Royal Historical Society* 22 (2012): 3–35. https://doi.org/10.1017/S0080440112000047.

Jones, Malcolm. *The Secret Middle Ages: Discovering the Real Medieval World*. Westport, CT: Praeger, 2002.

Kelley, Robin D. G. *Hammer and Hoe: Alabama Communists during the Great Depression.* Chapel Hill: University of North Carolina Press, 1990.

Keynes, John Maynard. *Essays in Persuasion*. Basingstoke: Palgrave Macmillan, 2010.

Kilgour, Frederick C. *The Evolution of the Book*. Oxford: Oxford University Press, 1998.

Kirkland, Caroline Matilda. *See* Clavers, Mary.

Kornblug, Joyce L., ed. *Rebel Voices: An IWW Anthology*. Oakland, CA: PM Press, 2011.

Kotin, Joshua. *Utopias of One*. Princeton, NJ: Princeton University Press, 2018.

Kriloff's Original Fables. Translated by I. Henry Harrison. London: Remington, 1883.

Krugman, Paul. *The Return of Depression Economics and the Crisis of 2008*. New York: Penguin, 2015.

Kuhns, L. Oscar. "Bestiaries and Lapidaries." In *1852–1853*, n.p. Vol. 4 of *A Library of the World's Best Literature*. Edited by Charles Dudley Warner et al. New York: International Society, 1896. https://bestiary.ca/etexts/kuhns-bestiaries-and-lapidaries.pdf.

Kwan, Natalie. "Woodcuts and Witches: Ulrich Molitor's *De lamiis et pythonicis mulieribus*, 1489–1669." *German History* 30, no. 4: 493–527.

Ladsaria, Seema K., and Rajni Singh. "The 'Semiotic Animal' in Roland Barthes: A Reflection on Calculating the Self as 'Difference in Man.'" *Rupkatha Journal on Interdisciplinary Studies in Humanities* 8, no. 3 (2016): 24–34. https://doi.org/10.21659/rupkatha.v8n3.04.

Landrin, Alexandre. *Le chat.* Paris: George Carré, 1894.

Laurie, Clayton D., and Ronald H. Cole. *The Role of Federal Military Forces in Domestic Disorders, 1877–1945*. Washington, DC: United States Army Center of Military History, 1997.

Lea, Henry Charles. *A History of the Inquisition of the Middle Ages*, vol. 3. New York: Harper and Brothers, 1887.

Le Blanc, Paul. "Lenin and Luxemburg: Through Each Other's Eyes." *Socialist Viewpoint* 13, no. 2 (Mar.–Apr. 2013). http://www.socialistviewpoint.org/marapr_13/marapr_13_42.html.

Lefebvre, George. *The Coming of the French Revolution*. Translated by R. R. Palmer. Princeton, NJ: Princeton University Press, 1947.

Lenin, Vladimir Ilyich. "Conspectus of Hegel's *Science of Logic*." In Vol. 38 of *Collected Works*, 86–237. Edited by Stewart Smith. Translated by Clemence Dutt. Moscow: Progress Publishers, 1976.

Lenin, Vladimir I. *Materialism and Empirio-criticism*. In Vol. 14 of *Collected Works*, 17–358. Moscow: Progress Publishers, 2010.

Lenin, Vladimir Ilyich. "Preface to the French and German Editions." In *Imperialism, the Highest Stage of Capitalism*, 667–74. Vol. 1 of *Lenin's Selected Works.* 1917. N.p.: Lenin Internet Archive, 2005. https://www.marxists.org/archive/lenin/works/1916/imp-hsc/pref02.htm.

Lenin, V. I. *Socialism and War*. Moscow: Foreign Language Press, 1970.

Lenin, Vladimir I. *State and Revolution*. In Vol. 25 of *Collected Works*, 381–492. 1918. N.p.: Lenin Internet Archive, 1993. https://www.marxists.org/archive/lenin/works/1917/staterev/.

Linebaugh, Peter. *The London Hanged*. 2nd ed. London: Verso, 2003.

Lipton, Sarah. *Images of Intolerance: The Representation of Jews and Judaism in the Bible Moralisée*. Berkeley: University of California Press, 1999.

Luxemburg, Rosa. "In a Revolutionary Hour: What Next?" In *Collected Works,* vol. 1., 554. New York: Verso, 2014.

Luxemburg, Rosa. *The Junius Pamphlet: The Crisis in German Social Democracy*. In *The Rosa Luxemburg Reader*, edited by Peter Hudis and Kevin B. Anderson, 312–41. New York: Monthly Review Press, 2004.

Luxemburg, Rosa. *The Letters of Rosa Luxemburg*. Edited by Georg Adler, Peter Hudis, and Annelies Laschitza. Translated by George Shriver. London: Verso, 2013.

Luxemburg, Rosa. "The Questions at Issue." In *Imperialism and the Accumulation of Capital*, edited by Kenneth J. Tarbuck and translated by Rudolf Wichmann, 45–150. London: Penguin, 1972.

Luxemburg, Rosa. *Reform or Revolution*. In *The Essential Rosa Luxemburg*, edited by Helen Scott, 41–104. Chicago: Haymarket, 2008.

Machiavelli, Niccolo. *The Prince*. Edited by Quentin Skinner and Russell Price. Cambridge: Cambridge University Press, 1988.

Mallery, Garrick. "Picture-Writing of the American Indians." *Tenth Annual Report of the Bureau of Ethnology to the Secretary of the Smithsonian Institution 1888–89*. Washington, DC: US Government Printing Office, 1893.

Mandel, Ernest. *Late Capitalism*. Translated by Joris De Bres. London: New Left Books, 1975.

Mann, Barbara Alice. *The Land of the Three Miamis: A Traditional Narrative of the Iroquois in Ohio*. Toledo, OH: University of Toledo Urban Affairs Center Press, 2006.

Mann, Barbara A. "The Lynx in Time: Haudenosaunee Women's Traditions and History." *American Indian Quarterly* 21, no. 3 (Summer 1997): 423–49. https://doi.org/10.2307/1185516.

Marcuse, Herbert. *Counterrevolution and Revolt*. Boston: Beacon, 1972.

Marcy, Mary E. "Letters of a Pork Packer's Stenographer: Letter No. III." *International Socialist Review* 5, no. 3 (Sept. 1904): 300–303.

Marglin, Stephen, and Juliet Schor. *The Golden Age of Capitalism*. Oxford: Oxford University Press, 1992.

Marx, Karl. "Bourgeoisie and the Counter-Revolution." In *Marx and Engels: 1848–1849*, 154–78. Vol. 8 of *Karl Marx, Frederick Engels: Collected Works*. Translated by Richard Dixon et al. New York: International Publishers, 1975.

Marx, Karl. *Capital*, vol. 2. Vol. 36 of *Karl Marx and Frederick Engels: Collected Works*. Translated by Richard Dixon et al. London: Lawrence and Wishart, 2010.

Marx, Karl. *The Civil War in France*. In *Marx and Engels, 1870–1871*,

307–56. Vol. 22 of *Karl Marx, Frederick Engels: Collected Works*. Translated by Richard Dixon et al. New York: International Publishers, 1985.

Marx, Karl. *Contribution to the Critique of Hegel's Philosophy of Law*. In *Marx and Engels , 1843–1844*, 3–129. Vol. 3 of *Karl Marx, Frederick Engels: Collected Works*. Translated by Richard Dixon et al. New York: International Publishers, 1975.

Marx, Karl. *A Contribution to the Critique of Political Economy*. In *Marx: 1857–1861*, 5–420. Vol. 29 of *Karl Marx, Frederick Engels: Collected Works*. Translated by Richard Dixon et al. New York: International Publishers, 1987.

Marx, Karl. *Critique of Hegel's "Philosophy of Right."* Translated by Annette Jolin and Joseph O'Malley. Cambridge: Cambridge University Press, 1970.

Marx, Karl. "Critique of the Gotha Programme." In *Marx and Engels, 1874–1883*, 75–94. Vol. 24 of *Karl Marx, Frederick Engels: Collected Works*. Translated by Richard Dixon et al. New York: International Publishers, 1987.

Marx, Karl. *Economic Manuscripts, 1857–58*. In *Marx: 1857–1861*. Vol. 28 of *Karl Marx and Frederick Engels: Collected Works*. Translated by Richard Dixon et al. London: Lawrence and Wishart, 1986.

Marx, Karl. *The Eighteenth Brumaire of Louis Bonaparte*. New York: International Publishers, 1963.

Marx, Karl. *The Eighteenth Brumaire of Louis Bonaparte*. Translated by Saul K. Padover and Progress Publishers. Marxists Internet Archive, 2006. https://www.marxists.org/archive/marx/works/1852/18th-brumaire/index.htm.

Marx, Karl. *Ethnological Notebooks*. Translated by Lawrence Krader. Assen, The Netherlands: Van Gorcum, 1974.

Marx, Karl. *Grundrisse*. Translated by Martin Nicolaus. London: Penguin, 1993.

Marx, Karl. "Layard's Inquiry." In *Marx and Engels, 1855–1856*, 57–58. Vol. 14 of *Karl Marx, Frederick Engels: Collected Works*. Translated by Richard Dixon et al. New York: International Publishers, 1985.

Marx, Karl. *Letters on Capital*. Translated by Andrew Drummond. London: New Park Publications, 1983.

Marx, Karl. "North American Civil War." In *Marx and Engels, 1861–1864*, 32–42. Vol. 19 of *Karl Marx, Frederick Engels: Col-

lected Works. Translated by Richard Dixon et al. New York: International Publishers, 1976.

Marx, Karl. "The Poverty of Philosophy." In *Marx and Engels, 1845–1848,* 105–212. Vol. 6 of *Karl Marx, Frederick Engels: Collected Works.* Translated by Richard Dixon et al. New York: International Publishers, 1985.

Marx, Karl. *The Process of the Production of Capital.* In *Marx: Capital,* vol. 1, 45–155. Vol. 35 of *Karl Marx, Frederick Engels: Collected Works.* Translated by Richard Dixon et al. New York: International Publishers, 1996.

Marx, Karl. *The Process of Capitalist Production as a Whole.* In *Marx: Capital,* vol. 3, 461–900. Vol. 37 of *Karl Marx, Frederick Engels: Collected Works.* Translated by Richard Dixon et al. New York: International Publishers, 1998.

Marx, Karl. "Speech at Anniversary of the *People's Paper.*" In *Marx and Engels, 1855–1856,* 655–56. Vol. 14 of *Karl Marx and Frederick Engels: Collected Works.* Translated by Richard Dixon et al. London: Lawrence and Wishart, 2010.

Marx, Karl. "Theses on Feuerbach." In *Marx and Engels, 1845–1847,* 3–14. Vol. 5 of *Karl Marx, Frederick Engels: Collected Works.* Translated by Richard Dixon et al. New York: International Publishers, 1985.

Marx, Karl. *Value, Price and Profit.* In *Marx and Engels, 1864–1868,* 101–43. Vol. 20 of *Karl Marx, Frederick Engels: Collected Works.* Translated by Richard Dixon et al. New York: International Publishers, 1985.

Marx, Karl. *Writings of Young Marx on Philosophy and Society.* New York: Hackett Publishing Company, 1997.

Marx, Karl, and Frederick Engels. "Address to the Central Authority. In *Marx and Engels, 1849–1851,* 371. Vol. 10 of *Karl Marx, Frederick Engels: Collected Works.* Translated by Richard Dixon et al. New York: International Publishers, 1985.

Marx, Karl, and Frederick Engels. *The Civil War in the United States.* Edited by Andrew Zimmerman. New York: International Publishers, 2016.

Marx, Karl, and Frederick Engels. *The German Ideology.* In *Marx and Engels: 1845–1847,* 19–450. Vol. 5 of *Karl Marx, Frederick Engels: Collected Works.* Translated by Richard Dixon et al. New York: International Publishers, 1976.

Marx, Karl, and Frederick Engels. *The Manifesto of the Communist Party*. In *Marx and Engels, 1845–1848*, 477–519. Vol. 6 of *Karl Marx, Frederick Engels: Collected Works*. New York: International Publishers, 1976.

McKay, Claude. "If We Must Die." In *Complete Poems*, edited by William J. Maxwell, 117. Champaign: University of Illinois Press, 2004.

Metzler, Irina. "Heretical Cats: Animal Symbolism in Religious Discourse." *Medium Aevum Quotidianum* 59 (2009): 16–32.

Mills, Robert. *Seeing Sodomy in the Middle Ages*. Chicago: University of Chicago Press, 2015.

Mommsen, Theodore. "Petrarch's Conception of the 'Dark Ages.'" In *Medieval and Renaissance Studies*, edited by Eugene F. Rice Jr, 106–29. Ithaca, NY: Cornell University Press, 1959.

Montaigne, Michel de. "An Apology for Raymond Sebond." In *The Complete Essays of Montaigne*, translated by Donald M. Frame, 318–457. Stanford, CA: Stanford University Press, 1958.

Morais, Herbert M. "Marx and Engels on America." In *A Centenary of Marxism*, 3–21. New York: Science and Society, 1948.

Morgan, Edmund S. "Slavery and Freedom: The American Paradox." *Journal of American History* 59, no. 1 (June 1972): 5–29.

Morgan, Henry L. *Ancient Society, or Researches in the Lines of Human Progress from Savagery through Barbarism to Civilization*. 1877. Chicago: Charles H. Kerr, 1907.

Morgan, Henry Lewis. *The American Beaver and His Works*. Philadelphia: Lippincott, 1868.

Morson, Gary Saul. *The Words of Others: From Quotations to Culture*. New Haven, CT: Yale University Press, 2011.

Müntzer, Thomas. *Hochverursachte Schutzrede*. In *Politische Schriften, Manifeste, Briefe 1524/25*, edited by Manfred Bensing and Bernd Rüdiger, 140–62. Leipzig: VEB Bibliographisches Institut, 1970.

Nelson, Craig. *Thomas Paine: Enlightenment, Revolution, and the Birth of Modern Nations*. New York: Viking, 2006.

Netanel, Neil Weinstock. "Maharam of Padua v. Giustiniani: The Sixteenth-Century Origins of the Jewish Law of Copyright." *Houston Law Review* 44, no. 4 (2007): 821–70.

Nettl, J. P. *Rosa Luxemburg*, vol. 1. London: Oxford University Press, 1966.

Newton, Huey P. "The Women's Liberation and Gay Liberation Movements: August 15, 1970." In *The Huey P. Newton Reader*, edited by David Hilliard and Donald Weise, 157–59. New York: Seven Stories Press, 2002.

Oeser, Erhard. *Katze und Mensch: Die Geschichte einer Beziehung.* Darmstadt: Wissenshaftliche Buchgesellschaft, 2005.

Oswald, John. *The Cry of Nature; or, an Appeal to Mercy and Justice, on Behalf of the Persecuted Animals.* London: J. Johnson, 1791.

Paine, Thomas. *Rights of Man, Common Sense, and Other Political Writings.* Edited by Mark Philip. Oxford: Oxford University Press, 1995.

Pedley, Colin. "Blake's Tiger and Contemporary Journalism." *Eighteenth-Century Studies* 14, no. 1 (March 1991): 45–49.

Pendergast, James F. "The Kakouagoga or Kahkwas: An Iroquoian Nation Destroyed in the Niagara Region." *Proceedings of the American Philosophical Society* 138, no. 1 (March 1994): 96–144.

Petrarch, Francesco. *Apologia cuiusdam anonymi Galli calumnias.* In *Opera Omnia.* Basel: n.p., 1554.

Pettman, Dominic. "Get Thee to a Phalanstery, or, How Fourier Can Still Teach Us to Make Lemonade." *Public Domain Review*, April 30, 2019. https://publicdomainreview.org/essay/get-thee -to-a-phalanstery-or-how-fourier-can-still-teach-us-to-make -lemonade/.

Polo, Marco. *The Travels of Marco Polo.* Translated by Ronald Latham. New York: Penguin, 1958.

Poovey, Mary. *A History of the Modern Fact.* Chicago: University of Chicago Press, 1998.

Rajnovich, Grace. *Reading Rock Art Interpreting the Indian Rock Paintings of the Canadian Shield.* Toronto: Natural Heritage/Natural History, 1994.

Rancière, Jacques. *Proletarian Nights: The Workers' Dream in Nineteenth-Century France.* Translated by John Drury. New York: Verso, 2012.

Read, Christopher. *Lenin: A Revolutionary Life.* London: Routledge, 2005.

Reclus, Élisée. 2013. *Anarchy, Geography, Modernity: Selected Writings of Élisée Reclus.* Edited by John Clark and Camille Martin. Oakland, CA: PM Press.

Robbins, Louise E. *Elephant Slaves and Pampered Parrots: Exotic Animals in Eighteenth-Century Paris.* Baltimore, MD: Johns Hopkins University Press, 2002.

Robespierre, Maximilien. "Réponse de Maximilien Robespierre à l'accusation de J. B. Louvet." In *Oeuvres de Maximilien Robespierre*, vol. 9, edited by Marc Bouloiseau, Georges Lefebvre, and Albert Soboul, 79–104. Paris: Presses Universitaires de France, 1958.

Rogers, Katharine M. *Cat*. London: Reaktion Books, 2006.

Rolnick, Arthur J., and Warren E. Weber. "New Evidence on the Free Banking Era." *American Economic Review* 73, no. 5 (Dec. 1983): 1080–91.

Romilly, Samuel. *The Life of Sir Samuel Romilly Written by Himself with a Selection from His Correspondence*, vol. 1. London: John Murray, 1842.

Rosemont, Franklin. "Karl Marx and the Iroquois." *Arsenal: Surrealist Subversion* 4 (January 1989): 201–13. https://files.libcom.org /files/Franklin_Rosemont_Karl_Marx_and_the_Iroquois.pdf.

Ross, Kristin. *Communal Luxury: The Political Imaginary of the Paris Commune*. New York: Verso, 2016.

Rousseau, Jean-Jacques. *Emile*. Translated by Barbara Foxley. London: J. M. Dent, 1911.

Rousseau, Jean-Jacques. *The Social Contract*. Edited by Victor Gourevitch. Cambridge: Cambridge University Press, 1997.

Russell, Frederic William. *Kett's Rebellion in Norfolk; Being a History of the Great Civic Commotion That Occurred at the Time of the Reformation in the Reign of Edward VI*. London: Longman's and Roberts, 1859.

Sahlins, Peter. *1668: Year of the Animal*. New York: Zone, 2017.

Saint-Just, Antoine. *Oeuvres Complètes de Saint-Just*, vol. 1. Edited by Charles Vellay. Paris: Librairie Charpentier et Fasquelle, 1908.

Saitō, Kōhei. *Karl Marx's Ecosocialism: Capital, Nature, and the Unfinished Critique of Political Economy*. New York: Monthly Review Press, 2017.

Samuelson, Paul A., and William D. Nordhaus. *Economics*. New York: McGraw-Hill, 1985.

Scott, James C. *The Art of Not Being Governed: An Anarchist History of Upland Southeast Asia*. New Haven, CT: Yale University Press, 2009.

Seale, Bobby. *Seize the Time: The Story of the Black Panther Party and Huey P. Newton*. New York: Random House, 1968.

Séguin, Philippe. *Louis Napoléon le Grand*. Paris: Bernard Grasset, 1990.

Sheehan, James J. *German History, 1770–1866*. Oxford: Clarendon Press, 1989.

Shukin, Nicole. *Animal Capital*. Minneapolis: University of Minnesota Press, 2009. Kindle.

Singer, Peter. *Animal Liberation*. New York: Avon, 1975.

Sparrow, Jeff. "Mimi and Rosa." In *Man and Beast*, edited by Andrew Rule, 99–102. Melbourne: Melbourne University Publishing, 2016. ProQuest Ebook Central.

Specht, Joshua. *Red Meat Republic: A Hoof to Table History of How Beef Changed America*. Princeton, NJ: Princeton University Press, 2019.

Spence, Thomas. *The Important Trial of Thomas Spence, for a Political Pamphlet, Intitled "The Restorer of Society to Its Natural State."* 2nd ed. London: A. Seale, 1803.

Spence, Thomas. *The Rights of Infants, or, the Imprescriptable Right of Mothers to Such a Share of the Elements as Is Sufficient to Enable Them to Suckle and Bring Up Their Young*. 1st ed. 1797. N.p.: Marxists Internet Archive, 2017. https://www.marxists.org/history/england/britdem/people/spence/infants/infants.htm.

Stahl, P. J. *Public and Private Life of Animals* [*Scènes de la vie privée et publique des animaux*]. Illustrated by J. J. Grandville. Translated from the French by J. Thompson. London: S. Low, Marston, Searle, and Rivington, 1877.

Taylor, Sunaura. *Beasts of Burden: Animal and Disability Liberation*. New York: New Press, 2017.

Theweleit, Klaus. *Male Fantasies*. Vol. 1 of *Women, Floods, Bodies, History*. Translated by Stephen Conway. Minneapolis: University of Minnesota Press, 1987.

Thompson, E. P. *The Making of the English Working Class*. New York: Vintage, 1968.

Thoreau, Henry David. "A Week on the Concord and Merrimack Rivers." In *A Week on the Concord and Merrimac Rivers; Walden, or Life in the Woods; The Maine Woods; Cape Cod*. New York: Library of America, 1985.

Thoreau, Henry David. *A Year in Thoreau's Journal, 1851*. New York: Penguin, 1993.

Timofeena, Oxana. *The History of Animals: A Philosophy*. London: Bloomsbury, 2018.

Tratner, Michael. "Derrida's Debt to Milton Friedman." *New Literary History* 34, no. 4 (Autumn 2003): 791–806.

Trotsky, Leon. "Hitler's 'Disarmament' and Prospects of War with Soviet Union." *Militant* 6, no. 41 (Sept. 1933). https://www .marxists.org/archive/trotsky/1933/06/hitler1.htm.

Trotsky, Leon. *My Life: An Attempt at an Autobiography.* New York: Pathfinder Press, 1970.

Trotsky, Leon. *The Third International after Lenin.* New York: Pathfinder Press, 1957.

Tuchman, Barbara W. *A Distant Mirror: The Calamitous Fourteenth Century.* New York: Ballantine, 1978.

van Renswoude, Irene. "The Art of Disputation: Dialogue, Dialectic and Debate around 800." *Early Medieval Europe* 25, no. 1 (Feb. 2017): 38–53. https://doi.org/10.1111/emed.12185.

Vatlin, Alexander, and Larisa Malashenko, eds. *Piggy Foxy and the Sword of Revolution: Bolshevik Self-Portraits: Annals of Communism Series.* Translated by Vadim A. Staklo. New Haven, CT: Yale University Press, 2006.

Vitalis, Ordericus. *The Ecclesiastical History of Orderic Vitalis,* vol. 4. Edited and translated by Marjorie Chibnall. Oxford: Clarendon Press, 1973.

Wallace, Robert G. *Dead Epidemiologists: On the Origins of COVID-19.* New York: Monthly Review Press, 2020.

Warner, Charles Dudley. "Calvin: A Character Study." In *The Complete Writings of Charles Dudley Warner,* vol. 1, edited by Thomas R. Lounsbury, 119–34. Hartford, CT: American Publishing Company, 1904.

Webb, Constance. *Not Without Love: Memoirs.* Hanover, NH: Dartmouth College Press, 2003.

Weber, Max. *The Protestant Ethic and the Spirit of Capitalism.* Translated by Talcott Parsons. London: Routledge, 1992.

Weir, Harrison. *Our Cats and All about Them.* London: Fanciers Gazette, 1892. https://www.gutenberg.org/files/35450/35450 -h/35450-h.htm.

Weld, Theodore Dwight, Angelina Grimke, and Sarah Grimke. *American Slavery as It Is: Testimony of a Thousand Witnesses.* Boston: American Anti-Slavery Society, 1839.

Wilder, Laura Ingalls. *Little Town on the Prairie.* New York: HarperCollins, 1969.

Wilentz, Sean. *Chants Democratic: New York City and the Rise of the Working Class, 1788–1850.* New York: Oxford University Press, 1984.

Wipplinger, Jonathan O. *The Jazz Republic: Music, Race, and American Culture in Weimar Germany*. Ann Arbor: University of Michigan Press, 2017.

Wolfe, Cary. "Human, All Too Human: 'Animal Studies' and the Humanities." *PMLA* 124, no. 2 (March 2009): 564–75.

Young, Katherine E. "Herbert's Herbivore: One-Dimensional Society and the Possibility of Radical Vegetarianism." *New Political Science* 38, no. 4 (2016). https://doi.org/10.1080/07393148.2016.1228582.

Žižek, Slavoj. "The Spectre of Ideology." In *Mapping Ideology*. London: Verso, 1994.

INDEX

colonialism 230; American, 98, 100, 104–5, 107, 109–12; English, 104–5; European, 18; French, 151, 168; settler, 18, 110. *See also* imperialism

commodity, 301, 334–35, 337; fetishism, 240; form, 325, 334–35; exchange, 8, 40, 185, 301

commons, the, 30, 92; elimination of, 17, 30, 92

communism, 223, 241; emergence of, 21, 54, 242, 297; interspecies, 236, 257; and veganism, 241

comradeship, 256–57, 327; interspecies, 16, 257, 284, 326–27, 337

Comyn, Marian, 246–47

Contat, Nicolas, 143, 222

Corrothers, James David: *The Black Cat Club*, 267

COVID-19 pandemic, 78, 329–30

credit, 88–90, 101, 282; evolution in Venice, 88–90. *See also* debt; imperialism

Crockett, Davy, 183, 188

Crusades, the, 17, 29, 40–42, 51, 60, 70, 75

Cuban Revolution, 297, 308

d'Abrantès, Laure Junot, 167

Darnton, Robert, 142, 143

Daston, Lorraine, 28

Davidson, Neil, 107

da Vinci, Leonardo, 90

Davis, Angela, 22, 108, 303–4, 309–10, 325–26, 333, 336; and the Communist Party, 309–10; education of, 303–4; on farm

animals, 325–26; and veganism, 304, 333

Dean, Jodi: on comradeship, 256, 327

Debord, Guy, 7, 299

debt, 60–61, 75, 88–89, 96, 101, 117, 282, 294; jubilee, 123; national, 60–61, 88–89, 101, 117; of Paine, Thomas, 121, 200; prisons, 195; and sharecropping, 294

Defense Production Act, 330

Deleuze, Gilles, 298, 299

democracy, 102, 216; "American paradox" of, 100, 102; bourgeois, 270–71, capitalist, 96, 99–100; economic, 121; French, 225, 235; parliamentary, 275–76; workers', 241, 256, 294, 321. *See also* age of democracy

de Rochefort, Garnier, 74

Derrida, Jacques: "The Animal That Therefore I Am," 7, 322; on his cat, 7, 298, 321–22; and Friedman, Milton: 322; on phallogocentrism, 321

despair, 126, 281, 298, 303

Dessalines, Jean-Jacques, 166–67

dialectic, the, 21, 54, 168, 277, 288; and Aristotle, 74; and the cat, 75; of cat-comrade, 257, 288–93, 298; of cat-mouse, 207–11; of lion-cat, 21, 55–57, 61, 86, 108, 168; of lord-bondsman, 55–57, 61; of "Marx for cats," 334–36; of tiger-tyger, 124–28, 168

Dodge Revolutionary Union Movement (DRUM), 310–11

domestic cats, 3, 4, 15, 17, 18, 29,

33, 48, 58–92, 118, 135, 180, 190, 212–47; and the American Revolution, 117, 118, in bestiaries, 48; and the bourgeoisie, 133, 142, 243, 245, 253–54; and the CIA, 315; and colonization, 96; and heresy, 58–92; and Leclerc, Buffon George-Louis, 142–43; and lions, 55–57, 61–62, 86, 168; and peasants, 52; persecution of, 69–70, 78; as symbols of social disorder, 53, 331; symbolic value of, 53, 81

Douglas, Emory, 308

Douglass, Frederick, 177–78, 229; *Narrative of the Life of Frederick Douglass, an American Slave*, 177

Dreyfus, Jack, 323

Du Bois, W. E. B., 231, 256, 308

Eagleton, Terry: on polyvalence, 292–93

Edward, Duke of York, 58, 66

Edwards, Stewart, 234

Eisenstein, Sergey: *Strike!*, 277

Emerson, Ralph Waldo, 192–93

Engels, Friedrich, 6, 181, 201; on abstraction and fact, 209; on the American bourgeoisie, 107, 193; on class struggle and history, 52, 142, 153; on class struggle and religion, 41; *The Communist Manifesto*, 11, 52, 181, 203, 223; *The Condition of the Working Class in England*, 202; *Dialectics of Nature*, 207–8; on diet and evolution, 207–8; on feudalism and heresy, 64, 69; on French and German nonsense, 221; *The*

German Ideology, 8, 209, 268; on Hegel, G. W. F., 210; *Outline of the General Plan*, 211; on peasants, 37; *The Peasant Wars in Germany*, 84–85; on species-being, 211, 285

Everett Massacre, 268

exchange value, 185, 190, 214, 301, 325–26

farce, 10, 12, 18, 225, 271

fascism, 126, 280, 297, 300, 301

fat cats, 271–72, 291

February Revolution, 222

Federici, Silvia: *Caliban and the Witch*, 13, 68–71, 73

feudalism, 4, 17, 21, 32, 63–64, 135, 140, 190; absence in America, 100, 107; limits of, 59–60; and lions, 51; transition to capitalism, 21, 28, 51, 54, 68–70, 87, 144, 149, 153, 319

Feuerbach, Ludwig, 209

finance, 13, 14, 63, 80, 92, 97, 272, 297, 315, 323

First Nations peoples, 17, 96, 97, 101–2, 104–5, 111, 189

Flinders, Matthew, 243–44

Flynn, Elizabeth Gurley: *Rebel Girl*, 261

Ford, Henry, 262–64

Fordism, 263, 297, 311

Foucault, Michel, 7

Fourier, Charles, 221, 300

Frankfurt School, the, 299–300, 303. *See also* Adorno, Theodor W.; Benjamin, Walter

freedom, 9, 28, 30, 79, 90, 99, 101, 180, 193, 286, 303, 336; American, 101, 112, 114–15; animal, 133, 193, 293, 262, 285;

Linebaugh, Peter, 83, 124
lions: and bestiaries, 15, 29, 43, 48, 50–52; in early America, 18, 96, 99, 108–9, 112, 116–18, 131; under feudalism, 29–43; and industrialization, 195; lion-cat dialectic, 21, 55–57, 61, 86, 108, 168; and nobility, 15, 25–52; as symbols of freedom, 178, 180; as symbols of imperialism, 11, 17, 28, 31, 35, 37–38,
livestock, 105, 326
Llortente, Renzo, 338
Louis XIV, 138, 150
Louis XV, 150, 151, 160, 215
Louis XVI, 150, 152, 160, 218
Louverture, Toussaint, 18, 166–68
love, 21, 29, 121, 151, 199, 220, 229, 239, 276, 285, 290, 313, 314, 338
Luxemburg, Rosa, 1–2, 6, 254, 271, 273, 281–86, 299–300, 336; *The Accumulation of Capital*, 282; on captivity, 285; correspondence of, 1–2, 282
lynxes, 9, 15, 51, 95–96, 102–5, 111–12, 133, 137; extermination of, 192–93; in First Nations creation myth, 17, 102–3, 105; otherness of, 55
Lyons, Ingelram de, 36
Lyons, Nicolas de, 36
Lyons, Richard, 80–81, 86, 119

Machiavelli, Niccolò, 6, 38, 173
Madison, James, 109
Mandel, Ernest, 319, 321
Mann, Barbara, 103, 104
Mao, Zedong, 4, 307
Map, Walter, 66
Marat, Jean-Paul, 129–30, 155, 160

Marcuse, Herbert, 300, 303–4, 309
Marcy, Mary E., 262
Maréchal, Nicolas, 151
Marie Antoinette, 153, 160
Marx, Eleonor "Tussy," 247
Marx, Karl; on the acceleration of historical time, 233; on accumulation, 185; on the American Civil War, 232–33; on boom and bust cycles, 187; on the bourgeoisie, 110, 114, 115, 214; *Capital*, vol. 1, 334–35; *Capital*, vol. 2, 210–11; *The Civil War in France*, 236; on Cobbett, William, 201, 318; on the commodity, 280, 334–35; *The Communist Manifesto*, 11, 52, 181, 203, 223; *The Eighteenth Brumaire of Louis Bonaparte*, 223–27; on the emergence of the proletariat, 152; on feudalism, 190; on the French revolution, 156–57; *The German Ideology*, 8, 209, 268; and Hegel, G. W. F., 10, 210; on history, 11–12, 32, 79, 160, 207, 226; on human exceptionalism, 194; on industrial farming, 194; on the leap of capital, 279; lineage of, 84–92; methodology of, 335; on national debt, 88–90; on the Paris Commune, 235; on the proletariat, 214; on public debt, 117; on revolution, 110; on Robespierre, Maximilien, 156–57; on Shelley, Percy Bysshe, 198–99; on slave uprisings, 229; on sorcery and capitalism, 63–64, 106–7; on species-being, 207;